The Broken Scythe
Death and Immortality
in the Works of J.R.R. Tolkien

Roberto Arduini & Claudio A. Testi (eds.)

# The Broken Scythe

Death and Immortality
in the Works of J.R.R. Tolkien

2012

Cormarë Series No. 26

Series Editors: Peter Buchs • Thomas Honegger • Andrew Moglestue • Johanna Schön

Editor responsible for this volume: Thomas Honegger

Library of Congress Cataloging-in-Publication Data

Roberto Arduini & Claudio A. Testi (eds.):
The Broken Scythe
Death and Immortality in the Works of J.R.R. Tolkien
ISBN 978-3-905703-26-9

Subject headings:
Tolkien, J.R.R. (John Ronald Reuel), 1892-1973
Death and Immortality
*The Lord of the Rings*
*The Hobbit*
*The Silmarillion*

Cormarë Series No. 26

First published 2012

© Walking Tree Publishers, Zurich and Jena, 2012

All rights reserved. No portion of this book may be reproduced, by any process or technique, without the express written consent of the publisher

Cover illustration *The Departure of Boromir* by Anke Eißmann. Reproduced by permission of the artist. Copyright Anke Eißmann (2003).

Set in Adobe Garamond Pro and Shannon by Walking Tree Publishers
Printed by Lightning Source in the United Kingdom and United States

BOARD OF ADVISORS

ACADEMIC ADVISORS

Douglas A. Anderson (independent scholar)

Dieter Bachmann (Universität Zürich)

Patrick Curry (independent scholar)

Michael D.C. Drout (Wheaton College)

Vincent Ferré (Université de Paris 13)

Thomas Fornet-Ponse (Rheinische Friedrich-Wilhelms-Universität Bonn)

Verlyn Flieger (University of Maryland)

Christopher Garbowski (University of Lublin, Poland)

Mark T. Hooker (Indiana University)

Andrew James Johnston (Freie Universität Berlin)

Rainer Nagel (Johannes Gutenberg-Universität Mainz)

Helmut W. Pesch (independent scholar)

Tom Shippey (University of Winchester)

Allan Turner (Friedrich-Schiller-Universität Jena)

Frank Weinreich (independent scholar)


GENERAL READERS

Johan Boots

Jean Chausse

Friedhelm Schneidewind

Patrick Van den hole

Johan Vanhecke (Letterenhuis, Antwerp)

## About the editors and contributors

Roberto ARDUINI (*1970), president of the Roman Society of Tolkien Studies, is a journalist and independent scholar. He is also a member of *Tolkien e dintorni*, the Scientific Review Committee for Marietti publisher, and contributed to *The J.R.R. Tolkien Encyclopedia: Scholarship and Critical Assessment*, ed. Michael Drout, (Routledge University Press, 2006). He edited *Il Kalevala. Poema nazionale finnico* (Il Cerchio, 2007); together with Claudio Antonio Testi, he edited for Marietti *La trasmissione del pensiero e la numerazione degli Elfi* (2008), *La Falce spezzata. Morte e immortalità in J.R.R. Tolkien* (2009) and *Tolkien e la Filosofia* (2011). He is one of the authors of *La biblioteca di Bilbo* (Effatà, 2011).

Simone BONECHI (*1966), graduated in History at the University of Florence and obtained a PhD in History at the Sacro Cuore University of Milan. He is a passionate reader of Tolkien since the 1980s, a member of the Tolkien Society, and collaborates with the Italian magazine *Endòre* and works for Marietti 1820 as a translator of Tolkien-related studies such as Brian Rosebury's *Tolkien: a Cultural Phenomenon*.

Giampaolo CANZONIERI (*1959) obtained a degree in Computer Science and earns his living in this field. He discovered *The Lord of the Rings* at the age of fifteen and Tolkien has been part of his life ever since. He is a member of the committee that stands behind the Italian *Tolkien e dintorni* book series, to which he contributed first by participating in the translation of Tom Shippey's *The Road to Middle-earth* and then by supervising the translation of Joseph Pearce's *Tolkien: Man and Myth* and of *La Trasmissione del pensiero e la numerazione degli elfi*, a collection including J.R.R. Tolkien's "Ósanwe-kenta", "Notes on Óre" and "Eldarin Hands, Fingers and Numerals".

Lorenzo GAMMARELLI (*1972) contributed in 2003 to the revision of the Italian translations of *The Lord of the Rings* and *The Hobbit*. In 2005 he was the editor of the new Italian editions of *Farmer Giles of Ham* and *Smith of Wootton Major*, and in 2007 he translated and edited John Garth's *Tolkien and the Great War*. He is a member of the scholarly committee for the books series *Tolkien e dintorni* and collects Tolkien-related books and magazines.

Alberto LADAVAS (*1978) graduated in Electronic Engineering in Milan in 2004. He is a Tolkien Society member and member of the scholarly committee for the books series *Tolkien e dintorni*. He is a Tolkien fan since he was 10 years old and growing up he widened his interests from epic and fantastic literature to Northern history and mythology.

Franco MANNI (*1960) obtained two degrees in Philosophy and Theology respectively. Since 1999 he has been editing a Tolkienian journal, *Endòre*, and several Tolkien-related books: *Introduzione a Tolkien, Tolkien e la Terra di Mezzo, Mitopoiesi, Lettera a un amico della Terra di Mezzo*, and the Italian translation of Shippey's *Tolkien Author of the Century*. He also published two papers in English, one in the Proceedings of the 2005 Birmingham Tolkien Conference, and one in *Mallorn*.

Andrea MONDA (*1966) obtained a degree in Religious Science at Pontifical Gregorian University. His thesis on theological meanings of *The Lord of the Rings* has been published by Rubbettino Editore under the title *L'Anello e la Croce* in 2008. He works as a teacher of the Catholic religion in the high schools of Rome, the Pontifical Gregorian University, and the Pontifical Lateran University. He has furthermore published, together with Saverio Simonelli, *Tolkien, il Signore della Fantasia* (Frassinelli, 2002) and *Gli Anelli della Fantasia* (Frassinelli, 2004), with Paolo Gulisano *Il Mondo di Narnia* (SanPaolo 2005) and with Giovanni Cucci *L'Arazzo rovesciato. L'Enigma del Male* (Cittadella Editrice, 2010).

Claudio Antonio TESTI (*1967) obtained his PhD in Philosophy at the University of Bologna, is member and cofounder of the Philosophical Institute of Thomistical Studies where he teaches logic and cosmology. His publications (more than thirty articles or books) range from exegetical studies of Thomas Aquinas's metaphysics to essays in formal logic and epistemology: recently the work of J.R.R. Tolkien has become the focus of his studies. He is co-director of the series of *Le Quaestiones* (concerning Philosophy and Literature) and of the series *Tolkien e dintorni*, a collection of critical studies and translations concerning Tolkien and the Inklings.

# Contents

Series Editor's Preface

List of Abbreviations

Verlyn Flieger
Preface … xxiii

Roberto Arduini & Claudio A. Testi
Introduction … 1

Franco Manni
A Eulogy of Finitude:
Anthropology, Eschatology and Philosophy of History in Tolkien … 5

Claudio A. Testi
Tolkien's *Legendarium* as a *meditatio mortis* … 39

Roberto Arduini
Tolkien, Death and Time: the Fairy Story within the Picture … 69

Lorenzo Gammarelli
On the Edge of the Perilous Realm … 103

Alberto Ladavas
The Wrong Path of the Sub-creator:
from the Fall to the Machine and the Escape from Mortality … 117

Simone Bonechi
"In the Mounds of Mundburg":
Death, War and Memory in Middle-earth … 133

Andrea Monda
Death, Immortality and their Escapes: Memory and Longevity … 155

Claudio A. Testi
Logic and Theology in Tolkien's Thanatology … 175

Giampaolo Canzonieri
A Misplaced Envy: Analogies and
Differences between Elves and Men on the Idea of Pain … 193

Bibliography … 211

Index … 227

# Series Editor's Preface

It is always an adventure to try and translate a work from one language into another – not least since it also means, to some extent, a 'translation' from one national academic tradition into another. The 'adventure' of *The Broken Scythe* began with the submission of the manuscript in Italian. Luckily, we could rely on some truly polyglot members of the Board of Advisors who were not deterred by the task of reading and assessing the volume submitted. The translation, then, does not deny its origin in the Italian tradition and especially in the scholarly study-group which met to discuss, criticise and comment on each other's essays (see the Introduction by the two editors on this).

The focus on the problem of death and mortality in the works of J.R.R. Tolkien has proved to be a fortunate choice and the contributions by the several authors bear witness to their thorough training in and intimate acquaintance with (Catholic) theology and philosophy. It may be no coincidence that such a contribution comes from Italian scholarship and we are all the more proud to make their results accessible to an English-speaking readership.

As before, I would like to thank my co-series-editors, those members of the Board of Advisors who evaluated the initial project submission, and the students who served part of their internship as proofreaders and layouters for WTP and wish, in the name of WTP, an enjoyable and stimulating reading!

Thomas Honegger<br>
Jena, April 2012

# List of Abbreviations

## Abbreviations for works by J.R.R. Tolkien

*ATB*: *The Adventures of Tom Bombadil and Other Verses from the Red Book*, London: George Allen & Unwin, 1962.

AW: "Ancrene Wisse and Hali Meiðhad", in *Essays and Studies* 14 (1929), pp. 104-126.

BMC: "*Beowulf*: the Monster and the Critics", in *Proceedings of the British Academy* 22 (1936), pp. 245-295, reprinted in *MC*.

EW: "English and Welsh", in *Angles and Britons: O'Donnell Lectures*, Cardiff: University of Wales Press, 1963, pp. 1-41, reprinted in *MC*.

*FGH*: *Farmer Giles of Ham*, edited by Christina Scull and Wayne G. Hammond, London: HarperCollins, 1999.

*FH*: *Finn and Hengest: The Fragment and the Episode*, edited by Alan Bliss, London: George Allen & Unwin, 1982.

GN: "Guide to the Names in *The Lord of the Rings*", in *A Tolkien Compass*, edited by Jared Lobdell, La Salle (Illinois): Open Court, 1975, pp. 153-201.

*GPO*: *Sir Gawain and the Green Knight, Pearl and Sir Orfeo*, translated by J.R.R. Tolkien, edited by Christopher Tolkien, London: George Allen & Unwin, 1975.

*H*: *The Hobbit: or, There and Back Again*, 1937, edited by Douglas A. Anderson, London: HarperCollins, 2001

HBBS: "The Homecoming of Beorhtnoth Beorhthelm's Son", in *Essays and Studies*, N.S. 6 (1953), pp. 1-18, reprinted in *TL*.

*HoMe*: *The History of Middle-earth*, 12 volumes containing: *LT I-II, LB, SME, LR, RS, TI, WR, SD, MR, WJ, PME*.

*Letters*: *The Letters of J.R.R. Tolkien*, edited by Humphrey Carpenter and Christopher Tolkien, London: HarperCollins, 1999.

*LB*: *The Lays of Beleriand*, (*HoMe* 3) edited by Christopher Tolkien, London: HarperCollins, 2002.

*LN*: "Leaf by Niggle", first published in *Dublin Review*, January 1945, pp. 46-61, reprinted in *TL*.

*LotR*: *The Lord of The Rings*, 50th anniversary edition, Boston: Houghton Mifflin, 2004.

*LR*: *The Lost Road and Other Writings: Language and Legend before The Lord of the Rings*, (*HoMe* 5), edited by Christopher Tolkien, London: HarperCollins, 2002.

*LT I*: *The Book of Lost Tales: Part One*, (*HoMe* 1), edited by Christopher Tolkien, London: HarperCollins, 2002.

*LT II*: *The Book of Lost Tales: Part Two*, (*HoMe* 2), edited by Christopher Tolkien, London: HarperCollins, 2002.

*LTP*: *La trasmissione del pensiero e la numerazione degli Elfi*, Milano: Marietti 1820, 2008.

*MC*: *The Monsters and the Critics and Other Essays*, edited by Christopher Tolkien, London: George Allen & Unwin, 1984.

*MR*: *Morgoth's Ring* (*HoMe* 10), edited by Christopher Tolkien, London: HarperCollins, 2002.

*OFS*: "On Fairy-Stories", first published in *Essays Presented to Charles Williams*, London: Oxford University Press, 1947, pp. 38-89, reprinted in *TL*.

*OOE*: *The Old English Exodus: Text, Translation and Commentary*, edited by Joan Turville-Petre, Oxford: Clarendon, 1981.

*P*: *Pictures by J.R.R. Tolkien*, London: George Allen & Unwin, 1979; London: HarperCollins, 1991.

*PME*: *The Peoples of Middle-earth*, (*HoMe* 12), edited by Christopher Tolkien, London: HarperCollins, 2002.

Preface: "Prefatory Remarks" to *Beowulf and the Finnesburg Fragment: A Translation into Modern English by J.R. Clark Hall*, London: George Allen & Unwin, 1940, pp. ix-xliii, reprinted in *MC* as "On Translating *Beowulf*".

*RGEO*: *The Road Goes Ever On: A Song Cycle*, (poems by J.R.R. Tolkien, music by Donald Swann), London: HarperCollins, 2002.

*RS*: *The Return of the Shadow*, (*HoMe* 6), edited by Christopher Tolkien, London: HarperCollins, 2002.

*S*: *The Silmarillion*, edited by Christopher Tolkien, London: George Allen & Unwin, 1977; reprinted London: HarperCollins, 2001.

*SD*: *Sauron Defeated*, (*HoMe* 9), edited by Christopher Tolkien, London: HarperCollins, 1992.

*SGGK*: *Sir Gawain and the Green Knight*, edited by J.R.R. Tolkien and E.V. Gordon, Oxford: Clarendon Press, 1925.

*Sigurd*: *The Legend of Sigurd & Gudrún*, edited by Christopher Tolkien, London: HarperCollins, 2009.

*SME/Shaping*: *The Shaping of Middle-earth*, (*HoMe* 4), edited by Christopher Tolkien, London: HarperCollins, 2002.

*SP*: *Songs for the Philologists*, by J.R.R. Tolkien, E.V. Gordon and others, printed by the Dept. of English, University College, London 1936.

*SWM*: *Smith of Wootton Major*, edited by Verlyn Flieger, London: HarperCollins, 2005.

*Tales*: *Tales from the Perilous Realm*, containing *FGH*, *ATB*, and *SWM*, London: HarperCollins, 2002.

*TI*: *The Treason of Isengard*, (*HoMe* 7), edited by Christopher Tolkien, London HarperCollins, 2002.

*TL*: *Tree and Leaf*, London: HarperCollins, 2001; containing: HBBS, OFS and LN.

*UT*: *Unfinished Tales of Númenor and Middle-earth*, edited by Christopher Tolkien, London: HarperCollins, 2001.

*WJ*: *The War of the Jewels*, (*HoMe* 11), edited by Christopher Tolkien, London: HarperCollins, 2002.

*WR*: *The War of the Ring*, (*HoMe*, 8) edited by Christopher Tolkien, London: HarperCollins, 2002.

*YWES*: *The Year's Work in English Studies*, containing the chapter "Philology, General Works", vols. 4-6 (1923-1925) cited by no. of volume and page.

## Abbreviations for parts of *The Silmarillion*

Ainul:   Ainulindalë

Val:     Valaquenta

Qu:      Quenta Silmarillion

Ak:      Akallabêth

RiPo:    Of the Rings of Power and the Third Age

## Abbreviations for parts of *The Lord of the Rings*

FR:      The Fellowship of the Rings

TT:      The Two Towers

RK:      The Return of the King

App:     Appendix

# Abbreviations for texts from *The History of Middle-earth* (in chronological order)

## 1917-25

*LT*: *The Book of Lost Tales*, written in 1917-20 and published *LT I-II*.

## 1926-30

Sk: Sketch of the Mythology, written in 1926, published in *SME*.

Q: Quenta Noldorinwa, written in 1930 (*SME* 76), expansion of Sk, published in *SME*.

AV1: Annals of Valinor, written in 1930 (*SME* 262, 294; *WJ* 3) as a chronology for Q, published in *SME*.

AB1: Annals of Beleriand, written in 1930 (*SME* 262, 294; *WJ* 3) as a chronology for Q, published in *SME*.

MuB: Music of the Ainur/Ainulindalë, written in the 1930s (*MR* 3-7, 432), published in *LR*.

## 1930-37

QS: Quenta Silmarillion, written in 1930-37 (*SME* 7, *LR* 199), expansion of Q, published in *LR*.

AV2: second version of AV1, written in 1930-37 (*LR* 107-109; *MR* 47; *WJ* 3) as a chronology for QS, published in *LR*.

AB2: second version of AB1, written in 1930-37 (*LR* 107-108; *MR* 47; *WJ* 3) as a chronology for QS, published in *LR*.

FN1: The Fall of Númenor, written in 1936-37 (*LR* 9, 34), inserted in "Lost Road" and published in *LR*.

FN2: written in 1937-41 but after FN1 (*LR* 9, 34) and published in *LR*.

FN3: written in 1937-41 but after FN2 (*SD* 331) containing some corrections related to DA1-2 and NCP, published in *SD*.

Lost Road: The Lost Road, unfinished tale written in 1936-37 (*LR* 7-9), published in *LR*.

**1937-56**

DA1: The Drowning of Anadûnê, typescript of extreme roughness written in 1945-46 (*SD* 147, 340, 357), published in *SD*.

DA2: typescript written with care of The Drowning of Anandûnê, written in 1945-46 (*SD* 147, 340, 357), published in *SD*.

NCP: The Notion Club Papers, written in 1945-46 (*SD* 147), containing FN3, published in *SD*.

LQ1: The Later Quenta Silmarillion, revision of QS, dated 1950-51 (*MR* 141, 433), published in *MR*.

AAm1: The Annals of Aman, written in 1951-52 as a revision of AV2, chronology for LQ1 (*MR* 433; *WJ* 3), published in *MR*.

GA1: The Grey Annals, written in 1951-52 (*WJ* 3-4), a revision of AB2, chronology of LQ1, published in *WJ*.

GA2: written in the early 1950s, clean manuscript, second version of GA1 (*WJ* 3-4), published in *WJ*.

AB3: see GA1 (*WJ* 3-4).

MuC*: Ainulindalë, already in existence in 1948, drastic revision of MuB (*MR* 432), published in *MR*.

MuC: Ainulindalë, written after MuC* (*MR* 4, 7, 432) and before 1951, published in *MR*.

MuD: Ainulindalë, written after MuC and before 1951 (*MR* 432), published in *MR*.

**1957-60**

FM1: The Tale of Finwë and Míriel, written in 1957-58 (*MR* 300, 433) before LawsA, published in *MR*.

LawsA: Laws and Customs among the Eldar, manuscript written in the late 1950s (*MR* 300), published in *MR*.

FM2: The Tale of Finwë and Míriel, written in the late 1950s, after FM1 and before LawsB (*MR* 141, 199, 300, 433), published in *MR*.

LawsB: typescript written in the late 1950s, after LawsA (*MR* 300) published in *MR*.

FM3: The Tale of Finwë and Míriel, written in the late 1950s, after LawsB (*MR* 141, 199, 300, 433), published in *MR*.

FM4: final text of The Tale of Finwë and Míriel written in the late 1950s after LawsB (*MR* 141, 199, 300, 433), published in *MR*.

LQ2 : Later Quenta Silmarillion, written in 1958 as revision of QS (*MR* 141, 433), published in *WJ*.

AAm2: typescript written in 1957-58 of the Annals of Aman (*MR* 432; *WJ* 4), published in *MR*.

GA3: The Grey Annals written 1957-58 connected to LQ2 (*MR* 432; *WJ* 4), published in *WJ*.

OK: Ósanwe-kenta, written in 1959-60 as appendix to Quendi and Eldar, edited with introduction, glossary, and additional notes by Carl F. Hostetter and published in *Vinyar Tengwar* 39, July 1998, pp. 21-34 (Italian translation in *LTP*).

Aman: Aman, written about in 1959, before Athrabeth (*MR* 361, 424), published in *MR*.

Converse: Converse between Manwë and Eru, written in 1959-60 and before the Commentary to Athrabeth (*MR* 361, 424), published in *MR*.

AthrabethB-C: amanuensis typescripts for Athrabeth Finrod ah Andreth, written in 1959-60 (*MR* 303-304, 352, 433), cited in *MR*.

Athrabeth: Athrabeth Finrod ah Andreth, manuscript written in 1959-60 (*MR* 303-304, 352, 433), published in *MR*.

Commentary: commentary to Athrabeth, written in 1960 (*MR* 303-304, 352, 433), published in *MR*.

Reincarnation: essay on the reincarnation of Elves written in 1960, after Athrabeth and Commentary (*MR* 363), cited in *MR*.

**1961-73**

NOO: Note on Óre, written in 1968, published in *Vinyar Tengwar* 41, July 2000, pp. 11-19 (Italian translation in *LTP*).

## Abbreviations conventions for citations

For *S* and *LotR*, the reference indicates the part and the chapter of the part:
- e.g. (*S*, Qu.1) indicates the first chapter of the Quenta Silmarillion, contained in *The Silmarillion*;
- e.g. (*LotR*, FR.II.3) indicates the third chapter of the book two of *The Fellowship of the Ring*, contained in *The Lord of the Rings*;
- e.g. (*LotR*, App. A.5) indicates the fifth part of Appendix in *The Lord of the Rings*, that is The Tale of Aragorn and Arwen.

For *Letters*, the reference is to the number of the letter:
- e.g. (*Letters* no. 131) indicates the letter no. 131 in *The Letters of J.R.R. Tolkien*;
- e.g. (*Letters* nos. 131, 156) indicates the letters no. 131 and no. 156, in *The Letters of J.R.R. Tolkien*.

For all the other references the last number indicates the number of the page.
- e.g. (*MR* 195) indicates p. 195 of *Morgoth's Ring*, volume 10 of *The History of Middle-earth*;
- e.g. (*MR*, Athrabeth 332) indicates p. 332 of Athrabeth Finrod ah Andreth in *Morgoth's Ring*;

- e.g. (Flieger 2002, 28) indicates p. 28 of Verlyn Flieger's *Splintered Light*;
- e.g. (*ibid.* 30) indicates p. 30 of the immediately preceding source, e.g. Verlyn Flieger's *Splintered Light*.

# Verlyn Flieger

## Preface

In 1936 J.R.R. Tolkien made a comment about *Beowulf* that could as easily be applied to his own work. Assessing the state of *Beowulf* criticism at the time, he said, "It is possible [...] to be moved by the power of myth and yet to misunderstand the sensation, to ascribe it wholly to something else that is also present" (*MC* 15-16). Tolkien was challenging the (at that time) current critical opinion that *Beowulf* was an important poem in spite of its fantastic content, which featured battles with ogres and a dragon where the critics would have preferred more realistic human foes. His point was that the power lies precisely in those monsters *rather than* mere human opponents, which best embody and support the poem's pervasive theme that *lif is læne: eal scæceð leoht and lif somod* (*MC* 19; 'life is loaned [transitory]: all perishes, light and life together'), the inevitability of death as the central tragedy and ultimate foe of human life. In short, said Tolkien, readerly response to *Beowulf* was unforced and genuine, while critical assessment was based on the mis-assumption that it ought to have been something else.

We have only to turn to a certain school of negative critical response to *The Lord of the Rings* to see how the same comment might apply to Tolkien's own work. Critics skeptical of the power of his mythos have deplored its fantastic content, ascribing its popularity precisely to the kind of fantastic elements the critics of *Beowulf* deplored, to the enchantment and arresting strangeness of Hobbits, Elves, Dwarves, wizards, and talking trees which are its surface and most salient features. And it is true that readers meeting at first hand a work so full of marvels could and often do "misunderstand the sensation," their attention captured by the fantasy as such with little awareness of its more serious implications. Nevertheless, as with the early audience of *Beowulf*, they are in fact responding at a deeper level than they realize to a more profound content than they are consciously aware of, to a narrative content that transcends the novelty of fantasy to touch the heights and depths of human hope and despair.

As the fantastic nature of the monsters of *Beowulf* tended to obscure their deeper representation of the "hostile world and the offspring of the dark," so the fairy tale aspects of Tolkien's *legendarium* tend to overshadow their contribution to that story's more serious level of meaning. Both stories are ultimately about loss and death. The fantasy elements of Tolkien's imagination are, like the monsters of *Beowulf*, valuable not just because they are fantastic, but because their fantasy is the vehicle for the more somber, indeed tragic theme of mortality, of death as the end of human life. For all its beer-and-mushroom hobbitry, its epic battles and fairy tale adventures in mysterious woods, the real strength of *The Lord of the Rings* resides in its dark side, its concern – carried over from its parent mythology of *The Silmarillion* – with death and deathlessness.

Like a deeply buried substrate of ore, loss, mortality, and death lie beneath the surface of Tolkien's entire corpus, and without this deeper level the surface would collapse, for it is the encounter of Tolkien's characters, even his immortal Elves, with the loss and impermanence of life on earth that gives his work its substance. The need for serious study of this substrate is obvious and indeed overdue, and it is to address this need that the present essays have been gathered. They are a major contribution to our growing understanding of Tolkien's fiction and our appreciation of its importance not just for his own time but beyond.

The essays in this collection, all by serious scholars in the field, are part of a current and very welcome wave in Tolkien criticism. Until recently much of the scholarship devoted to Tolkien has focused on the variety of his invention, the completeness and integrity of his Secondary World, the complexity of his languages, and the relationship of his mythos to medieval epic, romance and fairy tale. Though the situation has changed for the better in recent years, there has been as well a general tendency to focus on Tolkien's magnum opus, *The Lord of the Rings*, with less attention paid to fitting that into the larger *legendarium*, and still less attention given to the shorter stories and poems which, though different in form, nevertheless are concerned with the same theme. All these writings are part of a web of relationships woven into one another and into the larger issues of history and theology and philosophy, and it is these larger issues with which the present collection is concerned.

The collection begins with Franco Manni's densely packed and carefully argued "An Eulogy of Finitude. Anthropology, Eschatology and Philosophy of History in Tolkien". This is an examination of the relationship between the circumstances of Tolkien's life (early deaths of parents and close friends, two World Wars) and the deeply philosophical currents which, though seldom if ever explicitly named as such, inform his work, currents which Manni describes as "themes which are central to the philosophical tradition: ethics, aesthetics, anthropology, history, and religion."

Claudio A. Testi's essay on the *legendarium* as a *meditatio mortis* closely examines the entire corpus, from the earliest and most mythic *Lost Tales* of 1917 to such post-*Lord of the Rings* writings as the late "Athrabeth" (the most overtly theological discussion in all Tolkien's stories) and the more anthropological "Laws and Customs Among the Eldar". Testi sees these late, philosophical writings as addressing the question raised in the earlier writings by the existence of Tolkien's two races of Elves and Men, races with conflicting attitudes toward death. His essay provides a consideration of the emotional, practical, and philosophical issues thus raised.

Roberto Arduini's essay "Tolkien, Death and Time: The Fairy Story Within the Picture", matches Tolkien's theory with his art by showing the interconnection between the essay "On Fairy-stories" and his short story, "Leaf by Niggle". This approach is further amplified in Lorenzo Gammarelli's analysis of the theme of loss and bereavement in Tolkien's shorter works, a miscellany including "Aotrou and Itroun"; "Imram"; "The Stone Troll"; "The Mewlips"; the two "Man in the Moon" poems, and some of the darker poems from *The Adventures of Tom Bombadil*, "The Sea-bell"; "The Hoard"; "Shadow-bride"; and "The Last Ship". *Smith of Wootton Major* and "Bilbo's Last Song" round out the discussion.

Taking as his text Tolkien's comment in the letter to Milton Waldman that his work was concerned mainly with "Fall, Mortality, and the Machine", Alberto Ladavas illustrates "The wrong path of the sub-creator" through Tolkien's treatment of the people of Númenor and the Ringwraiths, all of whom are prey to the evil of possessiveness, both of life and of art, which leads to the "Machine", domination, the exertion of power of which the Ring is the supreme example.

Moving between the Primary World and Tolkien's Secondary World, Simone Bonechi places Tolkien's treatment of his fictive dead within the context of Britain's commemoration of its dead from the two great wars of the 20th century, and uses this perspective from which to consider the variety of funeral rites enacted in *The Simarillion* and *The Lord of the Rings*.

Andrea Monda's essay focuses on Escape from death, and on Memory as a kind of Escape, examining these in the context of Tolkien's treatments of longevity, or *longaevitas*, in *The Lord of the Rings*. Elves, Hobbits, Denethor, Saruman, Treebeard, Tom Bombadil, and the Ring itself embody aspects either positive or negative of Escape and Memory, and all are parts of Tolkien's theme.

Returning to the "Athrabeth" in his second essay in the collection, Claudio A. Testi addresses the logical structure of Tolkien's dialectic in this most dialectical of all Tolkien's stories, a very late writing and surely the most explicit example of argumentation in the whole *legendarium*. This thanatology is not so much a summing-up as an unresolved debate between Finrod and Andreth representing Elves and Men, raising but not answering each other's questions about death and deathlessness. Resolved or unresolved, the "Athrabeth" is an important text, both theologically and philosophically, as Testi shows: "a synthesis of profound literary and theoretical importance."

Giampaolo Canzonieri's essay, the last in the volume, takes a somewhat different approach, analyzing, in terms of differences between Tolkien's Men and Elves, the dualism of death and pain in place of the more conventional dualism of death and immortality as treated in the other essays.

These contributors, and the editors who brought them together, are to be congratulated on making available to a wide audience of Tolkien readers and scholars a collection whose strength lies in its variety within consistency: not simply in the authors' varying approaches to Tolkien's theme of death and immortality, but in the range of works considered in that context – from minor and little-read poems and stories in defunct periodicals, often now difficult of access, to the more popular works by which his name is known.

In his Foreword to the 1977 *Silmarillion* Christopher Tolkien observed that the old legends of his father's mythos became over time the carriers of his most profound reflections, while the later writings tended to replace mythology and poetry with more theological and philosophical concerns. The present volume strives to bring together the poetic and philosophical aspects of Tolkien's work, further to connect both to Tolkien's own comments on death and immortality in his letters, and finally to show all three as various components of the same essential concept – all the offspring of Tolkien's thought, as the Ainur were the offspring of Eru's.

# Roberto Arduini & Claudio A. Testi

## Introduction

*The Broken Scythe*, of which we here present the English edition, is first of all the answer to a need; an initial and hopeful attempt to introduce a serious and accurate approach to the study of J.R.R. Tolkien in a country, Italy, that despite being in 1970 the fourth in the world to see a translation of *The Lord of the Rings*, followed in a few years by most of the works of Tolkien available at the time, has seen very few translations of critical texts since then, and even fewer contributions from Italian critics at the extent that both are now difficult to retrieve not only in bookshops but even in libraries.

The main reason for this state of affairs, which lasted more or less till the release of the first Peter Jackson movie, was that in Italy, unlike in Anglo-Saxon countries, Tolkien was overlooked if not ostracized by the academic world, that branded him for an author of *juveniles* stamping his works as marginal, as though Lewis Carroll, Jonathan Swift or Rudyard Kipling should not be thoroughly studied because their books are read mostly by children.

Things fortunately started to change in 2001, when, after the release of the first movie, the feeling began to arise, not without resentful reactions by the usual die-hard critics, that Tolkien's works were certainly meant for young people but also as certainly *not only* for them. So it was that, mostly thanks to the efforts of some "happy few" editors, translators and enlightened publishers like Marietti 1820, it became possible to read Italian versions of the most important critical texts dedicated to J.R.R. Tolkien's fiction, life, and vision. To get an idea, one just has to skim through the *Tolkien e Dintorni* book series, that lists such seminal works as Tom Shippey's *The Road to Middle-earth* (translated in 2005) and Verlyn Flieger's *Splintered Light* (2007), as well as other important texts such as John Garth's *Tolkien and the Great War* (2007), Brian Rosebury's *Tolkien. A Cultural Phenomenon* (2009) and Joseph Pearce's *Tolkien. Man and Myth* (2010), not to mention a short anthology of writings by Tolkien himself (2008), originally published by Carl F. Hostetter in *Vinyar Tengwar*.

Without trying to claim roles that are not theirs, the editors of the series have successfully struggled to keep the difficult balance between popularization and culture, publishing primary critical texts while, at the same time, avoiding to scare away readers approaching these kind of texts for the first time. The published books cover a wide range of the themes presented or suggested in Tolkien's works, and show the diverse viewpoints and approaches of the different foreign scholars. The road goes ever on but, at least, the journey has started and the largest gaps have been filled.

Only in 2009, however, could the series present a book, *The Broken Scythe*, written by Italian scholars, the first critical text about Tolkien ever to be fully centred on the themes of death and immortality in his whole work. A book in which the authors tried to place their considerations and analyses in the framework of a rapidly developing international scholarship. The very method adopted to give the book its final shape is widespread in Anglo-Saxon countries, including the United States where it is used by universities and research centres. A preliminary work performed by a group of study led to an open invitation to several Italian Tolkienian communities, as well as to some scholars that had in recent years distinguished themselves by their research in the field. Then, the enlarged group started organizing quarterly meetings in different Italian cities (Rome, Modena and Florence), aimed at sharing and discussing among participants work methods as well as research lines. Finally, drafts of the essays in progress were read during the meetings, resulting in great improvements and enhancements deriving from mutual stimulus and advice.

The meetings took place in 2008 and first half of 2009 and were coordinated by the *Istituto Filosofico di Studi Tomistici* of Modena and the *Associazione Romana Studi Tolkieniani* of Rome, two cultural communities that have been working for years on spreading philosophical (mainly Thomistical) and Tolkienian culture, respectively. The same communities, building also on the positive experience of the *Broken Scythe* group of study, organized in 2010 the first Italian international meeting on Tolkienian studies that, under the theme "Tolkien and Philosophy", saw the participation of such important names as Tom Shippey, Verlyn Flieger, Christopher Garbowsky, Franco Manni, Andrea Monda and Wu Ming 4.

Despite the effort, the absence of J.R.R. Tolkien from the academic world is nonetheless still a gap to be filled. We hope that even in Italy this will be possible one day.

# Franco Manni

## An Eulogy of Finitude: Anthropology, Eschatology and Philosophy of History in Tolkien

*"I'm not a philosopher, but an experimenter"*
Tolkien, "The Notion Club Papers"

## 1. An undeclared love and a latent polemic

In his works Tolkien never refers to philosophers by name,[1] neither classical figures such as Socrates, Plato, Aristotle, St. Augustine, Thomas Aquinas, Descartes, Kant, Hegel, Schopenhauer or Marx, nor his contemporaries such as Freud, Bergson, Croce, Dewey, Wittgenstein, Husserl, Popper or Ryle. However, although he never openly cites Kant, he does make use of the Kantian neologism "noumenon" (*Letters* no. 131); the ideas of "perennis philosophia" (a syncretic compound of ancient and medieval traditions) are also frequently employed, but without reference to sources. Tom Shippey thinks that Tolkien did not mention philosophers like Plato, Boethius and others – in spite of his knowledge of them – because of his anti-classicistic bias, and, moreover, because – since he wanted to bring the native English literature out – he could not find English philosophers before Chaucer's times.[2] In my opinion a clear example may be found in Note 8 of the self-commentary Tolkien made on

---

[1] Not in those published during his lifetime; among posthumous works, Plato appears once in the "Notion Club Papers" in the context of the myth of Atlantis, which is connected with that of Númenor (*SD* 249), and there is also a passing reference to the little-known German philosopher Theodor Haecker (*Letters* no. 338), but the context of the quotation – where Haecker is associated to the philologist Bazell and the "normativeness" of Latin language is recalled – makes it more likely that Tolkien was referring to Haecker's book on Virgil, a literary essay, not a philosophical one (Haecker 1934).

[2] Email to FM (Franco Manni), August 21st, 2009. Shippey added (in his presentation "Tolkien between Philology and Philosophy" at the Conference "Tolkien and Philosophy", Modena, May 22nd, 2010): "I refer to the famous image of the soup, and the bones of the ox from which the soup has been boiled. Tolkien said, very firmly, that we should be content with the soup and not demand to see the bones of the ox. He was rejecting the utility of source-study, and as he often did, overstating his case to make a point. I think source-study can be useful, and that philosophers were no doubt among Tolkien's sources. But Tolkien was right in that it is very difficult to analyse soup into its component parts."

"Athrabeth Finrod ah Andreth" ("The Debate of Finrod and Andreth"); the note discusses "desire" and distinguishes three kinds: "natural" desire which is shared by all members of a species, "personal" desire ("the feeling of the lack of something, the force of which primarily concerns oneself, and which may have little or no reference to the general fitness of things") and "illusionary" desire, which obstructs the understanding that things are not as they should be and leads to the delusion that they are as one would wish them to be (*MR* 343). This distinction is the same as the one made by Thomas Aquinas in an article[3] in *Summa Theologiae*, a work which Carpenter says was present on Lewis's bookshelf during the Inklings' evening meetings[4] and which Claudio A. Testi tells me that he knows Tolkien to have possessed.[5]

There is another undeclared Thomistic point: the difference between the two kinds of "hope", "Amdir" and "Estel". In the "Athrabeth", Andreth reflects about the nature of Hope:

> "What is hope?" she said. "An expectation of good, which though uncertain has some foundation in what is known? Then we have none." "That is one thing that Men call 'hope'," said Finrod. "Amdir we call it, 'looking up'. But there is another which is founded deeper. Estel we call it, that is 'trust'. It is not defeated by the ways of the world, for it does not come from experience, but from our nature and first being. If we are indeed the Eruhin, the Children of the One, then He will not suffer Himself to be deprived of His own, not by any Enemy, not even by ourselves. This is the last foundation of Estel. [...] Among the Atani [...] it is believed that healing may yet be found, or that there is some way of escape. But is this indeed Estel? Is it not Amdir rather but without reason: mere flight in a dream from what waking they know: that there is no escape from darkness and death?" (*MR* 320)

In the *Summa Theologiae* Aquinas distinguishes "spes" as a pre-moral "passio" (feeling) – which belongs even to drunk people and brute animals and whose

---

3 *Summa Theologiae*, pars prima secundae partis, quaestio 34, art. 2. Aquinas distinguishes three kinds of "pleasure" ("pleasure" is the feeling which follows a fulfilled desire of a "good thing" [bonum]!) based on three kinds of "bonum": a) "bonum per se", i.e. "per suam naturam"; b) "bonum conveniens secundum dispositionem" (not universally, always) but in relation to some "not natural" circumstances. For example some plants work as medicine for a sick man while they are poisonous for a healthy man; c) "apparens bonum", when a man is wrong in his thought and thinks good what is evil instead. For me the following parallels between Tolkien and Aquinas are evident: between Tolkien's "natural desire" and Aquinas's "bonum per se", between Tolkien's "personal desire" and Aquinas's "bonum secundum dispositionem", between Tolkien's "illusionary desire" and Aquinas's "apparens (false) bonum".
4 Carpenter 1978, chapter 3.
5 Claudio A. Testi has purchased Tolkien's copy on the collectors' market and received a positive *expertise* by Carl Hostetter and Christopher Tolkien (see his second article in this volume).

content is "bonum futurum arduum possibile adipisci"⁶ – from "spes" as a theological virtue, of which he writes:

> Hope does not trust chiefly in grace already received, but on God's omnipotence and mercy, whereby even he that has not grace, can obtain it, so as to come to eternal life. Now whoever has faith is certain of God's omnipotence and mercy [...] That some who have hope fail to obtain happiness, is due to a fault of the free will in placing the obstacle of sin, but not to any deficiency in God's power or mercy, in which hope places its trust. Hence this does not prejudice the certainty of hope.⁷

Further references to ancient and medieval philosophers have been pointed out by Tolkien scholars: Plato,⁸ Plotinus and Augustine,⁹ Boethius.¹⁰

But Tolkien never uses the word "philosophy" in his fiction, and amongst other published works only thrice in the lecture "On Fairy-Stories" and thrice in the lecture on *Beowulf*. Thereafter this lexical ostracism – consciously wished for, I think – continues into Tolkien's scholars: in the two massive, erudite and up-to-date "Tolkien encyclopedias" by Drout and by Hammond & Scull there is no place – in the midst of hundreds of others – for the entry *Philosophy* (cf. Drout 2007; Hammond & Scull 2006b).

---

6 *Summa Theologiae,* pars prima secundae partis, quaestio 40, art. 1, 3, 6.
7 *Summa Theologiae,* pars secunda secundae partis, quaestio 18, art. 4, ad secundum et ad tertium. On Aquinas as a source for Tolkien, see Birzer 2007, 21.
8 Cf. Nagy 2007 and Gregory Bassham: "Tolkien's repeated use of the term "demi-urgic" (e.g., *MR* 332) to describe the creative/shaping activity of the Valar (borrowed from Plato's *Timaeus*); Númenor as based on Plato's story of Atlantis in *Critias*; the Ring as based on Gyges's ring in *Republic*, Book 2; reincarnation of the elves (likely borrowed from Plato, esp. the *Phaedo*)" (from an email to FM, June 15th, 2009).
9 Cf. Houghton 2003 and 2007.
10 Shippey 2000a, 128-142 and Gregory Bassham: "The question of how much philosophy Tolkien read is probably unanswerable. However, two philosophical works he almost certainly would have had in his library are (1) Alfred's translation of Boethius's *Consolatio* and (2) Chaucer's translation of the same. In fact, Boethius seems to have influenced Tolkien fairly heavily. His solution to the freewill/divine foreknowledge problem in *Ósanwe-kenta* and elsewhere is identical to Boethius's (God is outside time, so strictly there is no foreknowledge). Also, Tolkien's use of the term "consolation" for one of the three benefits of fantasy-reading (escape, recovery, consolation) likely derives from Boethius. Also, Tolkien's insistence that evil is a *privatio* is likely due mainly to Boethius (though Boethius himself borrowed the idea from Plotinus and Augustine). Some of Tolkien's ideas on "chance" and "luck" may also be indebted to Boethius's *Consolatio*. Tolkien certainly had Chaucer's translation of Boethius's *Consolatio* in his personal library. For many years Tolkien served as co-editor of the Clarendon Chaucer, but eventually had to bow out prior to publication (see Hammond & Scull 2006a, 121f.). He wanted to produce a new text of Chaucer but was obliged by the Press to use Skeat's *Chaucer's Poetical Works*. That edition includes the whole of Chaucer's translation. As for Alfred's translation: as one of the world's leading Anglo-Saxon scholars, Tolkien surely would have had essentially every surviving Anglo-Saxon text in his personal library" (from an email to FM, June 15th, 2009).

With regard to writings not intended for publication, this word appears a few times in his *Letters*, usually as a synonym for "religion" (*Letters* no. 26, 49, 153, 156, 183) or with the meaning of generalized "theory" (*Letters* no. 15, 49, 52), but also at times in a more strict sense, such as when he writes that the word "ent" has slightly philosophical overtones, or that he does not believe that there can be philosophers able to deny the possibility of reincarnation (*Letters* no. 153, implicitly showing, it seems to me, that he knew some of them!), or when he explains the significance of the Ring of Power or speaks of the moral corruption present in Eddison's novels (*Letters* no. 157, 211, 199). Sometimes, though, philosophy as rational knowledge is explicitly distinguished from religion, e.g. when he says that the Hobbits might have misunderstood Aragorn's miraculous healings because of their lack of philosophical and scientific knowledge, or when he makes it clear that although religion had a minor role among the Faithful of Númenor the same could not be said regarding philosophy and metaphysics, or when he observed that in *The Lord of the Rings* evil and falsity are represented mythically whereas good and truth are represented in a fashion more "historical and philosophical" than "religious" (*Letters* no. 155, 84, 156).[11] The "home" of philosophy is, according to him, "in ancient Greece" (*Letters* no. 84) (and not in Germany, which he considered the "home" of philology),[12] for the reason that "southern" mythology rests on deeper foundations than that from the north, and so must lead "either to philosophy or anarchy" (*MR* 25). In the aborted "Notion Club Papers" the word appears twice: once in reference to the character Rupert Dolbear (who is also interested in psychoanalysis and often falls asleep during discussions) and once in reference to the character Michael Ramer (a philologist alter-ego of Tolkien), who says that he is *not* a philosopher, but rather an "experimenter" (*SD* 159, 178).

These occurrences (or, better, non-occurrences) of the names of philosophers[13] or the word "philosophy" bring to mind Carpenter's reconstruction of a typical

---

11 In the latter, it is interesting to note that "religion" is equivalent to "myth" ("story" in Greek) and to tangible "representativeness", as he also says more than once in his work "On Fairy-Stories" (but without ever giving explanations).
12 Shippey 2007a, 114-136.
13 Wholly deliberate, I think. In the preparatory versions of the lecture "On Fairy-Stories" for example, Tolkien writes the name of Carl Gustav Jung, while in the definitive one he only quotes the word "archetype" but omits Jung's name (see Flieger & Anderson 2008, 129, 170, 307).

Inklings-session.[14] When they are together, the friends talk of many things: the war under way, *The Lord of the Rings*, the philosophy of history, literary criticism, Shakespeare, religion, ethics. But when they refer to thinkers by name, they do so polemically, disparaging "contemporary thought".[15] They also make me think of Tom Shippey – an intellectual often identified with his hero Tolkien – who says he knows nothing of philosophy, but also demonstrates a certain (latent) polemical attitude towards it, calling philologists "tough minded" and philosophers "tender minded".[16] Perhaps both Tolkien and Shippey were thinking of the abstruse and often essentially empty philosophy of 19th-century German idealism and 20th-century French and German existentialism on the one hand, and the differently abstruse and differently empty "Oxbridge Analytical Philosophy" which was already strong before the Second World War and afterwards dominant in the English-speaking academic world, on the other.[17] In Tolkien we find respect (though not *declared* love) for ancient and medieval philosophy, together with scepticism or at least lack of interest regarding modern and contemporary philosophy.

And maybe this happened – as I hinted at – because of rather extrinsic circumstances, I mean of social context and interpersonal relations, as Shippey thinks:

> Philosophy – why does Tolkien not mention it? I suppose I can only say that unlike Lewis he never took the philosophy part of the Oxford Classics course, so maybe he felt that he was professionally ill-equipped – Oxford is always full

---

14 Set in Magdalene College in the evening at a date between autumn 1940 and December 1941; see Carpenter 1978, chapter 3.
15 They are against Karl Marx and the theologian Karl Barth. (Carpenter 1978, chapter 3)
16 Several personal communications with Shippey.
17 See Shippey's (I think rightly) critical comment concerning the father of Anglo-American analytical philosophy G.E. Moore (Shippey 2000a, 158), and also this personal experience: "I intervened in an interview among philosophers at Oxford once, querying a point about language – the thesis was about the distinction in Augustine between 'God' and 'a god', and I said 'but Augustine wrote in Latin, where there is no such distinction. How can you tell?' – and this caused a most violent inter-college and inter-disciplinary dispute. W.H. Auden, Tolkien's friend, wrote a sarcastic verse about Oxford philosophers" (from an email to FM, July 14th, 2009). And Shippey said (at the Conference "Tolkien and Philosophy" in Modena): "Now, in our time, academic philosophers have ceased to have much to do with ordinary people. They do not talk the same language, and the language of academic philosophers is more and more impenetrable. So are ordinary people to be left to their own thought? It was one aim of the Inklings, I believe, and especially of Tolkien's great friend C.S. Lewis, to bridge this gap. I looked at the index of Lewis's book *The Problem of Pain* (one of the great philosophical questions, why is there suffering in the world? Especially if you believe in a benevolent and loving God?), and he mentions all the ancient philosophers whom Franco will tell us about in a moment – but never for themselves, only for what they had to say, and that is explained in a deliberately clear and simple and non-academic fashion."

of philosophers. Maybe he felt that that was Lewis's business. Or he could just have decided to keep his thoughts to himself.[18]

Furthermore, Ross Smith writes that even if there are no mentions of Tolkien on analytical philosophy, Tolkien was nevertheless a close friend of C.S. Lewis who opposed it, and especially A.J. Ayer (Smith 2007, 140-141).

But – as we already saw and shall see below – we find in Tolkien an attraction towards themes which are central to the philosophical tradition: ethics, aesthetics, anthropology, history and religion.

To sum it up, Tolkien showed a strong concern for philosophical themes,[19] combined with a latent polemical attitude towards the way in which these are treated by recent and contemporary philosophers!

## 2. Anthropology

Which themes, then? Verlyn Flieger agrees with Tolkien's assertion: the principal theme is death; Charles Nelson considers other subjects to be central;[20] W.A. Senior thinks that the central concern is the "sense of loss" of which death is but one form (Senior 2000, 173); Tom Shippey observes that although to Tolkien it "seemed that the central theme was death" (Shippey 2005, 301), he himself sees the "ideological" and "philosophical" core of Tolkien's work as being about providence (Shippey 2007a, 317 and 383).

---

18 Shippey at the Conference "Tolkien and Philosophy" in Modena (from an email to FM, June 27th, 2009).
19 Patrick Curry's opinion is similar (though not identical) to mine: "I have never heard from anyone that Tolkien ever read any philosophy, I'm afraid; and that is my subjective impression too. If you are looking for a direct connection, I think you will be disappointed. (Of course, his work has deeply philosophical implications, but that's another matter!)" (from an email to FM, dated March 21st, 2009). John Garth said: "I've seen none of these names in Tolkien's writings, published or unpublished; I've never seen a philosophical title among lists of his books; and I can't think of any of his papers at the Bodleian which have a philosophical bent. The closest, I suppose, is "On Fairy-Stories"" (from an email to FM, dated March 26th, 2009). Also Dimitra Fimi stated: "I am afraid I do not know enough to help you. I have looked at Tolkien's books in the Bodleian and in the English Faculty at Oxford, but I cannot remember any philosophy books within them (although I was looking for different things so I might have overlooked them)" (from an email to FM, April 5th, 2009). This has been corroborated by a visit of mine to both libraries mentioned where I consulted the manuscripts and books available.
20 As noted by Senior 2000, 173.

Tolkien is of course a great storyteller and – for example on the subject of death – presents us with expressive images such as that of Gildor Inglorion and the other High Elves, who in the woods of the Shire are aware they are meeting "mortals" (Hobbits), but he also loves to philosophize "behind the scenes", for example in the *Letters* and other writings not intended for publication, such as "Laws and Customs among the Eldar" and "Athrabeth Finrod ah Andreth" and in his various explanatory comments on these fictional writings (*Morgoth's Ring*). And here he discusses traditional anthropological and theological themes of body and soul and God's plan for these; death for him is always the "severance" of the two "components", which should remain united. The elf Finrod says to the wisewoman Andreth: "Do you not think that the separation of soul and body could be experienced as a liberation, as a returning home?" and Andreth replies: "No, we do not think so because this would be to disparage the body and is a thought of Darkness, for in the incarnate world it is unnatural" (Shippey 2007a, 317).

As Ralph C. Wood writes, this is a "radical non-Platonic turn."[21] Claudio A. Testi, too, writes: "[Philosophically] approximately one could say that it seems to be an Aristotelian element in a Platonic context."[22] Damien Casey agrees: theologically Tolkien is aware that the heart of Christianity is the incarnation, notwithstanding the atrophy of this heritage in the Platonic tradition.[23]

---

21 Wood 2003, 159. Anne Mathie (2003) comments: "The body and the world of matter are not something to be escaped or transcended as such. To separate the body from the spirit, the dweller from the house, is considered to be a terrible thing."
22 Claudio A. Testi, "Tolkien's *Legendarium* as a *Meditatio Mortis*", pp. 39-68 in this volume.
23 "Here we touch upon what I believe one of the most important challenges for Christian theology; our Platonic heritage has meant that the radically incarnational insight that is at the heart of Christianity has remained underdeveloped or atrophied. The incarnation's radical affirmation of the material world, however, lies at the very heart of Tolkien's theological anthropology" (Casey 2004). And Shippey observes: "The theology of 'body and soul' took some time to develop, but it was a favourite theme for Anglo-Saxon poets and homilists, and there is one mystery there. One of the most popular sermon collections of the Middle Ages is known as the 'sermones ad fratres in eremo', there are hundreds of manuscripts of it, but it is very poor both theologically and linguistically (the Latin is not distinguished). No-one knows where it came from, and the *Patrologia* editors suggest it must be Belgian, because it often mentions beer! But it is older than they think (because Anglo-Saxon homilists used it) and beer does not have to be Belgian (except to a French editor, perhaps). The point is, though, that by Aquinas's time the theology is clear: one should NOT say that the body is evil and the soul is good. But this terrible simplifying view is what sermons, and poems, creep back to. Good poets, like Andrew Marvell, are careful to keep the balance. Poor ones, or thoughtless ones, are likely to make it a fight between good and evil. I'm sure Tolkien knew the theology of this and was careful to give full value to the Incarnation, perhaps the more so because he had read works like the two Anglo-Saxon 'Soul and Body' poems" (from an email to FM, dated June 27th, 2009). I verified that among the books formerly owned by Tolkien (and now accessible at the English Faculty Library in Oxford) there is an *Old English Homilies* (edited by R. Morris), London, N. Trübner & Co, 1868, and among those homilies there is one entitled *Hic Dicendum est de Quadragesima* where the author underlines the idea that the

This "non-Platonic turn", Wood acutely explains, is also an implicit – but interesting and well-founded – explanation of the motivations behind Platonic dualism: it would seem that Men, or rather their "souls", possess the memory of "another world" from which they have become estranged and to which they seek to return (the Platonic soul which tends towards its original Hyperuranic homeland). *Yet* Andreth denies this, for her soul and body are each essential to the other, and thus their "severance" is a calamity caused by Melkor. So the "nostalgia" that the Elves have noticed in Men is *not* the desire for a world different to this one, but rather an effort to return to the harmony and unity between body and spirit which were lost by Men in the rebellion against Ilúvatar, and remain lost in corrupted Arda. Plato confuses the moral and theological problem with the anthropological and metaphysical, indicating "another world" for the "soul" when he should have indicated moral conversion for Men (Wood 2003, 158-160). Casey comments that the Platonic "salvation" to "another world" is merely an escape from evil and pain, but it does not in fact save Man's history, his identity, his own unique and unrepeatable human reality (which is in accordance with God's will); in order to save these things the salvation of *this* world must be included.[24]

Although the original Jewish/Christian message is both non-Platonic and in some respects anti-Platonic, it has for many centuries been spread widely by means of Platonic categories. Tolkien is, however, a Christian of the 20th century, a century in which theology and Christian spirituality have strongly criticized the fundamental category of Platonism, so-called "dualism" (a category which had already been philosophically opposed, in different ways, by both Hegelianism and 19th-century Marxist and positivist materialism), and he follows the debate which for him was contemporary, observing explicitly, for example, that his friend Lewis was not philosophically a dualist, but had a

---

body loves what the soul hates.

24 "Salvation makes no sense unless it includes the world. Salvation from the world is no salvation as much as an attempted flight from the disease. But the healing of the world will not simply restore the world to what it was in some imagined prelapsarian dawn, but will be something genuinely new. As Saint Paul explained in his epistle to the Romans: 'It is not for its own purposes that creation had frustration imposed on it, but for the purposes of him who imposed it – with the intention that the whole creation itself might be freed from its slavery to corruption and brought into the same glorious freedom as the children of God.' The difficulty with the Platonic flight from the world that is the more traditional path of sanctity is that it leaves Morgoth's ring intact. The salvation of the world entails that the ring of the world must also be taken up into God. And it is we who are to be the agents of the world's divinisation" (Casey 2004).

"dualist" imagination (*Letters* no. 291). And this was because, as Christopher Garbowski notes, "a general philosophical movement" had influenced Tolkien: in this the value accorded to psychosomatic phenomena had rendered obsolete a material conception of the separate "soul", thus permitting a return to biblical monism (Garbowski 2004, 157).

In "this" world happiness is difficult to achieve and – in practice – experienced only as "salvation". Shippey recalls an old Scottish tale – that Tolkien knew – in which an elf asks an aged human if salvation is possible for a being such as she, and he replies: "No, salvation is only for the sinful sons of Adam" (Shippey 2005, 238). Why only for the sinners? One might say by definition, as Jesus said: "I have not come to save the righteous, but the sinners" (*Matthew* 19,13); in other words everyone. Also remember that for many centuries Christianity considered the "second death" central: the death of the soul, spiritual death, and not the first ("Whosoever shall seek to save his life shall lose it" *Luke* 17,33).

In fact, mankind can think of death only as *quia est*, not as *quod est*, for we know that it exists, but not what it is, because we cannot form an idea based on experience, neither a conscious idea nor an unconscious one. Sigmund Freud – in all phases of his thought – was convinced of this. Summarizing and commenting upon Freud's notions of death, the Freudian psychoanalyst Franco de Masi (2202, 21) writes that the "idea" we have of death can be constructed only on the basis of experiences from life, for example on the basis of experiences of relationships which are all ultimately marked by separation or mourning.[25] This leads us to imagine death as a sort of life in which we perceive ourselves to be isolated from all other human beings, or in other words the idea we have of death is that of "psychic death", since our psychic life is formed, developed and maintained through interpersonal relationships. Many psychoanalysts have observed in relation to their clinical cases that such an "idea" of death may assume a devastating concreteness in psychotic patients; in these people physical death becomes a terrible prospect, because for them it constitutes the limit which puts an end to the possibility of correcting their

---

25 W.A. Senior (2000, 173) writes: "I would like to propose one concept that subsumes many of the others and that concomitantly provides Tolkien with his most pervasive and unifying component of atmosphere and mood; the sustained and grieved sense of loss, of which death is but one form, that floods through the history of Middle-earth." Concerning the problem of death and its connection with Freud's psychoanalysis see also the essay by Roberto Arduini in this volume.

psychic death – the notion that they are inconsistent and without significance for others.²⁶ Vincent Ferré, in the section "L' Aliénation et la Folie" of his book *Tolkien. Sur le rivage de la Terre du Milieu* rightly observes that in *The Lord of the Rings* the Ring either drives people mad or attempts to do so (Boromir, Gandalf, Galadriel, Aragorn, Bilbo, Frodo, Gollum) (cf. Ferré 2001, 253-255).

Amongst the psychotics to be found in Tolkien's stories are the kings of Númenor such as Ar-Pharazôn and the Nazgûl (former kings), who have in common the search for power and the search for immortality; in both groups the latter seems connected to the former. The evasion of death is sought for the personal and unconscious motive that the striving after power has led to an empty life, without meaning, and the character then tries to find more time because he is unable to accept his own "completion", unable to reach an end. Whereas, as Tolkien wrote in a letter:

> Death is not an Enemy! [...] the message was the hideous peril of confusing true 'immortality' with limitless serial longevity. Freedom from Time, and clinging to Time. The confusion is the work of the Enemy and one of the chief causes of human disaster. Compare the death of Aragorn with a Ringwraith. (*Letters* no. 208)

The paradoxical logical implication of this step is that "true immortality" coincides with death.

Immediately afterwards, Tolkien adds: "The Elves call 'death' the Gift of God (to Men). Their temptation is different: towards a fainéant melancholy, burdened with Memory, leading to an attempt to halt Time." For the Elves the temptation is not to seek to have more time, as Ar-Pharazôn and the Nazgûl try to do, but to stop time. There are hence two different "escapes" from that "Death" which coincides with "true Immortality": "serial longevity" (that of power-thirsty human kings) and the "hoarding memory" of the Elves (*Letters* no. 211).²⁷ Despite the pompous title of "Immortals" which other less long-

---

26 See de Masi 2002, 96, 129, 107-109. In his essay in this volume (pp. 193-208), Giampaolo Canzonieri examines the connection between physical and moral pain, and the fear of death.
27 With regard to this point, see also Peter Kreeft (although, in my opinion, there is some confusion here). In Tolkien there are two Immortalities: the false "serial longevity" and the true one, i.e. a natural desire to escape death, and this is the eucatastrophe described in *Leaf by Niggle*; true immortality is a self-purification, a self-sacrifice. There are also two Deaths; the good one is the death of selfishness and is associated with true immortality. Tolkien writes that the greatest acts of the human spirit are acts of self-denial (cf. Kreeft 2005, 96-100). See also "Death, Immortality and their Escapes. Memory

lived Middle-earth peoples accord to the Elves, this is not strictly true, for theirs is "strictly longevity co-extensive with the life of Arda" (*Letters* no. 212).

These two "escapes" from Death/Immortality – either by means of "serial" or "natural" longevity – have different aims: the slaves of power wish to have "more future" (albeit a future which is not unknown or open to change, but "serial") in order to increase power (and thus unconsciously deceive themselves that in this way their lives will acquire meaning). The Elves, on the contrary, desire to have "less future" due to their idealization of the past, since their memory of the past is not an instrument which serves the future, but rather a "hoarding", an avid treasuring. The slaves of power have no memory of the past; the Elves have a "burdened" memory. The common feature between the two groups is that neither believes in or hopes for an unknown future, open and new. And both are attracted to power! The Elves too seek a form of power, that of being able to stop change, which specifically means ageing, because they would like to keep things "fresh and fair". And this lesser power of theirs is tied to the greater power of Sauron and the slaves, and in fact when the latter fall, the Elves' power comes to an end (*Letters* no. 181). It is as if – when the power which tends always to dominate others' wills (and needs longevity to succeed) collapses – the idealization of the past and refusal of change (ageing) also come to an end.[28]

In summary, we can say that remembering the past is a good thing only if it serves to clarify future moral action ("historia magistra vitae"), as Nietzsche and Croce emphasized in their criticism of antiquarian historiography.[29] Since the Elves in Tolkien's fiction represent an aspect of real anthropology,[30] we might say that by means of the Elves' natural and the slaves' serial longevity

---

and Longevity" by Andrea Monda in this volume (pp. 155-173). Concerning the connection between fall, mortality and the machine see the study "The Wrong Path of the Sub-creator. From the Fall to the Machine and the Escape from Mortality" by Alberto Ladavas in this volume (pp. 117-132).

28 John D. Rateliff (cf. 2006, 87-88) summarizes this point. The common property shared by all the Rings of Power is their ability to slow down the decay of that which is loved and Tolkien judges this to be a fundamental error of the Elves. The Númenóreans want to live forever in an infinite present and the Elves want the past to last forever. Both errors seek to frustrate the capacity of the future to make its own contributions, but Ilúvatar gives time and death to Men which allow them to create; the present is not a blank slate, but a freshly cleaned slate (because the past must give way to the present). The Elves, who cling to the past, are forced to fade away with it.

29 See Nietzsche 1873 and Croce 1938.

30 "Elves are certain aspects of Men and their talents and desires, incarnated in my little world" (*Letters* no. 153).

he wishes to portray (amongst other things!) a pathological aspect of human nature (the "psychotic limit"); namely the distortions that a life which lasts 'too long' and avoiding contact with Death (which is the only 'true immortality'), may provoke.[31] This observation concerning the distortions caused by a life 'too long' is also supported, I think, by features of Tolkien's own life, as I will try to demonstrate below. At first, however, I will discuss the philosophical consequences of this anthropology, for example on the eschatology – the reflection on 'final things'[32] – or, as is also said, on the 'ultimate purpose'[33] of human life.

## 3. Eschatology

Franco de Masi rightly states that it is not easy to discern to what extent the *thought* of death is an obstacle to life and to which extent, on the other hand, it supports the reflection on the value and meaning of life (de Masi 2002, 23). It seems clearer that the *negation* of death leads to blindness to the real experience of the passage of time. This negation does not coincide with religious belief in 'immortality'; it is in fact necessary to understand exactly what is meant by this concept (de Masi 2002, 101). The great historical religions have at least two aspects: one profound and authentic, and one superficial and escapist. Garbowski observes with good reason that

> a very simplistic vision of afterlife in the common religious imagination causes many to think of immortality in terms of what Tolkien called serial living: a continuation of life as we know it, even if at a higher plane. This might be why instead of dealing directly with the problem of an afterlife in his mythology, the author proposes *the artistic construction of the Elf Beings themselves who demonstrate the shortcomings of immortality as simple deathlessness* […] This might

---

31 Harm Schelmhaas, in the context of the panel "Mortality and Immortality" held in Birmingham in 2005, replied to the question of why the righteous Men (such as Aragorn and the first kings of Númenor) are long-lived, that the more a person "can sustain the life, the more he appreciates the gift of Mortality at the end" (Wells 2008, 46). I do not agree, and offer the following reply. The idea of longevity as a 'reward' is an Old-Testament residue in Tolkien (the patriarchs) that is perhaps also present in the idea of the longevity of the Elves, a race which never forms an alliance with Melkor or Sauron; but it is an anodyne and aborted idea. In fact in many of Tolkien's stories righteous Men (and Elves) die prematurely, and Tolkien could not have forgotten the lives of many Christian believers and New Testament protagonists, first and foremost that of Jesus. It is clearly not necessary to be long-lived in order to appreciate the gift of immortality!
32 In the Christian tradition these 'final things' are Death, Judgement, Hell and Heaven.
33 The 'ultimate purpose' is also (from a different standpoint) known as the 'greatest good'. The subject is always Happiness, seen either as a principle (final cause) of human actions or as a criterion of preference for comparison between various 'goods' when these are in conflict and a choice must be made.

partially be understood as death being a rest from a world full of suffering and a life that ultimately does not offer full answers.[34]

Shippey notes that whereas in *Paradise Lost* Milton considers death to be a just punishment for sin, "the *Silmarillion* seems to want to persuade us to see death as a potential gift or reward."[35]

Paradoxical! For Tolkien the "reward" is not a sort of 'reawakening' followed by a sort of continuation of life, surrounded by lights, celestial music and in the embrace of loved ones, as in popular fantasies of immortality, but it *is* death ("true immortality")!

Here we should remember that through the philosophical tradition – even in the Christian one, as in Aquinas[36] – the so-called "eternity" is quite different from "endless time". Time concerns change, while eternity instead concerns immutability, "tota simul existens", and therefore, if immortality is meant as "eternal life", it is *not* a life lasting for an endless time. As Renée Vink rightly observes:

> Just like true immortality has often been confused with serial longevity, there is a related concept that has often been confused with neverending time. I am referring to eternity. Though Tolkien does not use the word, I would venture to say that "eternity" is the state of existence where what he calls true immortality has its proper place. Death may not be the enemy, but Time surely is. (Vink 2008, 127)

Tolkien writes that death is *not* punishment for sin, but inherent to human nature (biological *and* psychological), and attempting to avoid it is both *wicked*

---

34 Garbowski 2004, 168, italics added.
35 Shippey 2005, 237. But Gregory Bassham does not agree: "I must disagree with your claim that for Tolkien 'death is not punishment for sin, but inherent to human nature.' Rather, Tolkien presents men as originally immortal (*MR* 332) who, like elves, could die at will, but unlike the elves, could leave the walls of Arda by means of a bodily assumption (*MR* 333). This power was lost (taken away by Eru) when the primeval humans 'fell' and worshipped Morgoth in the depths of time. Thus, Tolkien's view is essentially the same as Paul's: 'the wages of sin is death.' Contra Shippey, there is no contradiction in seeing death as both a 'gift' (because a healing of world-weariness) and a punishment for sin (because a deprivation of the natural felicity that would have been the fate of unfallen man)" (from an email to FM, dated June 15th, 2009). In my reply I reminded him of *Letters* no. 156 and added: "But I agree with you that there is no contradiction in thinking that Death is *both* a gift *and* a punishment. It is a classic Augustinian and Thomistic doctrine saying that 'poena curat culpam.' And moreover, leaving aside Augustine and Aquinas, I think that this is what really happens in human life: the right punishment is a necessary (even if not sufficient) factor of the healing of the human sin." Claudio A. Testi also, in his second study in this volume, examines the connection between human nature and death.
36 *Summa Theologiae*, pars prima, quaestio 10, art. 1.

(because in conflict with nature) and *stupid* "because Death is a release from the weariness of Time" (*Letters* no. 156). Indeed, these two causes of escapism seem more likely to come to mind to those who are 'getting on in years': a young person might well disapprove of both, and particularly the second. And yet the young also die. John Garth commented that the poem *Kortirion*, which Tolkien wrote in 1915 at the age of 23, possessed typically Tolkienian melancholy for a world that was drifting away; the summer he regards with nostalgia could be seen as his childhood or the pre-war past, and the winter as the only (lethal) future offered to young people like himself.[37]

We know, though, that Tolkien's future was not to be war-time death, but marriage to Edith, children, philology at Oxford, writing tales and books and worldwide literary success. What we may imagine about the future is one thing; what it turns out to be is quite another. Two philosophers who were Tolkien's contemporaries, Croce (born in 1866) and Popper (born in 1902), have strongly emphasized that the future is completely unknowable, not a field to be studied, but open for the application of our will, for our programme of action.[38] Shippey, commenting upon the development of *The Lord of the Rings* with respect to the Mirror of Galadriel and the palantíri, notes that Tolkien wants to warn us of a great danger: "too much looking into the future can erode the will to action in the present"; one should not "speculate", but rather "get on with one's work" with determination and perseverance, and "this mental attitude may be rewarded beyond hope" (Shippey 2007a, 380-383).

The 'final things' are Death (the end of life), Judgement (of the significance of one's life), Heaven (if life had meaning) and Hell (if it had none), and all the four of them always (and only) are directed towards the future. And this is true both for the old and for the young. In the song that Frodo, who was

---

[37] Garth 2003, 109. This must be compared with a poetic note written by Sigmund Freud, also in 1915, for which he won the prestigious German literary prize named after Goethe, which was entitled *On Transience*. Freud wrote of a walk in the mountains in the company of a young poet who, whilst he admired the natural beauty which surrounded them, expressed a deep sadness at the thought of its impermanence (Freud 1976b, 173-176). In this volume Simone Bonechi examines the problems of death, war and memory in Middle-earth.

[38] Cf. Croce 1915; Popper 1957. Popper writes that he arrived at this conviction about the impossibility of predicting the future in the winter of 1919-1920 "through disappointment with the mythic, urgent advent of the worldwide Communist revolution" (Popper 1957, 7).

a young Hobbit, "just out of his tweens" (*LotR*, FR.I.2), sings in the Old Forest it is said – to *encourage* the wayfarer, not to deter him! – that "to east and west every forest ends" (*ibid.*). Shippey comments that it is difficult not to see a reference to life and death (the "end" of the forest) in these words; the travellers will set off towards the light of the sun (Shippey 2005, 190). In fact, every life has a beginning and an end, is defined by its limits. And why, according to Tolkien, does this finiteness serve to create hope? If it was only because our present ills will cease with death, this would be merely the Epicurean idea of ataraxia and would not be applicable to a young person in good physical and mental condition. Bill Davis suggests a more interesting motivation: life's finiteness can be considered good because it holds out the prospect of escaping the repetition of things already known, whether far off (for the young) or nearby (for the old).[39]

More profoundly, it may contain the message that non-transience itself would be a bad thing, because it would involve a necessary fixation of pride: anything which we believe to keep 'forever' is a source of pride or at least leads us to forget our limits,[40] our defects, and blinds us to seeing *other* things and *new* things. Other and new things turn up every day, but it is difficult to see them or, once noticed, to take them in; various fears and aspects of pride block us. At the end of his book on philosophers and death (their thoughts on death and their actual deaths!), Simon Critchley observes that it is as though the life of each one was held in the grip of pre-existing structures: the evolution of the species, the historical situation, the personal Freudian "family story"; and the desires which such structures provoke in us threaten to suffocate us. We cannot refuse these unasked-for gifts of nature and culture, but we can transform the way in which we accept them and we can stand more fully in the light that throws the shadow of our mortality: "It is my wager that if we can begin to accept our limitedness, then we might be able to give up

---

[39] Davis uses the metaphor of a house with no exit (the Elves' lives) and another house with an exit (Men's lives), and asks where this door leads – to a good place? To nothing? And he concludes: "Feeling trapped in a world with no escape, Elves envy even the possibility of annihilation. In uncertainty and despair most Men in Middle-earth fear that their fate is annihilation" (Davis 2003, 127).

[40] Towards the end of his long life, Norberto Bobbio wrote: "Everything that had a beginning has an end. Why should my life not have one? Should the end of my life, unlike that of other events, both natural and historical, be a new beginning? Only that which did not have a beginning has no end. But that which has neither a beginning nor an end is eternal" (Bobbio 1996, 41).

certain of the fantasies of infantile omnipotence; to be a creature is to accept our limitedness in a way that does not result in disaffection and despair; it is rather the condition for courage and endurance" (Critchley 2008, 280-281).

A sense of humility could therefore open us to 'final things' (to see different and new things), and an awareness of death could encourage such humility, as Christian and Buddhist traditions of asceticism have emphasized for centuries. With respect to two episodes in *The Lord of the Rings*, Shippey asks: what does it mean that Frodo in the Dead Marshes sees the faces of Elves and Orcs similarly covered in algae and dirt? And what does it mean that Merry in the barrow sees the face of the dead nobleman overlying that of the Barrow-wight? Perhaps that *all* glory decomposes (cf. Shippey 2005, 217)? It would seem so, at least for Tolkien, who wrote in a letter that the victors cannot enjoy the victory as they had imagined, for the more they struggle to achieve it, the more victory will be a delusion (*Letters* no. 181).

Perhaps in death there is not only the humility (and relief) of finiteness. Bearing in mind Tolkien's Christian belief, Shippey sees a connection between the theme of the Resurrection and a moment in the *The Lord of the Rings* (RK.V.4). At precisely the moment when Gandalf is about to be struck by the Lord of the Ringwraiths (who calls himself "Death") a cock crows and, as though in reply, the sound of war horns is heard. It is a reference to the New Testament account of the cock's crow which Peter heard and made him weep bitterly, immediately recalling Jesus's words. This sound means that the Resurrection has occurred and from that moment Peter's desperation and his fear of death have been overcome, that day follows night, that life conquers death, that a larger cycle exists above the smaller, that he who fears for his life will lose it and that dying fearlessly is not a defeat (cf. Shippey 2005, 214-215). Here Shippey suggests that the Resurrection coincides – in personal reality, not mythical fantasy – with the choice of death (the future martyr Peter) for love (of Jesus).

Bill Davis notes that Arwen prefers finiteness with love to infinity without, almost as though Tolkien were saying that it is impossible to have love without having death, and that even if death is not chosen for its own sake, then love is, and death accepted as the necessary price (cf. Davis 2003, 135). And Sam, says Shippey, returns to his home in the Shire not out of necessity, but despite having another option which he refuses – that of going to the Undying Lands with Frodo. He, just like Arwen, chooses mortality for love (love for Rosie, Elanor and the Hobbits of the Shire). This choice – according to Shippey – makes the ending of *The Lord of the Rings* sad, "but while on the one hand Sam has come to Death, for love, he has also come back to life, for he has his long and successful life ahead of him."[41] Arwen could have gone to the Undying Lands taking with her the *memory* of her love for Aragorn, but – writes Richard C. West – chooses to live this love and accept death that will take her beyond the "boundaries of the world" (West 2006, 326-327). These Undying Lands seem, then, to offer rest and escape from pain, but lacking in 'finiteness' because they are within, not outside, the "boundaries of the world"; death, on the other hand, seems tied to both 'finiteness' (beyond the "boundaries of the world") and love.

The word 'love' has many meanings, generally not incompatible with each other. In philosophical and religious traditions it is often emphasized that love is not only a sentiment, but also a concrete action for good, that it has both a content and a purpose: love for one's family, for one's country or for science are linked by the idea of having a task to perform, a mission. If "God so loved the world that he gave his only begotten son [...]" (*John* 3,16), then the Platonic idea of life as "exile" is mistaken; life is rather a 'mission'. Damien Casey observes: "The difficulty with the Platonic flight from the world that is the more traditional path of sanctity is that it leaves Morgoth's Ring intact. The salvation of the world entails that the ring of

---

41 Tom Shippey, email dated October 5th, 2008: "Turning to the other issue of sadness, why is 'Well, I'm back' so sad? I would say: 1) First, it is formally meaningless, in that it says nothing that needs to be said. Of course he's back, otherwise he would not be there to say 'well, I'm back.' So what he says demands another interpretation. This is what linguists call an 'implicature'. 2) What is meant to be implied is, perhaps, that he has come back when he had another option. And that option was to go with Frodo to the Undying Lands. 3) So he has come back to the land of mortality, and made, so to speak, *il gran rifiuto*, just like Arwen. This is in a way heroic of him, but taking that choice, as Elrond says, is a bitter one. 4) But while, on the one hand, he has come back to Death, for love, he has also come back to life, for he has his long and successful life ahead of him, Rose, children, grandchildren, Mayor of Michel Delving etc. 5) So it is also a very ambiguous moment. (And I think Tolkien perhaps should not have modified it by stating in the Appendices that Sam in the end takes the other choice and goes to the Grey Havens, once Rose has died. Better to leave it as he left the poem on St Brendan, with the person who has seen the Undying Lands nevertheless returning to and dying in Middle-earth. But Tolkien was always ambiguous about the voyage over the Sundering Sea. Some of his characters go, some refuse to go, some come back …) But I agree with Swanwick, or Swanwick's small son, that it is a very unexpected and non-Hollywood sort of ending, which Jackson did well to keep."

the world must also be taken up into God. And it is we who are to be the agents of the world's divinisation."[42]

And Shippey – commenting on the "walking songs" which appear throughout *The Lord of the Rings* up until when Frodo sings one before leaving Middle-earth – notes that they express a pain that is ancient, although soothed by the earth's beauty (Shippey 2005, 188-189). But why this suffering? For a world which does not die? And what world would that be? For Plato, it is something "other" from the one in which we live. But, if we take our distance from Plato, perhaps we can manage to see that the "world which does not die" – for which we experience this nostalgic pain – is none other than this one, or rather something *in* this one: the moral values which should be followed in this world, values for which we feel nostalgia since we live far from them as a result of our various defects. Our mission is to pursue them for love of themselves and of the world which needs them.[43]

Geoffrey Smith wrote to Tolkien on the occasion of the death of their mutual friend Robert Gilson that he did not care whether their friendly and intellectual fellowship achieved social success or received explicit recognition, because it was spiritual in nature and as such transcended mortality and was "as permanently inseparable as Thor and his hammer"; the influence to be exerted on the world was "a tradition which forty years from now will still be as strong to us (if we are alive, and if we are not) as it is today" (Garth 2003, 180).

On the other hand, the truth is that we all have a mission, even those considered "bad": Tolkien wrote in a letter that there are people who *appear* "damnable", but their "damnability" is not measurable on a macrocosmic scale (and in fact could be a force for good) (*Letters* no. 181). If even those who appear wicked to us have a mission, how can we visualize or understand *our* mission in life? Tolkien wrote, in a letter to his niece, "Why did God include us in his plan? We can only say that he has done,

---

42 Casey underlines how the reincarnated Elves normally remain in Aman, returning to Middle-earth only if they have a particular mission to carry out (cf. Casey 2004; see also Amaranth 2007).
43 I should like to recall here the views of Benedetto Croce (cf. Croce 1922) concerning the themes of death, immortality and the individual and his mission.

and therefore we cannot reply to the question of what is the meaning of life" (*Letters* no. 310).

This sentence of Tolkien's is full of humility, limpidly Socratic and open to 'last things' and 'ultimate purpose'. Anne Mathie observes that "the closing chapters of *The Lord of the Rings* are a portrait of mortality"; the Fellowship of the Ring has achieved its mission, Gandalf and the High Elves have won the war, Frodo has saved the world, and now they are leaving Middle-earth and many good things will be forgotten.[44] Thus the 'missionary' leaves, but the effects of the mission remain in the world. Shippey writes about the brooklet which runs through Mordor, seemingly for no purpose, but which is actually as useful as any water could be (to Frodo, Sam and Middle-earth): apparent failure, but success in practice (Shippey 2005, 219). That which seems to be the death of the streamlet becomes instead a cause of life; the death of each of us – Tolkien perhaps implies here – might seem to render useless the life of each of us, whereas a grain of wheat that does not die does not bear fruit. Our personal, individual life is finished, bounded by many things, especially death; but it is – perhaps! – part of a plan which includes it and extends beyond.

## 4. Philosophy of history

With reference to TCBS, their intellectual friendship club, Geoffrey Smith wrote to his friend Tolkien shortly before his death in the war:

> The death of one of its members cannot, I am determined, dissolve the TCBS. [...] Death can make us loathsome and helpless as individuals, but it cannot put an end to the immortal four! [...] May God bless you, my dear John Ronald, and may you say the things I have tried to say long after I am not there, if such be my lot.[45]

Similarly, after the death of their friend Rob Gilson, Christopher Weisman wrote to Smith: "I believe we are not now getting on without Rob; we are getting on with Rob. It is by no means nonsense, though we have no

---

44 Mathie (2003) adds "This has to be one of literature's saddest happy endings."
45 Letter of February 3rd, 1916, quoted in Garth 2003, 118-119, 177.

reason to suppose, that Rob is still of the TCBS."[46] In the words of these young men it is as if their aspirations and experiences of friendship were an immortal 'X' over and above the lives of human individuals.

This idea is transferred by Tolkien to *The Lord of the Rings*. In the novel we find with a sense of 'death' given by a continuing memory of people and episodes from the past, which structured and caused the events lived by the characters in their present, as Shippey has observed (cf. 2005, 308-317); and in the novel we also find (as in the letters to the friends of his youth) Tolkien's intention to consign to future generations (the "Red Book of Westmarch"!) the memory of present happenings which will become the past, as Ferré says.[47] And it is not merely remembering: the plot of the story and the characters' interpersonal relationships continually communicate and demonstrate to us how individual destinies are closely and necessarily interwoven, in life as in death; the relationship between Frodo and Sam (and Gollum!) is a good example of this.[48] This idea of the interpersonal quality of salvation is typical of twentieth-century Christian theology – it is not a coincidence that in the letter quoted above Weisman mentioned the "Communion of Saints", which strongly emphasized throughout the 20th century the biblical and patristic message of "collective eschatology".[49] Shippey notes that the entire story of Middle-earth is bound by a condition of interpersonality: it is like a limbo in which the un-baptised dead await the Day of Judgement (for Tolkien, the events he narrated were set in pre-Christian times) when they will be reunited with their baptised and saved descendants (Shippey 2005, 202-203).

---

46 Letter of August 30th,1916 that Smith later sent to Tolkien, quoted in Garth 2003, 185.
47 "Tombeau, monument, le texte de Tolkien perpétue la mémoire des victimes de la Guerre de l'Anneau, du passage à l'Histoire et du passage du temps, comme la chanson qui égrène le nom des disparus" (Ferré 2001, 274).
48 Cf. Ferré (2001, 197-199): alliances and groups are necessities of life, couples survive and those alone die, because individuals are overcome by hubris, "la solitude conduit avec certitude à la mort." Anne Mathie (2003) observes: "This fertility, this willingness to pass life on to a new generation rather than grasping for 'endless life unchanging' is the Hobbits' great strength, as it should likewise be mankind's proper strength. It makes them at once humbler than immortals, since they place less confidence in their own individual abilities, and more hopeful, since their own individual defeats are not the end of everything."
49 For a synthesis of this development – which in Catholic teaching culminated with Chapter VII (*The Eschatological Nature of the Pilgrim Church*) of the *Lumen Gentium* Constitution of the Vatican Council II on "God's People" – see the excellent book on historical and systematic theology by Ruiz de la Peña (1981).

But during the course of the 20th century, outside of the visible churches (perhaps earlier than inside them), the widespread sensitivity of the century for "interpersonality" was manifested in many fields: in political movements, pedagogy, clinical psychology, historiographical research and philosophy. Though he made no explicit references, Tolkien probably knew the philosopher Robin G. Collingwood;[50] they were in the same places at similar times (both Fellows at Pembroke College), and the latter was well known inside and outside academia for his writings on the philosophy of history and his specific historical research regarding Roman Britain. Collingwood's most important work[51] is *The Idea of*

---

50 See Alex Lewis 2009, 15, where the author suggests that the 1939 Andrew Lang Lecture ("On Fairy-Stories") was provided to Tolkien by Collingwood himself. And also Tom Shippey: "I know little or nothing about philosophy, but one philosopher (of history) whom Tolkien must have known and *may* have taken an interest in was Robin G. Collingwood. I think they were both at Pembroke College, and Collingwood certainly took close interest in fairy-tales, while Tolkien probably knew and respected his father, the Icelandicist (and writer of historical novels) W.G. Collingwood" (from an email to FM, February 7th, 2009). And also Dimitra Fimi: "Tolkien certainly knew R.G. Collingwood. In p. 264, note 1 of Collingwood's and Myres's *Roman Britain* the authors acknowledge Tolkien's help with the philology of the name Sulis, the Celto-Roman goddess of the hot springs at Bath. It also seems that Collingwood was the reason why Tolkien was consulted on the name "Nodens" found in inscriptions at the excavation of Lydney Park (Tolkien's piece has now been reprinted in *Tolkien Studies* 4, 2007, 177-183)" (from an email to FM, April 5th, 2009). And also Douglas Anderson, referring to his unpublished lecture of 2004: "Much of the work that I did do was on the similarity of interests between W.G. Collingwood, his son Robin, and JRRT, as well as what I could piece together of R.G. Collingwood's and JRR Tolkien's friendship. I barely touched on Collingwood's view of history, and there's a lot that could be said there" (from an email to FM, April 8th, 2009). And Claudio A. Testi came across the information in one of Tolkien's manuscripts (A 14/2, folios 28 and 29, at the Bodleian Library) where he, after quoting Bede on the name "Britain", observes that Collingwood is writing an introduction to the history of Roman Britain, but, being mainly a philosopher, he refers neither to literature (unless philosophical) nor to language (taken from an email to FM, August 7th, 2009). I note that in his book *Philosophy of Enchantment* (one section of which is entitled "On the Fairy Tale"), written at about the same time when Tolkien was preparing his lecture "On Fairy-Stories", Collingwood deals with themes such as the geographic and historical diffusion of the fairy tales, their relation to "archetypes" and their function for adults rather than for children. All these themes feature prominently in Tolkien's lecture, too. I think that the recent biography of Collingwood (Inglis 2009, 105, 201, 223), notwithstanding three mentions of Tolkien's name, is rather superficial on the relationship between the two authors.
51 Amongst contemporary philosophers, Collingwood's ideas correspond in particular to those of the Italian Benedetto Croce about whom he wrote several times and whose ideas (on aesthetics and especially philosophy of history) he spread, directly and indirectly, in the English-speaking world. William H. Dray, author of the most recent and complete study on Collingwood which documents his profound and lasting influence on Anglo-American philosophy of history (Dray 1995, 26), felt it necessary to underline that it was untrue that the English philosopher was "little more than a popularizer of Italian ideas." In his intellectual biography of Croce, Fausto Nicolini writes: "The English philosopher with whom Croce had the closest and most frequent exchanges of letters and personal contacts was R.G. Collingwood, who died at little more than fifty years old in 1943. Benedetto Croce began correspondence with him, then a young Fellow of Pembroke College, Oxford, in 1912-13, when Collingwood translated for the publisher Macmillan Croce's monograph on Vico. There followed the translations of *Contributo alla critica di me stesso, Iniziazione all'Estetica del Settecento, Frammenti di Etica* and also the article on Aesthetics for the 14th edition of the *Encyclopaedia Britannica*. These contacts further intensified in 1923 when Croce went to Oxford where he was subsequently to return twice (Nicolini 1962, 485).

*History* (1946). Its central idea is that of "re-enactment": historical thought (not only on the part of professional historians, but by everyone) consists of *re-living* the thoughts of people from the past.[52] This idea of re-living inspired the two 'time travel' novels which Tolkien left unfinished: "The Lost Road" and "The Notion Club Papers." Verlyn Flieger has discovered that in these Tolkien was directly inspired by a 1927 book, *An Experiment with Time*, by the non-academic philosopher J.W. Dunne (Flieger 1995, 39-44). The idea of 'immortality' which it contains – and which Tolkien abandoned in his novels – is exemplified by two persons who, in dreamlike or excited mental states, experience the reincarnation of persons or repetition of events from the past, however remote. The probable influence of Collingwood on Tolkien – if it should ever be proved – would have been different to that of Dunne, because he makes reference not to excited or dreamlike states, but to fully conscious and rational – critical – thought: Aragorn and Arwen "re-live" the stories of Beren and Lúthien inasmuch as they remember them and think about them, but they also judge them, and thus add to them in an original and creative way.

At the inception of the philosophy of history, several fundamental choices must be made: one must decide, for example, if history is cyclic and thus "nihil sub sole novum" as – more than Qohèlet – the ancient Gentiles thought (for example, with great clarity, the emperor and philosopher Marcus Aurelius); or, as the ancient Jews held and subsequently our Western Christian civilization

---

52 "The processes of nature can therefore be properly described as sequences of mere events, but those of history cannot. They are not processes of mere events but processes of actions, which have an inner side, consisting of processes of thought; and what the historian is looking for is these processes of thought. All history is the history of thought. But how does the historian discern the thoughts which he is trying to discover? There is only one way in which it can be done: by rethinking them in his own mind. [...] The history of thought, and therefore all history, is the re-enactment of past thought in the historian's own mind. This re-enactment is only accomplished, in the case of Plato and Caesar respectively, so far as the historian brings to bear on the problem all the powers of his own mind and all his knowledge of philosophy and politics. It is not a passive surrender to the spell of another's mind; it is a labour of active and therefore critical thinking. The historian not only re-enacts past thought, he re-enacts it in the context of his own knowledge and therefore, in re-enacting it, criticizes it, forms his own judgement of its value, corrects whatever errors he can discern in it. [...] Thought can never be mere object. To know someone else's activity of thinking is possible only on the assumption that this same activity can be re-enacted in one's own mind. In that sense, to know 'what someone is thinking' (or 'has thought') involves thinking it for oneself. [...] And this does not appear a satisfactory account of historical thought only to persons who embrace the fundamental error of mistaking for history that form of pseudo-history which Croce has called 'philological history': persons who think that history is nothing more than scholarship or learning, and would assign to the historian the self-contradictory task of discovering (for example) 'what Plato thought' without inquiring 'whether it is true'" (Collingwood 1946, 215f., 287, 300).

maintained, that history proceeds in a direction – perhaps unknown – and does not return and return again, so that there *is* something new under the sun.

The second option makes the theme of immortality relevant not so much for reincarnation or "re-enactment", but rather for the idea of the relay-race of generations. Every person and each generation leaves a unique and unrepeatable mark which irreversibly changes what will follow, and remains included within the new that – in any case – emerges.

Tolkien wrote that every event had at least two aspects: one regarding the history of the individual, the other the history of the world (*Letters* no. 181). Tolkien was concerned, at least in his fiction, with the 'history of the world'. In the aftermath of the powerful philosophies of history of the 19th century (Hegelian, Marxist, Positivist), Tolkien found himself living in a period – the first half of the 20th century – in which the 19th-century lesson was repeated and over-much varied. We find several classical and highly influential philosophies of history[53] such as those of Oswald Spengler (1918) and Arnold Toynbee (1934), together with others, intellectualist and extravagant ones such as that of Edmund Husserl (1935) or terrible and obscure such as that of Alfred Rosenberg (1934).[54] All somewhat pessimistic, perhaps not surprisingly given what was happening and was about to happen in Europe and the rest of the world. After the Second World War, this surfeit of philosophies of history contracted and disappeared. The appalling drama proved to be a decisive factor in the selection from and development of the 19th-century inheritance, which (like many others) was no longer considered and events took a different turn.

But Tolkien was a fully pre-war man and his *Silmarillion* and *The Lord of the Rings* are – amongst other things – stories about the philosophy of history. And in his letters he made explicit several of the links between this and actual

---

[53] Of which it is unlikely, given their diffusion in many different areas, that Tolkien knew nothing, as Michael Drout has also said: "The relationship between Tolkien and philosophers has not been explored as much as it should be (the focus has been almost entirely on Theologians), so your research is important. Unfortunately, I cannot help very much. There have been rumours over the years that a catalogue of Tolkien's personal library would be published, but that has not yet happened. I don't know of any direct evidence, but I would be shocked if he didn't know something about Spengler and Toynbee, but proving it is another story" (from an email to FM, dated March 22nd, 2009).
[54] See an interesting comparison between Rosenberg's philosophy of history and Tolkien's in Chism 2003, 72-75, and see the discussion of some shared themes in Tolkien and Rosenberg by Bachmann & Honegger 2005.

world history.⁵⁵ Shippey writes that one might have thought that Tolkien, with parents and friends dead and in the midst of the Great War, might have wanted to construct a myth to justify a dream of escaping death, but he had "motives that were much more than personal" for doing this: to elaborate a myth of England (*for* England) (Shippey 2005, 303). Meaning, I think, that this myth would have given nobility to the England of his time (as the *Aeneid* did to Rome at the critical moment of the end of the Republic), that of Churchill's "finest hour", in which the problem of personal life and death were grafted onto, and seek meaning from, the function of peoples in history.⁵⁶ Tolkien's "philosophy of history" is not as pessimistic as those in fashion at the time⁵⁷ (mentioned above): Tolkien does express a feeling of melancholy for the disappearance of elvish beauty in the Age of Men, but does not deplore moral decay or other forms of decadence! When he speaks of the fading of elvish beauty (or the ents) and the coming of the Age of Men, Tolkien – unlike Spengler, Rosenberg or Husserl – does not give us a message of "decadence", but instead one of "finiteness". His refusal to add to the already numerous "twilights of

---

55 See for example *Letters* no. 13, 211, 294 and 183. Tolkien gave considerable thought to the details: his own present and that of the readers of *The Lord of the Rings* (second half of the 20th century) corresponds to the end of the Sixth Age or the beginning of the Seventh Age and, since each Age lasts about 2000 years, between the beginning of the Third – and the events in *The Lord of the Rings* – and the book's publication there were about 6000 years. The idea of living at the end of the Sixth Age of the world or the beginning of the Seventh is not original to Tolkien, but first to be found in *De temporum ratione* of the Venerable Bede, an eighth-century English monk. Since Tolkien had marked the ends of the First, Second and Third Ages with grandiose events in Middle-earth in which the forces of good won over those of evil (the War of Wrath and the expulsion of Melkor; the War of Elendil and Gil-Galad against Sauron with Isildur who takes possession of the One Ring; the War of the Ring and the destruction of Sauron), it is interesting to ask which events might have corresponded to the ends of succeeding Ages. In a spirit of pure speculation, I propose: the Fourth Age finishes in about 2000 BC at the beginning of the Bronze Age, when the Indo-European Elamite people defeated and put an end to the Semitic Sumerian civilization, when the period of anarchy in the Egyptian Empire ended and the unified Middle Kingdom began, with its capital in Thebes, when the *Rigveda*, the oldest Hindu text, was written (Hinduism is the most ancient religion still in existence today). The Fifth Age finishes around the year zero, when Octavian defeated Anthony and Cleopatra at Actium (31 BC), checking the rise of the East; when Jesus of Nazareth was born as the incarnation of the Christian God (3 BC); when Jesus Christ was crucified, initiating universal redemption (AD 30). The Sixth Age finishes with the defeat of Hitler's plan to conquer the planet and enforce Nazi methods and ideology (AD 1945), or when de-colonization freed the peoples of the Third World from European dominion (1945-1965); or when, with Stalin's death and the 20th congress of the PCUS the irreversible de-totalitarization of the USSR and disintegration of the Third Communist Internationale began (1953). We should remember that Tolkien's letter no. 211 is from 1958.
56 For the links between England's "finest hour" and the composition of *The Lord of the Rings*, see Manni & Bonechi 2008, 33-51.
57 Even less pessimistic than that one of Christopher Dawson. Tolkien quotes Dawson several times in his lecture/essay "On Fairy-Stories", and the connection between the two authors is stressed by Bradley J. Birzer (2003) and by Gregory Bassham (email to FM, June 15th, 2009).

the West" then in vogue is made explicit, for example, in the dialogue between Gimli and Legolas at Minas Tirith.

As has been noted, the death of an individual for the preservation of his people is felt by many to be tolerable and just. Besides, as a young soldier, Tolkien saw the European nations' uncertain fate in the war through the lens of the early medieval period, when the destiny of small barbarian populations – like the Geats in *Beowulf* – hung by a thread. So, he focused his attention to the extinction of peoples in history, thinking that it was the rule rather than the exception; and so, in his Middle-earth, as in the European Great War, the principal theme is not the mortality (and desire for immortality) of individual persons – as in Goethe's *Faust* – but that of peoples. In the first half of the 20<sup>th</sup> century the nations of Europe, forgetting the idea of a universal empire of Christendom, sought "immortality in the mortal realm" with Wagnerian nationalism, just like Fëanor, Galadriel and the rebel Eldar in the First Age (Spengler (pseud.) 2003).

My comment on this opinion is as follows: all nations behaved thus during the First World War, but during the Second World War only some. England, for example, did not. It defended itself and in doing so defended the world, and afterwards accepted with good grace to lose, in this now changed world, its worldwide Empire. W.A. Senior shares this view: in Tolkien's "history of the world" we witness the destruction of Beleriand, Gondolin, Nargothrond and Doriath; Morgoth's slaughter of the Noldor, survived only by Galadriel, recalls the decimation of two generations of British men in two world wars, a loss which bled dry the British Empire and led to its gradual disintegration.[58] A disintegration of which Tolkien (like many other Englishmen) did not disapprove (*Letters* no. 53, 77)! The finite nature of the histories of peoples, like that of the lives of individuals, is viewed with sadness, but not with disapproval: 'true immortality' (it must be remembered!) coincides with finiteness, with death.

This meaning of "immortality" as a unique – and finite! – contribution that peoples and persons make to the history of the world, is applied in Tolkien's fiction to both Elves and Men. But there is another meaning of immortality, which

---

58 Senior 2000, 176. On the collective death of peoples and institutions in Tolkien's fiction, see also the chapter entitled "Le Déclin" in Ferré 2001, 253-255.

regards only the Elves. As I have tried to show in detail elsewhere (Manni 2009, 28-37), in Tolkien's world many events (wars, the fall of kings, cases of treachery etc.) occur without producing changes: a "generalized medieval period"[59] that lasts for thousands of years, devoid of the profound dynamics (Christianization, Renaissance, scientific revolution, birth of nation states, Enlightenment, political and industrial revolutions etc.) which make our actual history a true process of development. But Tolkien's world is that of the Three Ages dominated by immortal (or rather, long-lived) Elves. In fact, Tolkien's fiction tells us nothing about the Age of Men.

Why, I wonder. The historical immobility makes sense, I believe, because it refers to the Time of the Elves. A history of Men without cultural and social change would be meaningless and would lead to theological scepticism and desperation. Why would innumerable generations of individuals be born and die if it served no purpose for future generations, if it was part of no development, if it fulfilled no 'mission'? Real antiquity certainly did experience historical changes, but ancient historiography (that of the Gentiles, not the Jews) was not aware of it, for it held human nature to be unchangeable and time cyclical; hence the profound scepticism about the traditional gods and the sense of desperation which – like a karstic river – re-emerges, despite their best intentions, in Polybius and Tacitus.

Tolkien's Elves, on the other hand, live for thousands of years, so they can easily get a sense of the passage of time from their *individual* experiences; experiences of persons who, *during the course of their lives*, learn slowly and with effort, leave behind past errors, and mature morally. Through the Elves' immortality, Tolkien wants to talk about an aspect of human experience.[60] Not human *collective* experience, that which we call history, but the *single* experience of the individual, that which we call life. In fact, just as cultural and social change does not occur with the Elves collectively during the Three Ages, thus it is in the lifetime of each single man: his character does not alter, because the cultural and social characteristics of the world that formed it cannot be changed. A 13th-century man, be he Dante Alighieri or the most humble

---

59 See Honegger 2011b.
60 "Elves are certain aspects of Men and their talents and desires" (*Letters* no. 153).

servant of the manor, could never think, feel or act like one of the 18th or 20th centuries, as the historians of "mentality" are well aware.[61]

Although character does not change, the life of a man has meaning because he can modify his own response to it. 'Free will' does not involve trying to be another person and to live an external and internal reality different from that decreed by destiny, but instead consists of trying to understand it ("know thyself") and hence regard it *critically* – which are the good points and which the bad? – and adapt appropriately. The clearest example is Galadriel: in the First Age she is a proud Noldor princess who goes to Middle-earth against the wishes of the Valar, not to recover the Silmarils like Fëanor, yet neither to take on the leadership over the people like Fingolfin. In Middle-earth she sought "a realm at her own will" (*S*, Qu. 9).[62] Galadriel at the end of the Third Age is a woman who no longer leaves the side of her husband Celeborn,[63] who secretly conserves the ring Nenya, surveys the movements of the enemy, gives hospitality and encouragement to the Fellowship of the Ring, refuses – in a memorable scene with Frodo – every prospect of dominion, goes with Elrond and Gandalf to the Grey Havens and leaves Middle-earth forever.

And this is moral maturation, which for Tolkien is the only change recorded during the history of the Elves, for this story – it seems to me – does not recount history (at least not most importantly), but life. And since the life of Men is much briefer than that of the Elves, the former are much more "restless", because they are more urgently called by the conscious and unconscious demand for the achievement of moral maturity prior to death. Christopher Garbowski emphasizes that in "Athrabeth", Andreth interprets human restlessness negatively: unlike in the "Ainulindalë", for this woman death, which is not a gift of Ilúvatar, is the cause of this agitation; all human resources including reason cannot penetrate death and only obscurity remains (cf. Garbowski 2004, 156). But – says Tolkien – Andreth is wrong! As Matthew Dickerson observes,

---

61 "Mentality" is defined as that group of convictions held by *all* people in a certain historical and geographical context, irrespective of education, personal ability, sex, profession, wealth and age. See e.g. Vovelle 1990.
62 "'Nay,' she said. 'Angrod is gone, and Aegnor is gone, and Felagund is no more. Of Finarfin's children I am the last. But my heart is still proud. What wrong did the golden house of Finarfin do that I should ask the pardon of the Valar, or be content with an isle in the sea whose native land was Aman the Blessed? Here I am mightier.'" (*UT* 249, 263).
63 Unlike her previous behaviour; cf. *UT* 248-252, 256.

Men have a freedom which in some ways is more significant than that of the Elves, for whom the music of the Ainur is Fate; Men have the power to "give form to their lives" beyond music (Dickerson 2004, 109). In fact, for Tolkien free will is associated with mortality: "It is one with this gift of freedom that the children of Men dwell only a short space in the world alive" (*S*, Qu. 1).

Here as well then, we find the theme of "finitude": the lifetime of individuals is finite, the life of peoples is also finite, and finite, too, (though not equal to nought) is the capacity of a person to deal with his own destiny (or character).

## 5. A Moment in the life of Tolkien

A writer's sources and inspirational themes may (justifiably) be studied for their intrinsic value, although Tolkien, who in fact foresaw to what length academics would have gone with regard to his own works, thought that "it is the particular use in a particular situation of any motive, whether invented, deliberately borrowed, or unconsciously remembered that is the most interesting thing to consider" (*Letters* no. 337). Let us try, then, to examine more closely the 'particular situation' from which Tolkien drew most of his motives for death and immortality.

Claudio A. Testi calls the years 1957-1960 "the apex of Tolkien's reflection";[64] and in fact both in the unpublished works of fiction (now accessible in the volume *Morgoth's Ring*) and in his letters – especially those of 1957-1958 – we see a Tolkien who is more than ever a "philosopher". The fictional writings of this period are indeed largely discussions and philosophical analyses of themes such as the nature of evil, love and hope, sexuality and faithfulness, death and immortality. On the last of these subjects, the apex is reached in "Athrabeth" in 1959, the year Tolkien retired. Humphrey Carpenter writes in his biography that from the mid-fifties he ceased to meet his friends regularly. The Inklings' last years had revolved above all around reading *The Lord of the Rings*, by then finished, published and enjoying increasing international success. Now he passed his time mainly at home and wanted to dedicate himself

---

64 Cf. Claudio A. Testi's essay on the *Legendarium* in this volume.

to his beloved *Silmarillion*. But he was depressed and found his life tedious, almost a prison (cf. Carpenter 1977, 239-243).

When his young friend Rob Gilson died in the war, Tolkien wrote to his other friend Smith that the "destiny" of their TCBS was "greatness", to be an instrument in the hands of God, to be "a mover, a doer, even an achiever of great things"; now that Rob was dead, his "greatness" was revealed to have been that of a friend towards his companions. Tolkien still had those hopes and ambitions, but now felt himself to be an individual, not a member of that group, which had come to an end (*Letters* no. 5). In this letter written by Tolkien at the age of twenty-four we see a person sensitive and capable of affection, but not nostalgic, looking towards the future rather than the past of his adolescence.[65] At the end of the fifties the almost seventy-year-old Tolkien had been a "mover, a doer, even an achiever of great things". His *The Lord of the Rings* had been received with enthusiasm by many people and would be by many more. He had wedded Edith, his "Lúthien", had the family to which he had ardently aspired, met new and congenial friends, in first place C.S. Lewis, and had been able to express his philologist's vocation as professor at the University of Oxford. Why then the boredom, the prison?

Let's try looking at things from another perspective. Now his *magnum opus*, *The Lord of the Rings*, was finished and Tolkien had taken his leave of it; he was now retired and no longer a teacher, his children had grown up and left home, he but rarely saw Lewis and his other friends, he and Edith now began to experience directly the problems of old age. In his philosophical writings from those years he takes up again his thoughts on immortality; of which there are three sorts:

- the "true" variety which coincides with the death of those, like Men, who have a "short span of life";
- the "mad" sort of those who are long-lived but become slaves of power, such as the Nazgûl;
- the "melancholic" type of the long-lived who become progressively less interested in the future and more in the past, such as the Elves.

---

[65] On this crucial point in life Tolkien's orientation is substantially different to that of many of the Great War poets, idealist and nostalgic, who are well analysed by Paul Fussell in his interesting and perceptive book *The Great War and Modern Memory* (1975).

Tolkien was thinking of three kinds of lives, one brief and two long. What did he have in mind? Did the brief life remind him of his own parents and his TCBS friends who died young, with respect to whom he felt some guilt for having survived for so long? Did the long and extraordinary life confront him with the temptation to congratulate himself on the success of *The Lord of the Rings* and to try and increase his popularity (although this temptation seems to have been weak)? Did the long and melancholic life remind him of the important things in his life that were now in the past, now that he faced old age and increasing solitude?

Tolkien was not a narcissist like Heidegger (who made precise provisions in his will for the posthumous issue at regular intervals of his unpublished writings, so that he would continue to be talked about, a culture-infesting "serial spectre"!)[66] and in fact referred to the popularity he gained through *The Lord of the Rings* as a "deplorable cultus". He probably felt himself most at risk from the third sort of life – melancholic elvish longevity – that life of which he wrote in a letter of this period. Elvish immortality too has a weakness, because the Elves yearn for the past and have no wish to face change, so they also seek a (limited) power in order to preserve things from change (*Letters* no. 181).

Shippey underlines that Tolkien had always tried to prevent an important change in his own field of interest and activity: the academic extinction of the Venerable Comparative Philology (cf. Shippey 2007a, 139-156). But in the letter cited previously Tolkien wrote that with the fall of Sauron's power the Elves' efforts to preserve the past also fell to pieces! What does this mean? It occurs to me that with the fall of Hitlerian nationalism the efforts of philologists to preserve the academic and effective status of philology – which had been born and cultivated in its golden years for nationalistic purposes (Shippey 2007a, 80-96) – also disintegrated, or at least started to.[67]

---

66 See comments by Enrico Berti in his essay "Una metafisica problematica e dialettica" in Berti 1997, 45.
67 Tom Shippey tells me that in the English-speaking world Germanic philology is held in such poor repute that there are no longer young philologists able to produce critical editions of medieval texts written in any of the Germanic languages. And my old friend from the Pisa Scuola Normale and disciple of Gianfranco Contini – Father Saverio Cannistrà – recounts that the situation is the same today in France and Italy for Romance philology!

# An Eulogy of Finitude

It also comes to mind that Tolkien, in that he was an elf (i.e. an artist and scholar),[68] would have considered his own longevity to be "natural"; and Carpenter tells us that during these years and after, right up to the end, Tolkien continued indefatigably with his work both in fiction and philology. But as a man, did he also see it as "natural" (or, rather, as "serial"?) that he survived his long-lost TCBS friends, together with the multitude who died in the Second World War?[69] It is difficult to find answers to these questions, but it seems necessary to me at least to ask them in the context of a serious consideration of Tolkien's "artistic experiments" and "philosophical reflections" on Death and Immortality (that is, Not-Yet-Mortality).

In a 1958 letter, Tolkien makes clear that the elvish so-called immortality is not "true immortality", but "strictly longevity coextensive with the life of Arda" (*Letters* no. 212). Arda, or, in other words, *this* world! And – we know – the world continued to exist throughout the sixties and early seventies of the 20$^{th}$ century. Tolkien was of course "coextensive" at least to those decades, but did he perhaps feel himself "disappearing" or "fading" as he speculated about the Elves during the Age of Men?

A feeling, a temptation, probably. But – I believe – this was not dominant in his life. Carpenter writes that the later years of Tolkien's life were full, if not of interpersonal relations, at least of the *desire* for contacts with his wife, children, fans, ex-colleagues, even with passing guests at the Miramar Hotel. I am sure that he, as a man, was able until the end to come out of himself and his "hoarding memories" and – through others' love for him and his for them – to live in the present!

Before I draw my conclusion, I must briefly turn also to Tolkien's "elvish" side, as a scholar of the humanities and – especially – a great artist. Although he yearned to compose a "mythology for England", as John Rateliff points out, the result was a "mythology for our times", because *The Lord of the Rings* has been translated into thirty-eight languages. The majority of his readers have never been to England, and those in Germany – England's mortal enemy of

---

68 "The Elves represent, as it were, the artistic, aesthetic, and purely scientific aspects of the Humane nature" (*Letters* no. 181).
69 Including the greatest medieval scholar of the 20$^{th}$ century, Marc Bloch, murdered by the Gestapo because he belonged to the French Resistance.

sixty-five years ago – prefer his book to the Bible and the books of their fellow-German writer Thomas Mann.[70] Tolkien was able to witness at least a part of this great public appreciation and was amazed. After all, he had written *The Lord of the Rings* primarily for his own pleasure and as an "experiment" on the induction of "secondary beliefs" (*Letters* no. 328).

What did Tolkien mean by "experiment"? Carpenter has Tolkien say, on a typical Inklings Thursday evening: certain books reawaken desires that should not be reawakened, such as pornographic books, but the desires reawakened by books about fairies are of a different kind; he who reads pornography would like to live in reality situations similar to those described in print (and is disappointed when he does), whereas he who reads the chapter on Moria in *The Lord of the Rings* does not want to really "experience" the dangers of that mine. Lewis replies: the pornographic imagination empties reality and renders it less appetizing, whilst the story of an enchanted forest has the effect that a child can then appreciate real forests more (Carpenter 1978, chapter 3).

Tom Shippey writes a most interesting thing about philology in his historical itinerary. The flourishing of this discipline in the 19th century led to the discovery of the Goths, Huns and other Northern cultures, and to the philologists of the time (and to Tolkien) it seemed possible to at least get close to reconstructing the "Lost Worlds" of these peoples. The philological technique of "reconstructing" inspired in them a romantic desire of this sort, whereas the philologists of today, including Shippey, consider it to be impossible to achieve: too few documents survive. If a reconstruction may be made of these Dark Ages, it is only by means of a novelist's imagination, as William Morris and then Tolkien himself tried.[71] I personally suspect that when philology's limits became apparent to Tolkien, not only in connection with its declining academic and social role mentioned above, but also for the structural and intrinsic reasons recounted in this paragraph, he increasingly sought another path for the "re-enactment" which he desired to achieve in his fiction, the writing that at times he called "my real work".

---

70 According to a 2004 poll of 250,000 German readers (cf. Rateliff 2006, 89).
71 Shippey 2007a, 115-136. Now we have Tolkien's most explicit attempt to do that, *The Legend of Sigurd & Gudrún*, where he tries to solve – by his artistic means – the *Königsproblem* of Germanic Philology.

But things are not quite that simple. On the one hand, in 1961 he still worked as a philologist for the critical edition of *Ancrene Wisse*, and on the other, the continual additions and changes made to the endless *Silmarillion* no longer had the same meaning for Tolkien that the composition of *The Lord of the Rings* and the *Silmarillion* itself had had when, years before, he had wanted to publish it together with *The Lord of the Rings*. Youth is not like old age! All things change (and pass): Tolkien was continually more aware – and he expressed this – that things had also changed in himself as a novelist, and his resources were not infinite. Tom Shippey, in his analysis of the 1965 allegorical fable *Smith of Wootton Major*, emphasizes that Tolkien identifies with the blacksmith protagonist and adds that at that time Tolkien perceived that both philology and the World of Faërie (fiction, artistic creation)[72] had by now ceased contributing to Tolkien the individual, although not to the others who would cultivate and develop them in their own ways.[73] In other words – with respect to the nineteen-thirties, when Tolkien, in his lectures and writings on *Beowulf* and in "On Fairy-Stories", self-confidently proclaimed the power of philology and creative fiction (respectively) – now, in 1965, although continuing to praise their benefits, he also pointed out their limits, both intrinsic and as redeeming resources for individuals.

This too is, I believe, a Tolkienian "Eulogy of Finitude": both Philology and Fiction are good things, but finite, certainly to be appreciated, but not idealized.

I conclude with the consideration that this conviction, at which Tolkien arrived explicitly only after due philosophical reflection, in old age, he nevertheless 'acted out' or lived without explicit awareness throughout his entire life. In Tolkien, fantastic invention was *never* a substitute for real life (a form of 'pornography for intellectuals'); not with respect to interpersonal relationships, nor responsibilities in work, nor the seriousness of his academic research. Lúthien did not substitute Edith, Middle-earth was not a substitute for that

---

72 For the problem of death in Tolkien's shorter works, see the essay by Lorenzo Gammarelli in this volume.
73 "Defeat hangs heavy in *Smith of Wootton Major*. Smith is 'an old man's book', as Tolkien said in *Letters*, p. 389 [*Letters* no. 299]. But Alf is there *to put Smith in a longer history*. There were men who wore the star of inspiration before Smith; in a later age there will be others; in any case the star, that inspiration, is only a fragment of a greater world, a world outside the little clearing of Wootton" (Shippey 2005, 277).

Europe where he lived, and the Annals of the *Silmarillion* did not take the place of considered hypotheses based on medieval texts. But the creations ("sub-creations"!) of fantasy helped him to achieve a greater involvement in these experiences of his life. This process continued during the last stage of his life – that of old age and solitude – when Tolkien, however, continued to philosophize and write about the Elves' longevity and the mortality of Men. *De te fabula docet!*

# Claudio A. Testi

## Tolkien's *Legendarium* as a *meditatio mortis*

## Foreword

**Death and immortality:**
**Evolution of concepts in the *Legendarium*[1]**

The cultural climate in which we are immersed today avoids the theme of death intentionally and with attentive care. A great historian of civilizations, Philippe Ariès, has in fact defined the 20th century as the century of "forbidden death", a century in which death has replaced sex as the taboo peculiar to our times.[2] Evidence of this is the more and more evident "hospitalization" of death, which deprives both relatives and the dying person of the possibility of leaving life where and when they deem appropriate.[3] The 21[th] century now opens in complete continuity with the past era: the promethean spirit in each one of us prevents us from looking straight at our finiteness and instead elevates us to the rank of its conqueror while we aspire to making human life indefinitely long and young, in one word to gaining immortality. This perspective, already hypothesized by Edgar Morin (cf. Morin 2002), seems to have a chance of realization thanks to recent discoveries in the field of genetics.[4] It is a fact, however, that the world of contemporary culture still shows great indifference

---

1 For the essays here presented I owe much to the observations and considerations that all members of the group of study shared with me in these years we have been working together. Special thanks go also to Mrs Verlyn Flieger, for the patience and kindness she showed me in reading both my essays and suggesting precious changes that contributed to improve the original versions.
2 Ariès 2001, 68-80 and Ariès 1992, 659ff. On the history of death see also Vernant 2007; Vovelle 2009; Tenenti 1989.
3 Elias 1985, see Fulton and Bendiksen 1994; Jonas 1991.
4 In this regard see the clear analysis by Boncinelli and Sciarretta 2005. In this volume the authors show that today it is "scientifically" possible to envisage immortality thanks to four main developments: 1) prevention of illnesses, 2) prolongation of life, 3) substitution of decayed body parts with prosthetic parts, 4) prolongation of the psyche by means of transplantation into other bodies or electronic equipment. On the same theme see also Canonici and Rossi 2007.

towards the themes of death and immortality, as pointed out by Jankélévitch[5] in his impressive essay *La Mort*.[6]

Strangely enough, these topics have suffered the same fate in Tolkienian studies. Although they are central in the works by J.R.R. Tolkien, as stated on several occasions by Tolkien himself,[7] scholars have, in fact, neglected them almost completely.[8] It is hard to say if this is due to the "forbidden death" theorized by Ariès; it is in any case a significant oversight. Therefore this anthology is intended as a contribution to make up for it.

With this essay we wish in particular to provide the reader with a sort of historic introduction to the themes of immortality and death within the Tolkienian *Legendarium*, in the effort to find a common thread in the complexity of the matter.[9]

The word *Legendarium* was used in the past to indicate a collection of legends and lives of saints. Tolkien recovers the word with its original meaning and uses it as the title for his monumental collection of Middle-earth writings[10] amounting – *The History of Middle-earth* included – to more than 8,100 pages with more than two million words.

A careful analysis of Tolkien's texts has led us to identify at least six themes of great relevance on the subject of death and its denial, which will be examined as follows:

1) Death and immortality among the Elves:
    1.1) Elves and disease;

---

5 See Jankélévitch 1995, 27.
6 Jankélévitch 1977; see also Elias 1985.
7 *Letters* no. 181, 186, 203, 208, 211, 245; see Tolkien's interview of 1968 quoted in Hammond and Scull 2006b, 611.
8 To date there is only one volume explicitly dedicated to these themes and confined to *The Lord of the Rings* (Ferré 2001). For some articles of Tolkienian criticism on the same subject refer to the bibliography. We are talking in any case of a limited number of contributions, especially if compared to the huge quantity of essays written up to the present time which are in most part listed in the bibliography by Johnson 1987; Drout and Wynne 2000.
9 On the history of Tolkienian mythology, consult Chr. Tolkien 1980, Whittingham 2007; Kane 2009; Flieger and Hostetter 2000; Hammond and Scull 2006b, 906-917; see the somewhat dated but always useful Kilby 1977. For a synopsis on the shaping of the themes of death/immortality, consult Garbowski 2007; Hammond and Scull 2006b, 604-614.
10 Gilliver, Marshall and Weiner 2006, 153-154.

1.2) Death and the "fading" of the Elves;
1.3) Destiny and reincarnation of the Elves;

2) Death and immortality among Men:
2.1) Men's final destiny;
2.2) Envy for immortality and death;
2.3) Death: gift, fate, destiny or nature of Men?

Compiled over a period of fifty years the *Legendarium* has thus taken the shape of a true *meditatio mortis* for contemporary man which has developed through five main stages:

I. 1917-25: THE FIRST UNSORTED IDEAS, not yet consistently structured and rejected at a later stage, are set forth for the first time in *The Book of Lost Tales* (1917-20) and in the first versions of the poems on Túrin and Beren & Lúthien (1920-25).

II. 1926-37: THE FIRST ELUCIDATIONS in this regard begin to make their appearance throughout this period, as shown both in the first versions of "The Music of the Ainur/Ainulindalë" written in the 1930s and the so-called "Sketch of the Mythology" (Sk 1926) later to be expanded into the "Quenta Noldorinwa" (Q 1930) and the "Quenta Silmarillion" (QS 1930-37). "The Annals of Valinor" and "The Annals of Beleriand" provide the core of the Q and are later modified in the second version (1930-37) appended to QS. *The Hobbit* was also published during this same period (it was written between 1930 and 1936 and published in 1937) and the myth of Númenor is also to be 'discovered' for the first time in "The Fall of Númenor" (1936-37).

III. 1937-56: These are the years of THE STABILIZATION OF IDEAS which had been elaborated throughout the preceding period and were included in *The Lord of the Rings* (written at intervals between 1937 and 1949). The myth of Númenor's is now also fully developed, as attested by "The Fall of Númenor" in 1942 and "The Drowning of Anadûnê" (1943-46). After completing *The Lord of the Rings* Tolkien goes back to the primary ages of Middle-earth, with a revision of QS (the so-called "Later Quenta Silmarillion" of 1950-51: LQ), the corresponding evolutions of the annals (which are now called "Annals of Aman" and "Grey Annals"), three versions of the "Ainulindalë" written between 1946 and 1951 and a rewriting of Túrin's story. However, in the years between 1953 and 1955 Tolkien was engaged in writing the final version of the *The Lord of the Rings* and only after its completion was he able to go back to the primary ages of Arda for deeper evaluation.

IV. 1957-60: THE HIGHEST POINT OF TOLKIEN'S THOUGHT. During this exceptionally fecund period we have the first versions of the fundamental story of Finwë and Míriel (1957-59) and a series of elaborations on LQ (LQ2 1958) with the relevant source material from the Annals (AAm2, GA3). However, it is mostly in a series of new essays and dialogues that the themes of death and immortality are masterfully explored – first in "The Laws and Customs among the Eldar" (1957-58) and later in "Aman" (about 1959), both preceding the literary/philosophical masterpiece "Athrabeth Finrod ah Andreth" (1959-60), soon followed by "Converse between Manwë and Eru", by Tolkien's commentary on "Athrabeth" and lastly by a short essay on the reincarnation of the Elves (1960).

V. Writings and interviews from 1961 to 1973 show no significant developments on the themes of death and immortality but only HINTS OF CONFIRMATION (either direct or indirect) of the positions established by the end of the 1950s.

## 1. Death and immortality among the Elves

Among the many elements which make J.R.R. Tolkien unique within the history of Western literature,[11] "elvencentrism" is certainly one of the foremost characteristics to keep in mind when approaching Tolkien's writings (see *Letters* no. 181, 212, 131). Tolkien uses this term to point out not only that most of the stories of the *Legendarium* revolve mainly around Elves but also that even the narrator's point of view is mainly elvish rather than human.[12] What would the life of a people be if their lives were tied to the cycles of their

---

11 On the theme see Simonson 2008.
12 Within the *Legendarium* we also find non-elvencentric stories, primarily *The Hobbit* and *The Lord of the Rings*, which are written from the point of view of Hobbits or of Men, respectively (*Letters* no. 131; however, in the same letter, Tolkien equates Hobbits to Men). As far as the myth of Númenor is concerned, Tolkien makes a threefold distinction: while "The Fall of Númenor" is seen from an elvish point of view, the "Drowning" is written by men, whereas and in the later "Akallabêth" both perspectives are present (*SD* 406). On the theme of the different (and at times conflicting) points of view used by Tolkien see Flieger 2005a, 47ff. Pearce, too, examines the different approaches (elvish and human) to the theme of death (Pearce 1998, 122ff.).

world until its end? How would these immortals perceive the passing of time and the evolving of history? It would only be possible to answer these challenging questions by recurring to the sub-creation of a world within which an Elf would become believable. The answer to these questions are not simply fanciful narrative devices: "Elves and Men are just different aspects of the Humane, and represent the problem of Death as seen by a finite but willing and self-conscious person. [...] The Elves represent, as it were, the artistic, aesthetic, and purely scientific aspects of the Human nature raised to a higher level than is actually seen in Men" (*Letters* no. 181). Through them we have a neater and more precise vision of some of the mysterious aspects of mankind itself, beginning with the problem of death.

## 1.1 Elves and disease

Since the earliest drafting of the *Legendarium*, Elves were perceived as an immortal people destined to last as long as Arda.[13] This idea will represent a constant within the complex Tolkienian universe (see 1.3). But can such a people die solely because of extrinsic causes? And if they can die, how can they return to Arda? And further, can these 'immortals' fall ill and suffer? These are some of the many questions to which Tolkien has given various answers over the years.

### 1917-25: The first ideas – The possibility of disease outside of Valinor

That Elves *may die* is already explicitly stated in *The Book of Lost Tales*, where it is said that they can be slain or can die from grief (see footnote 13). Again, in the same period the first death of an Elf occurs in "Aman" when Fëanor's father is dramatically slain by Melkor (*LT I* 145).

As far as disease is concerned, it is admitted that *it is part of their destiny* unless the Elves stay in Valinor, where they live on the beneficial food of the Blessed

---

[13] "The Eldar dwell [in the world] till the Great End unless they be slain or waste in grief (for to both of these deaths are they subject), nor doth eld subdue their strength, except it may be in ten thousand centuries; and dying they are reborn in their children, so that their number minishes not, nor grows" (*LT I* 59).

Realm.¹⁴ In this first phase it is not specified whether the possibility of the Elves becoming ill might also entail a premature death once they have been affected by the illness. This question will be at the core of Tolkien's future considerations.

## 1926-37: Towards a first clarification – Between total immunity and exemption from deadly disease

Starting from 1926, Tolkien goes back to these first ideas and rethinks them significantly as is clearly attested in Sk. In fact, in one of his early drafts Elves are seen (unlike previously thought) as totally 'free from all sickness' ("free from all sickness", *Shaping* 21-22; see also 51-52). However, he soon abandons this idea and modifies the manuscript in the sense that Elves cannot die of illness ("free from death by sickness", *ibid*.).

A later version of the same passage contained in Q confirms the last version of Sk¹⁵ which will be used unchanged in QS (*LR* 246). However, the idea of total freedom from illnesses fleetingly reappears in the "Annals of Aman" (*MR* 117-118) and will be resolutely reaffirmed later as we will have the opportunity to see.

## 1937-58: Confirmation of immunity exclusively from deadly disease

Despite this continuous fluctuation of ideas, in these years we find confirmation of what was stated in Q and QS: in fact in LQ1 and LQ2 we find again the exemption from death by sickness only, a concept which will also be put forward in the *Silmarillion* published by Tolkien's son Christopher (*WJ*, LQ1-2 175; *S*, Q 12).

## 1958-60: The highest point of Tolkien's thought and the reinstatement of total immunity from sickness

During these years Tolkien again takes up his forty-year-long meditation over the theme and reaffirms the total exemption from sickness: this is stated in

---

14 As for the Elves flying from Valinor, "never would they have made the dreadful passage of the Qerkaringa had they or yet been subject to weariness, sickness, and the many weaknesses that after became their lot dwelling far from Valinor. Still was the blessed food of the Gods and their drink rich in their veins and they were halfdivine" (*LT I* 166).

15 "Immortal were the Elves, and their wisdom waxed and grew from age to age, and no sickness or pestilence brought them death. But they could be slain with weapons in those days, even by mortal Men, and some waned and wasted with sorrow till they faded from the earth" (*Shaping*, Q 100; see 172).

*Letters* no. 212 (never posted) of 1958,[16] in his late work "Aman" (*MR* 427) and in the extremely important commentary to the "Athrabeth" (*MR* 341).

In this final synthesis, the Elves seem to realize 'by their nature' one of the possible human paths of Men to immortality; in other words prevention of all pathologies, something which the recent advances in modern science have made possible for us to conceive (see Morin 2002). This complex evolution in the *Legendarium* is not simply a minor detail, but is the sign of something deeper. It is not only the expression of a spasmodic search for "consistency" in his imaginary world but is also a profoundly felt meditation on the relation between life and physical illness. A people destined to last until the end of the world must accordingly be exempt from physical illness, even though fatal wounds and sorrow might expose them to an early departure from Arda, to which however they are destined to return in a different body (see 1.3).

## 1.2 The "fading" of the Elves

Is it then possible that the only causes for the Elves' premature (albeit not permanent) death be physical wounds and grief? Could they not die of other causes related to that very same physical nature? It is a fact that since the time of *The Book of Lost Tales* Tolkien had been writing 'enigmatic' phrases that he would explain further only later.

### 1917-25: The first unsorted ideas on the fading of the Elves

It is in the first draft of the tale of Beren and Lúthien (both originally conceived as Elves) where quite unexpectedly we find for the first time the passage which states: "Tinúviel slowly fade[d], even as the Elves of later days have done throughout the world" (*LT II* 240). As quite correctly observed by Christopher Tolkien, it almost seems "as though in the original idea Elvish fading was a form of mortality. This is in fact made explicit in a later version" (*LT II* 250).

What does this fading consist of in concrete terms? In the *Book of Lost Tales* we find, although only barely hinted at, two different answers to the ques-

---

16 "The Elves were not subject to disease, but they could be 'slain': that is their bodies could be destroyed, or mutilated so as to be unfit to sustain life" (*Letters* no. 212).

tion. At first it seems that Elves may be destined to see their size shrink to that of the small fairies of the English folk tales (*LT II* 301, 326). This first hypothesis, however, will be soon abandoned (cf. Fimi 2009, 13-61). Again in the *Book of Lost Tales* we find the mention of a more plausible alternative according to which the Elves' *physical strength* is destined to *diminish* along with the passing of the centuries (see footnote 13): two incompatible ideas of which only the second one will find confirmation and adequate elaboration in successive writings.

## 1926-37: First elucidations – All Elves fade but perhaps only in Middle-earth

In Sk the parallel between Lúthien's fading and the Elves' future fading (*Shaping* 33) is reaffirmed and mention is also made of the fact that all Elves will sooner or later fade (*ibid*. 21). This idea will be strengthened in Q where it is added that when Elves fade they become like shadows, wraiths and memories (*Shaping* 99-100).

In QS Tolkien takes up the passages of Q, but at some points it seems that fading also only concerns the Elves as long as they stay in Middle-earth.[17] Additionally, we find the hint of a possible 'physical' explanation of this fading which is due to a mysterious consumption of the body by the spirit.[18]

Similarly, in AV1 it is confirmed that Fëanor's sons, even if they are not killed in battle, will in any case fade like all other Elves (and sooner than them) (*Shaping* 267). A destiny they share with the People of the Stars who remained in Middle-earth which will be confirmed in AV2 (*LR* 116).

---

17 "And outside Valinor [clarification not present in Sk and Q] they tasted bitter grief, and some wasted and waned with sorrow, until they faded from the earth. [...] In after days, when because of the triumphs of Morgoth Elves and Men became estranged, as he most wished, those of the Elf-race that lived still in the Middle-earth ["world" in Sk and Q] waned and faded [...] becoming as shadows and memories [compared with Q *wraiths* has disappeared], such as did not ever and anon set sail into the West, and vanished from the earth [which only in LQ1 will be replaced by "Middle-earth"]" (*LR*, QS nn. 85 and 87, 247; see *S*, Q 12).

18 "Yet their bodies were of the stuff of earth and could be destroyed, and in those days they were more like to the bodies of Men, and to the earth, since they had not so long been inhabited by the fire of the spirit, which consumeth them from within in the courses of time" (*LR*, QS 246-247). Steve Walker examines how Tolkien gives an entirely new semantic function to the word "fade" (Walker 2009, 125ff.).

## 1937-56: Confirmation and first hints of new ideas – Elves and their fading in Middle-earth

A mention of the Elves' fading is also made in *The Lord of the Rings*, when Treebeard, in a dialogue written at the beginning of 1942,[19] affirms: "*Laurelindórenan!* That is what the Elves used to call it, but now they make the name shorter: Lothlórien they call it. Perhaps they are right: maybe it is fading, not growing" (*LotR*, TT.III.4). It can be observed that the same verb is used to indicate both the fading due to the prolonged use of the Rings of Power (*LotR*, FR.III.2, two references) or the wound afflicted by Morgul's sword (*LotR*, FR.II.1) and the Elves' final destiny ("fade or depart": *LotR*, FR.VI.5).

In LQ1 then most of what had already been established is confirmed with a higher degree of congruity. The corresponding passage of QS is therefore modified accordingly ("earth" is replaced by "Middle-earth": see footnote 17) and will not be subjected to further changes in the revised version LQ2 (*WJ* 175). In the coeval "Annals of Aman" (*MR* 117-118) it is coherently and explicitly specified that fading only concerns those Elves who remain in Middle-earth.

## 1958-60: The synthesis of maturity – Elves are subject to fading only in Middle-earth because *fëa* is consuming their body

In his later essays "Laws and Customs among the Eldar" (*MR*, LawsB 212 and 219), "Aman" (*MR* 427), and in the commentary to the "Athrabeth" (*MR* 242-243), Tolkien at last arrives at a mature and definitive explanation for the fading of the Elves. Here it is said that it is the preserving force of the *fëa* by which the body (*hröa*) is consumed in such a way that the fading of the Elves of Middle-earth is bound to occur sooner or later. It is explained in a definitive form that this fading because of a slow consumption of the body is in part caused by the spirit which, due to Melkor's doing, corrupts the bodily matter. This status is therefore not natural (*MR* 342) if we take an 'ideal' state as our point of reference, although this process does not take place in Aman (*MR*, Aman 427). Nevertheless, fading is the exact opposite of death. In fading the Elves in fact become immortals. Once their bodies become a distant memory held safe by the spirit, the cause of the premature departure of the *fëa* from

---

19 *Treason* 1, 411-421; Hammond and Scull 2006b, 536.

Middle-earth is removed, so: "The Elves are indeed deathless and may not be destroyed or changed" (*MR*, LawsB 219) and their *fëar* will stay in Arda until its end (*MR*, LawsB 218-219; *MR*, Commentary 342-343).

## Tolkien's definition of mortality for mortals and immortals

Once established that only wounds and grief (not sickness or fading) may cause a 'violent' separation of the spirit from the body, Tolkien reaches the peak of his speculative maturity by the end of the 1950s, defining through Manwë's words the meaning of death and immortality for the Elves:

> We may say, therefore, that the Elves are destined to know 'death' in their mode, being sent into a world which contains 'death', and having a form for which 'death' is possible. For though by their prime nature, unmarred, they rightly dwell as *spirit and body* coherent, yet these are two things, not the same, and *their severance (which is 'death')* is a possibility inherent in their union. (*MR*, LawsA 244-245, italics added)

> the 'death' [is] the severing of these two [*fëa* and *hröa*]
> (*MR*, Athrabeth 316-317)

We have therefore a first precise definition of death, meant as separation of the spirit from the body; this notion – as we will later see – is also applicable to human death.

If the Elves can be afflicted by this fatal separation, how can they be defined as immortal? The answer to this question is given by Tolkien in "Athrabeth" in Finrod's words, where he affirms that

> [t]here are two deaths: the one is a harm and a loss but not an end, the other is an end without redress: and the Quendi suffer only the first
> (*MR*, Athrabeth 311)

It is the certitude of a *post mortem* return to Arda that makes the Elves 'immortal' and for this reason 'immortality' designates the perennial link between the elvish *fëa* and Arda, where the Elves will at some point return to:

> From their beginnings the chief difference between Elves and Men lay in the fate and nature of their spirits. The *fëar* of the Elves were destined to dwell in Arda for all the life of Arda, and the death of the flesh did not abrogate that destiny. (*MR*, LawsB 218)

Elvish 'immortality' is bound within a part of Time (which we would call the History of Arda), and is therefore strictly to be called rather 'serial longevity', the utmost limit of which is the length of the existence of Arda. (*MR*, Commentary 331)

This kind of immortality is not available to Men, and the reason is that they are the only creatures that are 'afflicted' by a second meaning of death, the death as departure from the History of Arda. This idea was already present before (see: *LT I* 59; MuB; *Letters* no. 131 and 156; *LotR*, App. A.5 cited in note 49), but is now distinguished from the death as a separation of body and soul with particular clearness:

[Human mortality implies a] short life span having no relation to the life of Arda. (*Letters* no. 212)

[Human mortality is] not being tied to the 'circles of the world'. (*ibid*.)

To sum up, there are two fundamental kinds of 'death':

- death as a separation of body and soul, affecting both Elves and Men, opposed to immortality as owned by superior beings not subject to this separation either because they do not own a body (Eru and the Ainur who did not enter Eä) or because their body is a mere raiment of their *fëa* (the Great Valar and the non-incarnated Maiar);[20]

- death as the departure from Arda (or from "the circles of the world"), affecting only Men who should seek beyond the Music of the Ainur. This, however, although almost always manifested through the separation of body and soul (except in the case of assumption: see *MR* 333 and my second essay), must nonetheless not be confused with the first kind. This second kind of death, as opposed to Elvish immortality or serial longevity, which is the possibility granted to the Elves: to return to Arda after the (rare) separation

---

20 See *MR*, LawsB 218. As for Eru, it would be more correct to talk of 'eternity'; even though Tolkien uses, at least in the letters (*Letters* no. 153 and no. 156), the concept of eternity as synonymous with a life span which – unlike elvish longevity – is not linked to the duration of Arda (which is in fact non-eternal: see *MR*, LawsA 251 and *MR*, Aman 424). In this sense Eru, the Ainur who did not enter Eä and the non-incarnated Valar are 'eternal'. It is still not clear where in this scheme the other Valar and Maiar should be placed.

of their body and soul. This creates a perennial link between the People of the Stars and our world.[21]

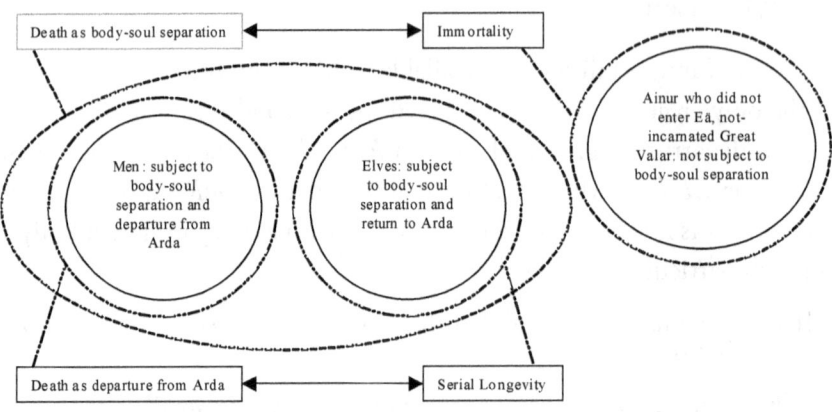

## 1.3 Destiny and the reincarnation of the Elves

When an Elf dies, how can his perennial dwelling in Arda be achieved in practical terms? When and how can he return to the world? In one word: what is the destiny of an 'immortal' people who can nonetheless be subject to death? The question is in itself paradoxical and – as all paradoxes – cannot but deeply commit whoever is trying to answer it. It is therefore no surprise that Tolkien had been unrelentingly elaborating on this theme for over sixty years, at times coming to solutions radically differing from each other.

### 1917-26: First ideas on the destiny of the Elves

In *LT I-II*[22] up to the changes brought to Sk, there were three possible destinies for an Elf: (a) he dies of wounds or grief, (b) he fades and nothing more is said

---

21 For Verlyn Flieger the idea of serial longevity recalls the serial time of Dunne (Dunne 1984), according to which an observer can 'ascend' the steps of the series of ages and get a wider and wider view of events (see Flieger 1997, 110-112).
22 "Thither in after days fared the Elves of all the clans who were by illhap slain with weapons or did die of grief for those that were slain – and only so might the Eldar die, and then it was only for a while. There Mandos spake their doom, and there they waited in the darkness, dreaming of their past deeds, until such time as he appointed when they might again be born into their children, and go forth to laugh and sing again" (*LT I*, 76; see the comment by Christopher Tolkien at page 90).

about what happens to him afterwards, or (c) he lives up to the end of Arda. In the first case he will wait in the Halls of Mandos (a.1) until Mandos (or all the Gods, according to Sk) proclaims his reincarnation into a new child (a.1.1.; it is not specified where this is going to take place).[23] This picture is only apparently clear, since Tolkien does not sufficiently elaborate on the nature of the fading of the Elves (see 1.2) or on whether the fading actually takes place in Valinor. To sum up, between 1918 and 1926 Tolkien envisages the three following possible destinies for an Elf which leave a few questions unanswered:

    a. death by being killed/of grief:
    a.1. the Elf goes to Mandos
        a.1.1. rebirth in the Children (where?)
    b. fading and possible afterlife (how and until when?)
    c. life in Valinor (without ever disappearing?)

## 1930-56: Confirmations and completion of previous ideas of the dwelling in the Halls of Mandos

In Q it is reaffirmed that all Elves eventually fade (*Shaping* 99). It is also specified that not only the ones who had been slain will go back to the Halls of Mandos but also those who had died of grief and those who had faded. Mandos himself will decide (contrary to what was stated before) whether they will be re-embodied (it is not said where) or return to Valinor[24] (it is not very clear how). The picture changes in QS, where it is said that only in the case of a violent death or a death of grief (and not because of fading) the spirit of the Elf will find itself in the presence of Mandos (a.1).[25] Here the spirit may be held back, as happened for the first time to Fëanor (a.1.2).[26] The norm is, however, that after a waiting time of a thousand years, Mandos will ask

---

23 "And then [slain or waste with sorrow] their spirits went back to the halls of Mandos and awaited a thousand years, or the pleasure of the Gods, before they were recalled to free life. [note 3: Added at the same time as the insertion given in note 2: and they were reborn in their children, so that the number grows not]" (*Shaping*, Sk 21).
24 "Slain or fading their spirits went back to the halls of Mandos to wait a thousand years, or the pleasure of Mandos according to their deserts, before they were recalled to free life in Valinor, or were reborn [later changed to "or sometimes were reborn"], it is said, into their own children" (*Shaping* 100).
25 "But if they were slain or wasted with grief, they died not from the earth, and their spirits went back to the halls of Mandos, and there waited, days or years, even a thousand, according to the will of Mandos and their deserts" (*LR*, QS 247). This passage, also confirmed in *WJ*, LQ1-2 174-175, is quite inexplicably absent in *S* (Q 12).
26 *LR*, QS 249. In the corresponding passages of Sk (*LR* 22) and Q (*LR* 101) nothing is said by Mandos about the destiny of Fëanor.

the Elf (a.1.1) which of the two destinies he prefers: either to be reborn in the Children (a.1.1.1), or to return as a spirit; the place of their rebirth, however, is not specified (Valinor[27] or Middle-earth: a.1.1.2).[28] It is also affirmed (and this answers the first question) that Elves are subject to fading only outside of Valinor. In the Ainulindalë versions from 1930 to 1951, references to rebirth are still present – although without any particular clarification.[29] Quite inexplicably, references to rebirth in the Children are totally absent in the published version of the *Silmarillion* (S, Ainulindalë and Qu 12).

Between 1930 and 1951 the destinies envisaged for the Elves are structured as follows and still leave many questions unanswered:

   a. death by being killed/of grief
   a.1 the Elf goes to Mandos
      a.1.1. Mandos asks him to choose:
         a.1.1.1 rebirth (where?)
         a.1.1.2 return as a spirit (where?)
      a.1.2 Mandos can keep him (e.g. Fëanor)
   b. fading in Middle-earth and life as shadows (until when?)
   c. life in Valinor without ever fading

## 1957-60: The highest point of meditation: Míriel, the Houseless, the Lingerers and the refusal to be reborn in the Children

In the "Laws" everything becomes more complex because Tolkien in the meantime had "discovered" that Míriel, after giving birth to Fëanor, decides to abandon the world thus leaving her body lifeless in Aman (although no wounds had been inflicted to her); an event which causes great distress among the Valar.[30] According to the "Laws" an Elf can therefore: (a) die of grief or wounds (either

---

27 This is what happened to Finrod (*LR*, QS 300; LB 358, *WJ*, LQ 243).
28 "Thence they are recalled at length to freedom, either as spirits, taking form according to their own thought, as the lesser folk of the divine race; or else, it is said, they are at times re-born into their own children, and the ancient wisdom of their race does not perish or grow less" (*LR*, QS 247). In MuB too (of the 1930s) it is said that "often" Elves are reborn in their Children (*LR*, MuB 163). QS seems to specify, in contrast to MuB, that in those other rare cases they either do not come back (Fëanor) or return as spirits.
29 *LR*, MuB 163; *MR*, MuC 21 and MuD 37.
30 Míriel makes her first appearance in the role of Fëanor's mother in LQ1 (*MR* 185) and in the contemporary AAm1 (*MR* 92). However, it is only around 1957-58 that she abandons her body as narrated in some marginal notes of AAm (*MR* 101, footnotes 1 and 4, see 205), in FM1 (*MR* 205-207) and in one of his successive revisions in 1958 included in QS (*MR* 271; see FM2 in *MR* 254-257). In "Laws" it is affirmed for the first time that Míriel is re-embodied into her own body after Finwë's death and that she decided to stay in Mandos (*MR*, LawsA 249-250).

in Valinor or in Middle-earth: *MR* 218, 221 footnote) or (b) fade, as is the case with the Lingerers who, by delaying their return to the West, had been left with their *fëa* only, which had consumed their body thus making them able to live as immortals in Arda until its end[31] [see 1.2]. In the case of separation of the body from the spirit the Elf is summoned to Mandos and can either accept the call (a.1) or refuse it (a.2) thus becoming a houseless spirit wandering as a shadow in the land of the living (*MR* 233). The destiny of the Elf who has accepted the summoning is entrusted into Mandos' hands, who in due time (*MR* 235) will decide whether he is going to keep the Elf with him (a.1.2)[32] or offer him (a.1.1) the double choice of being reborn in the Children (a.1.1.1)[33] or dwell in his Halls for ever (a.1.12).[34] The rather enigmatic reference made in QS to a possible return as a spirit is therefore abandoned. Instead it is affirmed that rebirth is the only possible way of returning.[35] An exception to a return by rebirth is provided to Míriel whose body had been kept untouched in the Blessed Realm, hence making it possible for the *fëa* to be reinstated in it (a.1.1.3; *MR*, LawsB 221). This synthesis introduces a threefold choice concerning the Elves' destiny (one for Mandos and the other two for the Elves) and a new unsettling event (Míriel's 'case'):

a. death by being killed/of grief: the Elf is called to Mandos' presence and
a.1. goes to Mandos:
    a.1.1. Mandos asks him/her to choose:
        a.1.1.1 be reborn in one of the Children (after that: re-embodiment by Manwë) or
        a.1.1.2 dwell in Mandos (e.g. Finwë) or
        a.1.1.3 return into his/her body (Míriel)
    a.1.2. Mandos keeps him/her with him (e.g. Fëanor, some married Elves);

---

[31] "The Lingerers are not houseless, though they may seem to be. They do not desire bodies, nor do they seek shelter, nor strive for mastery over body and mind. Indeed they do not seek converse with Men at all, save maybe rarely" (*MR*, LawsB 224-225).
[32] This happens for example if a married Elf dies and the spouse remarries before his or her return (*MR*, LawsA 234), or if a married Elf dies but he or she does not wish to remarry the same spouse (*MR*, LawsA 233).
[33] "Those who were healed could be re-born, if they desire it: none are reborn or sent back into life unwilling. The others remained, by desire or command, *fëar* unembodied, and they could only observe the unfolding of the Tale of Arda from afar, having no effect therein" (*MR*, LawsB 223).
[34] This often happens to those who died twice (*MR*, LawsB 222), but also Finwë decides to abide with Mandos forever (*MR*, LawsA 249).
[35] "A houseless *fëa* that chose or was permitted to return to life re-entered the incarnate world through child-birth. Only thus could it return" (*MR*, LawsB 221).

a.2 does not answer the call ("Houseless") and his *fëa* will dwell in Arda until its end;
b. fading in Middle-earth and life as shadow until the end of Arda ("Lingerers");
c. life in Valinor without ever fading.

The ideas exposed in the "Laws" will be maintained in Tolkien's successive writings[36] with the exception of only one fundamental change: the abandonment of the idea of the rebirth in the Children (a.1.1.1) in favour of a different mode of return upon which we intend to dwell for a closer analysis.

## Reincarnation and harmony between body and spirit

The discarding of the concept of rebirth in the Children, which had been a constant for over forty years in the *Legendarium*, is of particular significance, all the more so because the idea is also implicitly present during and after the composition of *The Lord of the Rings* (where, however, Tolkien never mentions the reincarnation of the Elves by rebirth in the Children). In fact, in 1954 Tolkien alludes to this possibility during a conversation with Mr Hastings, manager of a Catholic bookshop which was distributing *The Fellowship of the Ring*: the cause of great perplexity to Mr Hastings who then writes to Tolkien for elucidations. In a draft letter of 1954 Tolkien writes:

> 'Reincarnation' may be bad *theology* (that surely, rather than metaphysics) as applied to Humanity [...]. But I do not see how even in the Primary World any theologian or philosopher, unless very much better informed about the relation of spirit and body than I believe anyone to be, could deny the *possibility* of re-incarnation as a mode of existence, prescribed for certain kinds of rational incarnate creatures. This is a biological dictum in my imaginary world. (*Letters* no. 153)

Despite these peremptory statements, it is only during this period that Tolkien begins to strongly question the issue of reincarnation (most likely because of the numerous letters he received from his admirers). First in the "Laws" he strenuously attempts to provide a structure for the reincarnation theory. In

---

36 Especially in "Athrabeth" and in the commentary to it we find confirmation of Mandos's call, his judgement, the choice the Elves are left with to answer the call or not and the form of their return (*MR* 339), fading as some form of immortality (*MR* 342) and the Elves' connection with Arda until its end; in this respect it is explained that the history of the Elves will end with the end of Imbar (the Earth) or at least of Arda (the Solar System), but not necessarily with the end of Eä (the Universe), where other forms of intelligent life may exist besides Elves and Men (*MR* 337-338).

doing so he inevitably comes across the many incongruities implied by the theory which are at first aporias of a moral and social nature and concern the *fëa* of the married Elves. In order to avoid a sort of possible "bigamy", Tolkien introduces the judgement of Mandos, who will not allow the return of an Elf who is not willing to reunite with his living spouse (*MR*, LawsA 227; see footnote 32). Difficulties of a "psychological" nature will also surface: in the case of rebirth the Elf will gradually reacquire the memories of his past life thus finding himself with four different parents at the same time (two for each life) (*MR* 221-222).

In the "Converse between Manwë and Eru", we witness a first change after fifty years: the Valar will be, in fact, granted the power to let the Elves return to an adult body, shaped by the Valar themselves, whereas rebirth will become just "a" path – no longer the only one – which, if chosen by the Elf, will need approval by Eru in person (*MR*, Converse 362). However, what is going to be truly decisive and will lead Tolkien to reject the thesis of rebirth is the 'discovery' of the metaphysical principle of the harmony between *hröa* and *fëa*. This concept is peremptorily reaffirmed in the commentary to the "Athrabeth" (*MR* 330) and will represent the main cause for rejecting the idea of rebirth in the Children in "Reincarnation".[37]

These results will once again be confirmed more than ten years later in "Glorfindel" (1970-72) and in a contemporary note on reincarnation.[38] It is difficult to give a philosophical evaluation of this important principle (you may refer to my other essay on this subject published in this volume). What is certain is that Tolkien manages to do here what he had criticized in *Letters* no. 153, namely to philosophically elaborate on the relationship of body and soul to the point that he rejects the very idea of reincarnation.

---

37 "The most fatal objection [is that] it contradicts the fundamental notion that *fëa* and *hröa* were each fitted to the other: since *hröar* have a physical descent, the body of rebirth, having different parents, must be different" (*MR* 363).
38 In the story "Glorfindel I" it is said that "it was a duty, therefore, of the Valar to restore them" (*P* 378) and in "Glorfindel II" it is added that "it was a duty of the Valar, by command of the One, to restore them to incarnate life" (*ibid*. 380). No mention of the rebirth in the Children is present here. Moreover, it is defined as a misconception of human origins (*MR* 382-383). Also for the death of the Dwarves, a complex evolution of concepts is present in the *Legendarium* see Rateliff 2007, 720-723.

## 1.4 Conclusions on the Elves – The drama of immortality

If we review this fifty year plus process as a whole, it will be hard not to see in it the mighty speculative effort which, with the help of a literary device, is meant to explore the mysterious relationships between spirit and body, life and death. Tolkien's thought at its peak envisages that the People of the Stars are immune from any kind of sickness, their spirit consumes the body until it fades, they can also exert their freedom by choosing different destinies and, to return to Arda, they do not follow the path of being reborn in the Children.

We have thus a sort of higher 'spiritualization' of the Elves which makes their immortality far more plausible. It is exactly this spiritualization that enables us to understand better the dramatic aspects the idea of immortality entails. Without reincarnation (which interrupts the continuity of life) and sickness, Legolas's words in *The Lord of the Rings* which express the 'negative' side of immortality in fact acquire a stronger plausibility:

> 'Nay, time does not tarry ever,' he said; 'but change and growth is not in all things and places alike. For the Elves the world moves, and it moves both very swift and very slow. Swift, because they themselves change little, and all else fleets by: it is a grief to them. Slow, because they do not count the running years, not for themselves. The passing seasons are but ripples ever repeated in the long long stream. Yet beneath the Sun all things must wear to an end at last.' (*LotR*, FR.II.9)

This dialogue, which was written (and more than once rewritten) in 1941[39] and has been the subject of a masterful analysis by Verlyn Flieger (Flieger 1997, 89-116), clarifies that for Elves time passes very fast. As beings who have been destined to a life span just as long as that of Arda, they witness the death not only of animals or humans but also of plants and whole geological eras. The same concept can be found, reinforced, in "Aman" (written almost at the same time as "Reincarnation") where the nature of the Elves is made apt to the passing of life in Valinor, whereas one year of their life corresponds to 144 sun cycles in Middle-earth:

> [I]n Aman the world appeared to them as it does to Men on Earth, but without the shadow of death soon to come. Whereas on Earth to them all things in comparison with themselves were fleeting, swift to change and die or pass away,

---

39 *Treason* 363-364; see Hammond and Scull 2006b, 535.

in Aman they endured and did not so soon cheat love with their mortality. On Earth while an Elf-child did but grow to be a man or a woman, in some 3000 years, forests would rise and fall, and all the face of the land would change, while birds and flowers innumerable would be born and die in loar upon loar under the wheeling Sun (*MR*, Aman 426).

Due to these innumerable recurrences Elves have stopped the reckoning of seasons and years, thus making time stand almost still. Everything is worsened by the fact that the history of Arda (just as in 'our' Primary World: *Letters* no. 43) is bound to a progressive decline if compared to its luminous past (cf. Flieger 2002). Elves have therefore stopped counting the years and the centuries and are dramatically dragged by the generations towards a future which is behind them, while they are permanently turned towards more and more remote ages which they try to 'embalm'.

Besides these two metaphysical reasons (velocity/recurrences of history, remoteness from better times), we find a third reason, unexpectedly related to the romantic theme of love, which makes serial longevity even more intolerable. In Tolkien's writings we encounter three masterfully developed examples of Elves who give up their immortality. All three are elvish maidens driven by their feelings of love; we are referring to Lúthien (from 1926), Arwen (*LotR*, from 1948) and Míriel (FM1-2-3, since 1957).[40] Quite obviously these are three emblematic cases used by Tolkien to suggest two more "plausible" reasons to refuse a life without end on earth: the love for a mortal being (Lúthien and Arwen) and the forsaken love (Míriel).[41]

So is a never-ending life desirable? No, Tolkien seems to answer, and this is not because of a scarcely believable "tedium of immortality"[42] which might be due to the fact that "in an infinite period of time all things happen to all men" (Borges 1997b, 19), but rather because of the exact opposite, insomuch as:

---

[40] Bill Davis quite correctly maintains that Arwen's choice does not originate from her wish to escape the "tedium of immortality"(see footnote 42) but from her love for Aragorn, with whom she wishes to share in full the 'short' human life in Middle-earth (Davis 2003, 123-136). On the theme see also Greenwood 2005, 171-195; West 2006.

[41] It is necessary to recall that although Míriel decides to abandon her life as the consequence of a postpartum crisis (see *Letters* no. 212 and *MR* 267-268), she does not draw back from her decision after she realizes that her husband Finwë was not patient enough to wait for her and remarried quite soon (*MR*, LawsA 243). In fact, only after her husband's death does Míriel decide to return to Valinor in her own body (*MR*, LawsA 249).

[42] For a philosophical analysis of the problem, see Williams 1999, 82-101. On Williams's thesis and the subsequent debate see Steila 2009, 158ff.

1. the eternal bond to the cycles of Arda makes history too erratic and fugacious, in such way that events evolve at too fast a pace for an immortal being;
2. this flow of time inexorably moves the Elves away from a luminous and unrecoverable past which they in vain (and erroneously) try to embalm;
3. finally and in practical terms, a life without end makes it extremely arduous (Míriel/Finwë) or almost impossible (Lúthien/Beren, Arwen/Aragorn) to establish durable and authentic loving relationships.

All this transforms immortality into a burden which, under certain aspects, can also be found in the contemporary nightmare of longevity or in the expectancy of an indefinitely long old age subject to the most advanced but inhumane medical treatments which separate us from our dearest affections and will never bring back our youthful vigour (Heath 2009, 21ff.) We understand why even the gods might be envious of human death (see 2.2) although Men have not yet understood or are reluctant to understand why.

## 2. Death and immortality in Men

If Men, in Tolkien's conception, are led to cease aspiring for a never-ending life on earth, they still maintain the 'right' to ask themselves what awaits them after death and what the ultimate destiny of their world will be. The Tolkienian *Legendarium*, however, does not provide a precise and satisfying answer to this question. Certainly, the author, a Christian and a "Roman Catholic" (*Letters* no. 195), believes in the resurrection of the body and in the Final Judgement, but he rejects a didascalic narration and most of all carefully avoids (in an allegorical and explicit manner) resorting to elements of a strictly Christian faith within his mythology,[43] with the exception of a few rare and problematic cases.

---

43 "The Arthurian world [...] does not replace what I felt to be missing. For one thing its 'faerie' is too lavish, and fantastical, incoherent and repetitive. For another and more important thing: it is involved in, and explicitly contains the Christian religion" (*Letters* no. 131; see also *Letters* no. 153 and 156 cited in footnote 67; *MR* 354).

## 2.1 Men's final destiny

### 1917-25: First contradictory ideas – The destiny of Man within and outside Arda

One of these exceptions is the one related to the final destiny of Men, and belongs to the 'unsorted' first period of *The Book of Lost Tales*. Here Tolkien describes Fui Nienna (the spouse of Vefántur/Mandos) as the judge who assigns Men to different regions in Arda, roughly corresponding to Hell, Purgatory and Paradise. This not only violates 'Tolkien's razor' (i.e. his determination to avoid Christian allegories in his mythology) but – as was also said by Christopher Tolkien (*LT I* 90-91) – contradicts the almost contemporary "Music of the Ainur" from *The Book of Lost Tales*, which describes death as a radical separation from Arda (*LT I* 59).

### 1926-37: Towards clarification – Human death, the encounter with Mandos and the departure from the history of Arda

This mediocre mimicry of Christian beliefs is soon to be abandoned. Already in Sk, in a sort of 'negative theology', it is affirmed that no human dead go to Mandos and they are not reborn and no Valar can decide their final destiny.[44] The only change of perspective we find is in this same text, which Tolkien almost immediately rectifies by adding that Men too, once they die, have to face Mandos even though in different Halls than those destined for the Elves and that, besides Ilúvatar, possibly only Mandos knows the mysterious final destination: the only certitude is that the dead do not return to Arda with, of course, the exception of Beren.[45]

This last schema of Sk will be reconfirmed later in Q (*Shaping* 99-101), whereas in QS it will be also added that Manwë was privy to the dead's final destiny (*LR* 247).

---

[44] "What happened to their [Men's] spirits was not known to the Eldalië. They did not go to the halls of Mandos, and many thought their fate was not in the hands of the Valar after death. Though many, associating with Eldar, believed that their spirits went to the western land, this was not true. Men were not born again" (*Shaping*, Sk 21).

[45] *Shaping*, Sk 22 footnote 4. On this change see comments by Christopher Tolkien (*LT I* 78, 90-93; *Shaping*, Sk 51-52).

## 1937-56: Confirmation of previous stances

The passage in QS will be kept essentially unchanged in LQ1-2 (*WJ* 175). Starting from 1917 the destiny of Men will become more and more indefinite and uncertain: the *post mortem* survival of the soul will be confirmed, but no mention given to what exactly will happen to it.[46] Not even the following writings will unveil this mystery, leaving humankind in Middle-earth in a state of great disquiet and incertitude. This state will be masterfully and powerfully described in the more mature phase of the story of the Númenóreans (a subject illustrated in this anthology by Alberto Ladavas), where it will be explained that Man's envy is especially connected to the arduous trial of "believing" in a favourable after-death future (see 2.3).

## 1957-60: The peak of Tolkien's thought: from the Great End to Arda Remade. Further confirmation (1967)

Beyond the destiny of Mankind, what is the ultimate destiny that Middle-earth and the whole of Arda are heading to? In order to answer this question it is important to mention briefly the tradition concerning the 'Great End' of Arda, an event which undergoes remarkable changes throughout the progressive genesis of the *Legendarium* and recalls both the Ragnarök of Norse mythology and the Christian Apocalypse (on Tolkien eschatological conception see Franco Manni's contribution to this volume).[47]

The prospect of a Great End in which a grandiose battle involving all the Valar and also the spirits of some dead humans (among whom Túrin Turambar)[48] appears in *The Book of Lost Tales* (*LT I* 53) and will be taken up again in Sk (*Shaping* 40). In Q (*Shaping* 165) and QS (*LR* 333) a rebirth of Arda after the Great End is outlined and the theme of Arda Remade/Healed will be predominant in the years of maturity (*MR*, LawsA 245, 251; Athrabeth 405ff.). On the other hand, we find already in Aragorn's words to Arwen (written in 1948)[49] the hope for

---

[46] These positions are also shared by Purtill (2003, 131-132) and Grant (1997); Edoardo Rialti, in an essay on death, however, talks of an "almost tragedy" (Rialti 2004). Passaro, on the other hand, leans towards the rejection of any life after death perspective in Tolkien (Passaro and Respinti 2003, 55-56).
[47] See also Whittingham 2007, 170-200; Nelson 1998.
[48] *LT II* 115-116; *Shaping*, Sk 40 and 165; *LR*, QS 333; *P* 374. On Túrin's destiny see also Hammond and Scull 2006b, 606.
[49] "In sorrow we must go, but not in despair. Behold! We are not bound forever to the circles of the world, and beyond them is more than memory. Farewell!" (*LotR*, App. A.5).

a future world where Men and Elves can be reunited (see the essay by Andrea Monda in this volume). The same idea will be alluded to a few years later by the Elf Finrod at the end of a debate with the wise Andreth,[50] introduced as the bearer of an ancient tradition known only by a limited number of mortals, the existence of which will be confirmed in "The Problem of *Ros*" of 1967 (*PME* 374).

## 2.2 The Envy for Death and Immortality

Human death seen as the departure from Arda will always be an unresolved enigma for Men, Elves and the Valar,[51] whereas the immortality of the Elves and the gods, paradoxically, appears to be fully understood by everybody. It is exactly this asymmetric knowledge of death and immortality that creates an intricate warp and weft of relationships and mimetic attitudes among these three peoples where reciprocal envy is quite unexpectedly the dominant feeling.

### The Gods' envy for freedom and death as departure from Arda

The envy of the Gods towards Men appears as far back as *LT I-II*, if only under the prospect of the Valar envying and coveting human freedom, conceived as the possibility to go beyond the music of the Ainur.[52] From 1920 to 1936 this "human, too human" attitude disappears. However in *The Lost Road* (1936)[53] there will be the first appearance of the Gods' envy for human death, envy which will be reaffirmed in "The Drowning of Anadûnê" (*SD* 346 and 365) and in MuC (see footnote 62). In the versions of the "Music" from the years 1946-51 mention is also made of the envy of Melkor towards Elves and Men

---

50 "But you [Andreth] are not for Arda. Whither you go may you find light. Await us there, my brother [Aegnor, that Andreth loved] – and me [Finrod]" (*MR* 326). On these developments see Whittingham 2007, 170-200 and Drout 2007, 475.

51 "Since the point of view of the whole cycle is the Elvish, mortality is not explained mythically: it is a mystery of God of which no more is known than that 'what God has purposed for Men is hidden': a grief and an envy to the immortal Elves" (*Letters* no. 131).

52 "The giving of that gift of freedom was their envy and amazement" (*LT I* 59). The corresponding passages in Sk (*Shaping* 11-12), Q (*Shaping* 78), QS (*LR* 204, 247) and MuB (*LR* 163) do not contain this semi-divine envy; however a rough manuscript of MuB contains this idea (*LR* 165).

53 "But Death is not decreed by the Lords: it is the Gift of the One, and a gift which in the wearing of time even the Lords of the West shall envy" (*LR* 65). This is a pencil note added to the text and testifies a first appearance of the Gods' envy of human mortality; see the comment by Christopher Tolkien (*LR* 74).

for the special gifts they received from Eru.⁵⁴ Tolkien, however, does not linger on the subject nor does he adequately explain the reasons for this envy, as if he meant that we are not allowed to fully understand the motives of the Gods.

## Elves and human death – from amazement to envy

As far as the Elves are concerned, the first feeling they experienced when witnessing the death of Bëor the Old from old age (years 1930-37) was that of great sorrow (*LR*, AB2 131; QS 276). However, between 1938 and 1939 Tolkien, in his celebrated lecture "On Fairy-Stories", explicitly elaborates on the elvish desire to evade immortality, to the point that he quite oddly quotes his *Legendarium* which was at the time unpublished:⁵⁵

> Fairy-stories are made by men not by fairies. The Human-stories of the elves are doubtless full of the Escape from deathlessness. But our stories cannot be expected always to rise above our common level. They often do. Few lessons are taught more clearly in them than the burden of that kind of immortality, or rather endless serial living. (OFS 68)

In conformity with the ideas illustrated in this lecture, where for the first time he expounds the elvish desire to escape from the endless cycles of lives on earth, Tolkien is to modify his *Legendarium* accordingly. First in the "Grey Annals" he describes the sorrow for Bëor's death coupled with a feeling of astonished amazement;⁵⁶ later in LQ2 he will restrict the reaction to the death by old age to one of wonder only.⁵⁷ The elvish desire to be freed from immortality, which is also due to the halo of mystery surrounding it, is at last described by Tolkien as envy for human death in his note to the letter n. 156 of 1954: "Death [...] is the Gift of God (envied by the Elves)" (*Letters* no. 156).

---

54 "But he desired rather to subdue to his will both Elves and Men, envying the gifts which Ilúvatar promised to endow them" (*MR*, MuC 12); the text stays unchanged in MuC* (*MR* 30) and MuD (*MR* 40).
55 See Shippey 2007b, 4 on this self-quotation.
56 "The Eldar saw then for the first time [the death of weariness, without wound or sickness; *by late pencilled change*] the swift waning of the life of Men and the coming of death without wound or grief; and they wondered at the fate of Men, grieving greatly at the short span that was allotted to them" (*WJ*, GA2 52).
57 "And the Elves wondered much at the strange fate of Men, for in all their lore there was no account of it, and its end was hidden from them" (*WJ*, LQ2 225).

## Men's envy for immortality and serial longevity

This intricate relation is explicitly brought to completion starting from 1936, from the human point of view, when Tolkien 'discovers' the story of Númenor, which closes with a dramatic epilogue brought about by Man's envy for the immortality of Valar and Elves. Since the first versions of "The Fall of Númenor", Man "murmurs" against the Gods because of his mortality (*LR*, FN1 11, 32ff). This will remain a constant in the whole mythology related to the fall of Númenor. It is only between 1943-45 that Tolkien elaborates on the reason for this envy, that is the great effort to "believe" in this positive function of death.[58] In fact, while Elves have the reassuring certitude that they can return to Arda after their death (see 1.2), Men are bound to a blind act of faith in the positive outcome of life after death, something which requires an enormous and continuous 'existential' endeavour (as is well illustrated in the essay by Giampaolo Canzonieri). First in DA1 it is the immortals (the Avalai, that is the Elves and the Valar: *SD* 354) who infer that this "necessity of faith" is at the root of Man's envy (*SD* 345-346) and then in the second edition it is the turn of the Mortals (Adûnâi) to confirm this hypothesis (*SD*, DA2 365).

This envy is once again reaffirmed in Appendix A to *The Lord of the Rings* (App. A.1 cited in 2.3), in the crucial letter 131 of 1951, and persists up to the "Athrabeth", where the wise human Andreth addresses Finrod with particularly harsh words which are quite correctly interpreted by the Elf as a strong envy for his longevity (*MR* 310). No mention is made in the text of the Valar and the Elves envying Man. This is consistent with the crisis of the classical conception of death as a 'gift', as we will see.

It is also noticeable that even in this fundamental dialogue Tolkien uses a female character in order to exemplify the theme of death, which also on the human side (after Lúthien, Arwen and Míriel, see 1.3) is intertwined with the theme of love (cf. Flieger 1997, 161) as Andreth reluctantly reveals at the end of the debate; the true source of her envy for the elvish longevity being her love

---

58 A 'healthy' immortality wish does also exist, but it should be understood as an eternal life as opposed to the indefinite prolongation of the life present, as is very well shown by Kreeft 2005. On the wish of escaping death which is inherent in fairy stories, see also OFS 63ff.

for the Elf Aegnor, Finrod's brother, who years before had left her because he could not bear to see her growing old (*MR* 323).

To conclude, it should be noticed that the theme of envy towards death or immortality, respectively, essentially confirms an already remarked periodicity which, after the early ideas (1917-25), gives way to an elucidative period; leading to a complete interrelation of the envies in the years 1936-38 (FN1, OFS) which will receive further consolidation and elaboration in the following years (see *LotR*, DA1-2) until their completion between 1957 and 1960 with the episode of the haughty Andreth replying to the erroneous elvish opinion expressed by Finrod.

## 2.3 Death: gift, fate, destiny or Man's nature?

What value can death have for the short and dramatic human life? This seems to be the question which has mostly interested Tolkien during the creation of his *Legendarium*. A question which has found more and more articulated and elaborately different answers in different periods, according to the various points of view (elvish or human) of those who have pronounced them.

### 1918-20: Death as one of the gifts to Man together with freedom

In the "Music of the Ainur" which is part of *The Book of Lost Tales* it is stated that "to Men he [Ilúvatar] gave strange gifts" (*LT I* 57). It is also indicated that the first of these gifts is the freedom to go beyond the original Music, whereas Death is only later defined as the characteristic which "is however one with this gift of power" (*LT I* 59).[59]

### 1925-37: First elucidation and new ideas: first mention of death as 'the' gift to Man

Sk does not contain references to the gifts given to Man. In Q there is only unspecific mention of gifts given to both Man and Elves (*Shaping* 78), whereas

---

[59] This intrinsic link between freedom and mortality is also found in MuB and MuD (*LR* 163 and *MR* 37): the passage is also found in *S* (Q 1) where the Italian version is seriously faulty ("It is one with this gift of freedom" is translated into "*Uno di questi doni di libertà*" ("One of these gifts of freedom"). One of the best texts on freedom in the *Legendarium* is by Dickerson 2004; see also Fornet-Ponse 2006.

in MuB Tolkien returns, almost to the letter, to the version of 1918-20 (*LR* 163). Significant changes can be noticed from 1936. In FN2 *death* for the first time is pointed out as the unique gift given to Men,[60] and in the almost contemporary *Lost Road* death is explicitly defined as *the* Gift of the One to Man (cited in footnote 53). The theme will again occur in NCP, where eternal life is defined by Sauron as the gift which has been reserved for the Elves (*SD* 315). In the almost contemporary FN3 it is once again stated that death is a gift specific to Man (*SD* 333).

## 1937-56: Classical conception: death as gift, doom, fate and Man's nature — First hints of the fall

In his OFS, Tolkien affirms that "it is one of the lessons of the fairy-tale [...] that on callow, lumpish, and selfish youth peril, sorrow and the shadow of death can bestow dignity, and even sometimes wisdom" (OFS 63), almost a reprise of the hint made in *The Lost Road* where shadow and fear of death were linked together.[61] "The Drowning of Anadûnê" is also very important with respect to this "dark" conceptual development, in so much as for the first time death is referred to as "Man's doom" (*SD*, DA2 361); a few months later, in MuC and MuD, death is defined (still in connection with freedom) as "Man's fate", and the replacement of hope with the fear of death is ascribed as Melkor's doing.[62] This is possibly an allusion to the fall of Mankind, consistent with some notes related to the Drowning where we are reminded of the Fall of Man, originally destined to become Valar (sic!), but dragged into mortality because of Melkor's enticements (*SD* 401-403).

These 'progressive steps' in the way death has been conceived all merge in *The Lord of the Rings*. In Appendix A it is said, with regard to the story of Númenor, that death is "*the* gift of Men (or Doom of Men as it was called later)" (*LotR* App. A.1, italics added). Nonetheless Men aspire to "immortality within the life

---

60 "But Elrond and all his folk were mortal; for the Valar may not withdraw the gift of death, which cometh to Men from Ilúvatar" (*LR*, FN2 25).
61 "There is a shadow, but it is the shadow of the fear of death" (*LR* 68). On this theme see Devaux 2002 and 2008, Garbowski 2004, 140ff. Both Ferré 2001 and Sullivan 2000 show how the encounter with death deeply characterizes many of the characters in the *Legendarium*.
62 "Death is their fate, the gift of Ilúvatar unto them, which as Time wears even the Powers shall envy. But Melkor hath cast his shadow upon it, and confounded it with darkness, and brought forth evil out of good, and fear out of hope" (*MR*, MuC 21). The passage, absent in MuC* (*MR* 43) is present in MuD (*MR* 37) and is also included in S, Ainul.

of the world, which was the prerogative of the Eldar, and murmuring against the Ban" (*ibid.*). The peak of this classical conception of death as a gift is found in the wonderful story of Aragorn and Arwen, a fundamental part of the epic (*Letters* no. 181) where in a sort of romantic death-rite[63] death is reaffirmed as gift/doom.[64] The story is concluded with Arwen's bitter words[65] and a last hint of hope on the part of Aragorn (see footnote 53).

This position is also confirmed in the long letter no. 131 of 1951, where Tolkien states that death is Man's gift and doom, adding that immortality does not belong to human nature.[66] In Letters nos. 153 and 156 (of 1954) it is still denied that death be a punishment and it is affirmed for the first time that Men are mortal by nature (and Elves immortal).[67]

## 1958-60 The peak of Tolkien's thought –
## Death as consequence of the Fall and not inherent to human nature

In letter no. 212 of 1958 death (both as separation of body and soul and as the departure from Arda [see 1.2]) is once more defined as a gift and natural to Men (and serial longevity natural to the Elves), but it is also seen, in contrast to what was previously stated, as a punishment.[68] In my opinion this is the first sign of an exquisitely theological concern in Tolkien, who is rethinking

---

63 For funeral rites in Tolkien see Reynolds 2008; Paggi 1990, 56-59.
64 First through the words of Elrond: "I fear that to Arwen the Doom of Men may seem hard at the ending." (*LotR*, App. A.5) and then through those of Aragorn to Arwen: "The uttermost choice is before you: to repent and go to the Havens and bear away into the West the memory of our days together that shall there be evergreen but never more than memory; or else to abide the Doom of Men." (*LotR*, App. A.5). In the various versions of the story of Aragorn and Arwen a growing attention towards the theme of death can be noticed (*PME* 268ff.).
65 "For if this is indeed, as the Eldar say, the gift of the One to Men, it is bitter to receive" (*LotR*, App. A.5). It may also be noted that in the available Italian translation the fundamental "as the Eldar say" has been omitted.
66 "Doom or gift of God, of mortality, the gods of course cannot abrogate"; "the special doom or gift of Ilúvatar (God), and which their nature could not in fact endure" (*Letters* no. 131).
67 "Since 'mortality' is thus represented as a special gift of God to the Second Race of the Children (the *Eruhíni*, the Children of the One God) and not a punishment for a Fall, you may call that 'bad theology'. So it may be, in the primary world, but it is an imagination capable of elucidating truth, and a legitimate basis of legends" (*Letters* no. 153, in footnote); "the point of view of this mythology is that 'mortality' or a short span, and 'immortality' or an indefinite span was part of what we might call the biological and spiritual nature of the Children of God, Men and Elves" (*Letters* no. 156).
68 "*Immortality*, strictly longevity co-extensive with the life of Arda, was part of the given *nature of the Elves*; beyond the End nothing was revealed. *Mortality*, that is a short life-span having no relation to the life of Arda, is spoken of as the given *nature of Men*: the Elves called it the *Gift of Ilúvatar*"; "It should be regarded as an Elvish perception of what *death* – not being tied to the 'circles of the world' – should now become for Men, however it arose. A divine 'punishment' is also a divine 'gift', if accepted, since its object is ultimate blessing" (*Letters* no. 212, italics added).

his mythology in order to make it more in agreement with Catholic doctrine, which Tolkien wrongly presumes as not considering death as part of human nature, nor seeing it as a gift but rather as a punishment[69] (in my second essay I will examine this mistaken supposition by Tolkien concerning Catholic Theology, which, however, considers death as being natural for Men). Hence a first attempt to make gift and punishment coincide, which anticipates a radical revision of the concept of death as a gift and natural for Men.

Tolkien had indeed already suggested in the Laws that death is not natural in Arda Unmarred (*MR* 239-240), but it is only in the "Athrabeth" that, through the words of Andreth, an ancient human tradition surfaces in full and definitive form which envisages Man's death in form of a separation of body and soul as a consequence of a mythical and obscure fall (narrated in the "Tale of Adanel", *MR* 345-349), and therefore not pertaining to his nature. "Men are *not* by nature short-lived, but have become so through the malice of the Lord of the Darkness" (*MR* 309) and since that moment Man has experienced the fear of death (*MR* 333). If this death is not natural to Man, he must have been originally immortal by nature,[70] in the sense that he was not naturally destined to death as the separation of body and soul, but only to death as a departure from Arda (the second kind of 'death' [see the illustration on page 50]). Since 1958, therefore, only this death-departure can be considered as the 'natural' Gift of Ilúvatar.

## 1961-68: Subsequent confirmations of previous ideas

The concepts expressed in "Athrabeth", the apex of Tolkien's thought over the theme of death, will be reaffirmed unchanged in various successive writings, as attested for example in the "Notes on Óre" of 1968 and in an interview given to the BBC that same year, where Tolkien, quoting Simone de Beauvoir, affirms that death is not inherent to human nature.[71]

---

[69] "But it must be remembered that *mythically* these tales are Elf-centred [...] This is therefore an 'Elvish' view, and does not necessarily have anything to say for or against such beliefs as the Christian that *'death' is not part of human nature*, but a punishment for sin (rebellion), a result of the 'Fall'" (*Letters* no. 212, italics added).
[70] "But the Elves were on their part generally ignorant of the persistent tradition among men, that Men were also by nature immortal" (*MR*, Commentary 332).
[71] Tolkien quotes the author (de Beauvoir 2001, 102): see this text in Roberto Arduini's essay (who has brought this important reference to my attention); see also Vink 2008.

## 2.4 Conclusion: Man's Death and Immortality

If we go over this multifaceted phenomenology of human death with a synthetic vision, we see:

- a progressive increase of uncertainty over the future Man faces after his death (we may compare the 'Christian' certitudes of *The Book of Lost Tales* to the drama of the Númenóreans or to Aragorn's last words (2.1);
- a perception of death as an increasingly 'extrinsic' and negative separation of the *fëa* from the *hröa* to the point that death is defined first as a gift, then the gift and later fate, destiny and alien to human nature (2.3);
- these two aspects contribute to the 'existential' burden of death, which in order to become bearable requires a blind faith which is the main source of the envy for elvish serial longevity (2.2.).

However, a much more positive vision of the future of Arda begins to take shape in connection with these negative aspects of death. The unexpected perspective of an Arda Remade makes its appearance in the final phase of the Tolkienian mythology (2.2).

To summarize, we can affirm that in the *Legendarium* we observe a more and more concrete presence of mortality on the horizon of human existence, which paradoxically gives way to a new hope. This concept is admirably mirrored in the elvish spiritualization, which leads to the perfect longevity but at the same time nullifies any definite faith in present and future history (1.4). It seems then that we are confronted with a constant feeling of the presence of both death and hope. Indeed Tolkien himself affirms "Men had a shadow behind them, but the Elves had a shadow before them" (*MR*, Commentary 331),[72] almost suggesting an opposition to the modern death ban and the contemporary search for immortality (see Foreword). The more death is looming on the horizon of our lives, the more we open ourselves to a brighter and ultimate hope, whereas the more we ban death from our lives and look for perennial longevity, the deeper we sink into the darkest despair.

---

[72] See footnote 61. In LQ2 (1958) Bëor says for the first time that "A darkness lie behind us" (*WJ* 217); this idea is derived from GA2 (*WJ* 37) and is also present in *S* (Q 17).

# Roberto Arduini

## Tolkien, Death and Time: the Fairy Story within the Picture

> *Only in the field of fiction do we find that variety of life which we require. We identify with a hero's death, and still we survive him, willing to die in such a harmless way yet another time, with another hero.*
>
> S. Freud, "Thoughts for the Times on War and Death"
>
> *To ask what is the origin of stories [...] is to ask what is the origin of language and the mind.*
>
> J.R.R. Tolkien, "On Fairy-Stories"

## Introduction

J.R.R. Tolkien constantly questioned himself regarding the nature of death and how man can defeat it. His thoughts stray, touching on themes such as art, creativity, literature, the power of myths and fables, and dreams. As the years passed, however, the urgency of the theme of death became more and more pressing, to the point of emerging in many of his later writings. Death is the theme underlying his most strictly "autobiographical" works (Shippey 2005, 418): his grief and its inevitability, the impulse to flee from it, the duty and impossibility of resigning oneself to it.[1] "Death, [...] that which ends life, and demands the surrender of all and yet by the taste (or foretaste) of which alone can what you seek in your earthly relationships (love, faithfulness, joy) be maintained, or take on that complexion of reality, of eternal endurance, which every man's heart desires" (*Letters* no. 43). Awareness of his advanced age and a sense of exclusion seem to have slowly developed in the writer, be-

---

1 Traces of these thoughts are found in his later works and in drafts of works which, although unpublished, are the mirror of a subject vital for the author: "Imram", *The Adventures of Tom Bombadil*, "The Lost Road" and "The Notion Club Papers". They are seen also, though only indirectly, in the cycle constituted by *The Hobbit*, *The Lord of the Rings*, *The Silmarillion* and the other works making up his *Legendarium*. On the other hand, our analysis directly focuses on the *Letters* and the contents of *Tree and Leaf*. See Shippey 2005, 392-402.

coming stronger and stronger. "Little doth any man know what longing is his whom old age cutteth off from return" (*LR* 44), Tolkien writes in "The Lost Road". The theoretical climax of this theme, developed throughout his works, is reached in *Tree and Leaf*, a collection of writings which are very diverse as regards their genre, style and subject, but closely linked by the writer's reflections on art and on mythopoetics or, as he defines it, "sub-creative" activity. It is precisely thanks to his works that the artist lifts himself above other men, who often fail to understand him.[2]

I propose a logical thread to trace the essential elements of the concept of death in Tolkien that will permit us to add some observations to literary criticism regarding him and his works. I refer to the author's attempt to make his own death subjective, to answer questions regarding him not only as a writer, but also as a man (cf. chapter 1). This logical thread is linked to some significantly-recurring words: naturally "death" and "life" (cf. chapter 2), but also "time" (cf. chapter 1.1), "trip" (cf. chapter 1.2) and "dream".

Particularly relevant is also that point in which the concept of death is interwoven with that of art (cf. chapter 3): Tolkien affirms that his work springs from the need to face thorny themes like death and immortality, but not from a philosophical, physical or religious viewpoint (cf. *Letters* no. 208). He seems to favour a position satisfying a need for a creative strategy rather than an orientation: the invention of a clearly-existing non-human world whose sole guarantee of existence is the imaginative power of the human mind and writing. We will thus open those enchanted pages of Tolkien's works to some specific points in his narrative (cf. chapter 1), at the same time turning the pages of his life, starting from the biographical outline at our disposal (cf. chapter 2). After this, we will examine in detail his "On Fairy-Stories" (cf. chapter 3.1-3.2), "Leaf by Niggle" (cf. chapter 3.3-3.4) and the poem "Mythopoeia" (cf. chapter 3.5), in which the theme of death is interwoven with that of art and sub-creation.

---

[2] See Mr. and Mrs. Parish and Councillor Tompkins in "Leaf by Niggle" or the final lines of "Mythopoeia".

# 1. Death and Human Circumstances

## 1.1 Time and Narration: Some Reflections

Although time is a necessary and intrinsic part of life, when we ask ourselves what it really is, aside from the clichés, we find no certain answer: it slips through the fingers of any type of conceptual understanding. Does it exist? At the origins of the universe, be it real or fantastic, we find the intrinsic difference between past and future, without which we cannot think or speak or act. This is why death exists even in fairy stories, not only due to isomorphism with real life. "Truth cannot be recounted save in the form of a fable," writes Dürrenmatt (1982, 154-157). Between life and death or between life and immortality the dimension of a 'between-time' presents itself. And it is in this 'meanwhile' that we live moment by moment.

Even if a narrative follows temporal rhythms, reproducing scansions and sequences in terms of days and nights, minutes, hours, age and years, the relationship with time and thus with death operates according to a specific logic. First of all, a book can be opened at any moment: at the instant in which one glances at the page, another moment begins, that of reading, and by turning the pages we can move forward or backward in time every time we wish to ...

Real time is not like this: we cannot go back ... Time as an irreversible dimension is a function of the nature of death. We can remember, but past events remain in the past. On the other hand, writing engraves shreds of time on paper, and we have the opportunity to read and re-read them. "When the end nears," Borges comments, "no images of memories remain; only words are left. Words, words, uprooted, mutilated words, the words of others, were the poor alms left to him by hours and centuries" (Borges 1997b, 25).

It is understandable why traumatic experiences, separation and, above all, death are a source of anguish, another recurring theme in Tolkien's works:[3] in other words, they represent the experience of "irreversible temporal dis-

---

[3] *Letters* no. 64: "If anguish were visible, almost the whole of this benighted planet would be enveloped in a dense dark vapour, shrouded from the amazed vision of the heavens!"

continuity" (Lombardi 2008, 19-20). However, as Bergson says: "We do not imagine real time. We experience it, as it transcends intelligence."[4]

In fairy stories, as in dreams, something else occurs.[5] Bettelheim points out important differences between fairy stories and dreams, relevant as regards the transmissibility of the former. While in dreams gratification of a desire is concealed, in fairy stories it is openly expressed. We cannot control what happens in dreams; on the other hand, the fairy story derives not only from unconscious content, but is shaped and forged on the conscious level. In addition, it is the expression of the consensus not only of an individual but of all those seeing particular themes portrayed as universal problems and all those who accept the solution proposed in the story as being plausible. If these elements were not present in a fairy story, it would not be handed down from one generation to the next (cf. Bettelheim 1990, 39).

The oneiric process, which like the fairy story uses the metaphor, also follows the principle of pleasure. In this dimension, time becomes unconscious time, with no rules linking before and after; it is eternal time, as when one dreams of a deceased loved one as if he were still alive. Furthermore, as Modell (1994, 85) recalls, in the narrative, time has two fundamental dimensions: there is the time of the arrow in the universe, linear, "Chronos", and cyclical or human time, "Kairos", that is to say mythical time, both that of repeated tragedies but also that of the new beginnings celebrated by anniversaries, rites and religious ceremonies, time, in other words, that becomes human only to the extent that it can be narrated. Ricoeur suggests that the pleasure deriving from the narrative is precisely the pleasure obtained from the re-depiction of time (cf. Ricoeur 1984, 91). On the other hand, Chronos is objective and impersonal time, associated with logic and science, biological time, which marches on inexorably.

"I wish I had time!" Tolkien writes to his son (*Letters* no. 313). And a year later he repeats: "When you pray for me, pray for 'time'!" (*Letters* no. 315).

---

[4] In his rigorous analysis of time as it is perceived within the conscious mind, the philosopher demonstrates that time as it is assumed in physics, i.e. as constituted by a succession of perfectly homogeneous instants, is in reality only the product of intellectual abstraction. See Bergson 2002.
[5] For a discussion of fairy stories and the treatment of time, see Rak 2005, 33-34 and 105-112. On the theme of death in fairy stories, see Richter 2005, 159-168.

The English writer needed time to finish the work he had been working on for all his life, the *Silmarillion*. He did not in fact have time to complete it. Unlike the text published with the same title by his son Christopher, Tolkien's *Silmarillion* is a vast collection of stories and writings which he had started in 1917 and which was incomplete nearly seventy years later, in 1973. Tolkien's assertions are theorised in his essays and staged in his works, particularly in *The Lord of the Rings*. The Oxford Professor's reflections are along the same lines as those of other thinkers and philosophers, Schopenhauer, Bergson and Freud, who like him were living in a period of great changes and conflicts.

## 1.2 The Metaphor of the Journey

The human condition is objectively limited. Man encounters a series of insuperable obstacles, the last and most obvious of which is death. However, there are material, intellectual, and cultural limits, as well as those of individual knowledge. Setting out on a journey may be a way to overcome some of them: since antiquity, the journey has been the metaphor for man's search, for a new experience to be acquired and a broader perspective from which to observe what happens (cf. Rak 2005, 94-104). A man who travels is a man who learns, and when he returns home, he is different, more mature, 'superior' in a certain sense to one who has stayed at home, capable of having a point of view that elevates him above others. He might even be misunderstood, as happens to the Hobbits when they return to the Shire, transformed by their contact with "things deeper and higher" (*LotR*, RK.V.8), where they are scolded by Sam's father, the Gaffer, for having associated with "strange company":

> And while you've been trapessing in foreign parts, chasing Black Men up mountains from what my Sam says, though what for he don't make clear, they've been and dug up Bagshot Row and ruined my taters! (*LotR*, RK.VI.8)

The journey as experience, but also death as a journey. This too is a theme and model dating back to antiquity. It happened to Ulysses in the *Odyssey*: his continuous travels finally lead him to Hades. There the Greek hero has the opportunity to talk to the dead and learn more about the *dike broton*, the destiny of men after death, described by Ulysses's mother, Anticleia, a destiny implying a tenuous shape: after the destructive action of fire on the body and strength, only a "shape" and name remain. An idea of oneself, an identity, although mortified, persists among those who are no longer living. They are only appearance, smoke, says Homer, shadows and dreams. Here we have the extremely close link, existing since the beginning of Western civilisation, between the journey, death and dreams.

The unreal will be consolidated with Pindar, who sings "man is the dream of a shadow" (*Pitica* VIII), with Shakespeare, "we are such stuff as dreams are made on, and our little life is rounded with a sleep" (*The Tempest* IV.1), with Borges, "no face exists that is not about to be erased, like the face in a dream" (1997a, 164). A final moment, bearing with it earthly experience, which becomes an absolute experience in the Next World. Ulysses's visit to the Other World, however, makes him understand that death is not desirable. The answer given to the hero by the soul of Achilles is exemplary:

> 'As for you, Achilles, no one was ever yet so fortunate as you have been when you were alive. Now you are a great prince among the dead. Do not therefore take it so much to heart even if you are dead.' Thus I spoke and he answered me: 'Say not a word, illustrious Ulysses, in death's favour; I would rather be a paid servant in a poor man's house than king of kings among the dead.' (*Odyssey* XI.ll.484-491)

The descent to the Underworld is the hero's supreme test, as Campbell (2008) has pointed out. And the hero returns from this journey to the Underworld enriched, above all in spirit. Not even the protagonists of Tolkien's works can avoid this destiny. It happens to Bilbo in *The Hobbit*,[6] when his journey to the bowels of the earth leads him to obtain the One Ring; it happens to Aragorn in *The Lord of the Rings*, where the Paths of the Dead mark the first step towards the throne of Gondor, but above all to the fulfilment of the prophecy regarding the return of the king; it happens to Niggle, who will finally be able to see his picture completed only after his journey.

In his greatest work, Tolkien represents the connection between the journey and death extremely well in a universe embodying the final aspirations of life, in which, as Rosebury notes:

> We seek happiness in spite of a fuller sense of our mortality, and at the same time attempt to preserve our original joy in the world, or at least to maintain

---

[6] Various studies on *The Hobbit* put the theme of the journey alongside that of death. See Matthews 2000, 62-63.

an integrity between the freshness of the early experiences and the ripeness of the later. If (to impose an over-literal symbolism for the momentary sake of clarity) the Shire equals childhood, then the Hobbits' venturing beyond it represents facing up to adult responsibilities; their returning to it, though sadder and wiser, expresses the desire to maintain lifelong psychological contact with one's childhood, until one has to renounce it, along with everything else, in death. The purposeful and enriching journey "there and back again" (to quote the subtitle of *The Hobbit*) stands as an image for spiritual wholeness preserved through the vicissitudes of life. (Rosebury 2003, 58)

The relativity of the human condition is more deeply perceived by those who have overcome some of their limits and no longer have a restricted point of view of reality. Only he who has fought in and experienced war, can observe a man killed in combat and ask himself, as does Sam Gamgee, "what the man's name was and where he came from; and if he was really evil of heart, or what lies or threats had led him on the long march from his home; and if he would not really rather have stayed there in peace" (*LotR*, TT.IV.4). It is Tolkien himself who is speaking in these pages and who imagines himself once again in the trenches of the Somme, in that World War I which has rightly been called "The Great Slaughter".[7]

## 1.3 The Limits of Existence[8]

It was precisely World War I, with its grief, victims and the destruction of civic institutions, which may have made the English writer more sensitive to the theme of death. The same thing happened to another thinker, his contemporary Sigmund Freud, who wrote "Thoughts for the Times on War and Death". It is evident that a conventional attitude towards death is incompatible with war, which "treats life in an unnatural manner" and "produces" death as on an assembly line. Freud writes:

> It is no longer possible to deny death; we are forced to believe in it. Men actually die, not one by one but *en masse*, tens of thousands every day. This time we are not dealing with accidental death. Undoubtedly, it is mere chance when a bullet strikes one man instead of another; however, the latter may be struck by

---

7 For Tolkien's experience in World War I, see the essay by Simone Bonechi in this volume and Garth 2003. There is vast literature, on the other hand, regarding the inhuman life of soldiers in the trenches. For an overview, see particularly: Willmott 2004; Senardi 2008; Gibelli 2007; Lussu 2005.
8 I have taken this title from the volume by Franco de Masi, which has as its subtitle *A Psychoanalytical Contribution to the Problem of the Transience of Life*. See the essay by Franco Manni in this collection.

the following bullet. The great majority of deaths become incompatible with the notion of chance. (Freud 1976a, 140)

There are, on the other hand, eloquent indirect indications of the general disinclination at present to face death, using methods whose popularity depend on the extent to which they can exorcise it without even pronouncing its name, or rather denying it.[9] It is the discussion, currently becoming decidedly more widespread, regarding everything that moves the pointer on the scale towards the indefinite lengthening of life, the defeat of time, the promise of immortality. These are the "distractions", according to Pascal's definition, which are introduced to mitigate the torment of the death-conflict: "Men, unable to cure death, poverty and ignorance, have decided, in order to live happily, not to think about them."[10]

In reality, in the depths of our psyche, in our unconscious, the concept of death does not exist: man has the tendency to consider himself immortal, and if he grasps the possibility of death, it is always due to fate or some exterior evil force, a murder, which must and can be opposed. Freud specifies this:

> One's own death is unimaginable, and every time we attempt to imagine it, we realise that in reality we continue to remain present as spectators. Therefore, as psychoanalysis maintains, no one is thoroughly convinced of his own death or, and it is the same thing, in our unconscious, each of us is convinced of his own immortality. (Freud 1976a, 137)

Freud does not accept any discussion of death because, he affirms, no one has ever actually described it. No one has come back from the dead to tell about it. Therefore, everything said about it is a product of the imagination, impressions, fantasy or faith.

Man's psyche is shaped by life, not death. It is individual experience that moulds the psyche. We speak of the Hereafter using the terminology of this life: "life" after death, passing on to "a better life", a new "life". Death is a mysterious void which man fills with his earthly experiences. Any type of speculation on the Hereafter has its roots in life. Therefore, we have no experience of death and cannot discuss it.

---

9 On the removal of death from Western thought, see the essay by Claudio A. Testi in this volume.
10 Thought no. 348. See also those that follow: "Our nature lies in movement; absolute repose is death" (no. 350); "Despite all this misery, man only wants to be happy, and he cannot fail to wish to be so. But how can he do this? To succeed, he would have to make himself immortal; as he cannot, he has resolved not to think about death" (no. 351). See Pascal 1967, 150-151.

Freud himself, however, admits that humanity, in its tendency to eliminate death from the book of life, finds an outlet in stories to satisfy its yearning for immortality. And in this case as well the theme of the journey is closely linked to that of death:

> The Hanseatic banner proclaimed: *navigare necesse est, vivere non necesse!* Navigating is a necessity, living is not. And we are led, in an absolutely natural way, to search for what we have rejected during real life in the world of make-believe, literature, the theatre. There we still find men who know how to die and cause the death of others. Only there does the condition exist in which we might reconcile ourselves to death. Indeed, this reconciliation would be feasible only if we succeeded in convincing ourselves that, regardless of the vicissitudes of life, we will continue to live forever, but a life safe from every attack. In fact, it is extremely sad to realise that life is like a game of chess in which one wrong move is enough to make us lose, with the aggravating circumstance that during life, we cannot even count on a return match. However, in the field of fiction, we find that variety of life which we require. We identify with a hero's death, and still we survive him, willing to die in such a harmless way yet another time, with another hero. (Freud 1976a, 139)

Freud does not view man's mortal state as a limit, but rather as a fertile incentive: it is this feared mortality that fosters desire and creativity. In a brief essay, "On Transience", Freud contests the fact that the transience of what is beautiful implies its debasement:

> During the course of our existence, we see the beauty of the human face and body vanish forever, but this brief duration adds new enchantment to those sources of attraction. The fact that a flower blooms for only one night does not make its blossoms appear less splendid to us. In the same way, I could not see how the beauty and perfection of a work of art or of intellectual creation could be debased by its temporal limitations. [...] The value of all this beauty and perfection is determined only by its significance for our immediate sensibility; it has no need to outlive them, and for this reason, it is independent of absolute temporal duration. (Freud 1976b, 174)

It is by no means clear that immortality is a valid alternative to death. In some cases, it might be even worse, as happened in *Death with Interruptions* by José Saramago.[11] "Being immortal is a mere trifle: except for man, all creatures are immortal since they are unaware of death," Borges writes in "The Immortal", the "divine, fearful incomprehensible thing is to realise we are immortal" (1997b,

---

11 The book, set in an unknown country and at a point in the unspecified past, opens with the end of death. The common citizens generally enjoy their new-found immortality. But it soon becomes apparent that the end of death presents unique demographic and financial challenges. See Saramago 2008.

18). To illustrate this, the writer recounts the adventure of an explorer who, after having been lost in the desert, arrives in the City of the Immortals and discovers that they live in holes dug in the ground, in a state of lethargic apathy, totally indifferent to the world: "So absorbed that they were virtually unaware of the physical world" (Borges 1997b, 18). Their immortality has guaranteed complete, infinite satisfaction, as well as all possible human experiences, and, as a result, the death of every desire.

## 2. Tolkien and his Reflections on Death

### 2.1 A Slow Process

Tolkien expressed similar thoughts on death and war during the time he spent on the battlefield in 1916, but above all when his sons were doing military service during World War II. Thus war becomes "the utter stupid Waste," but most of all the only direct experience "which goes really to the heart" (*Letters* no. 64). Having lost more or less half of his friends in World War I, Tolkien refers to his personal experience: the traumatic collective demise of those dearest to him.

The writer himself, like Freud, thinks that death cannot be portrayed. He writes in a letter:

> Gandalf really 'died', and was changed: for that seems to me the only real cheating, to represent anything that can be called 'death' as making no difference. 'I am Gandalf the *White*, who has returned from death.' Probably he should rather have said to Wormtongue: 'I have not passed through death (*not* "fire and flood") to bandy crooked words with a serving-man.' And so on. I might say much more, but it would only be in (perhaps tedious) elucidation of the 'mythological' ideas in my mind; it would not, I fear, get rid of the fact that the return of G. is as presented in this book a 'defect', and one I was aware of, and probably did not work hard enough to mend. (*Letters* no. 156)

Starting above all in the 1960s, Tolkien is no longer so sure of his own ideas. It is difficult not to believe that in that period he saw himself (perhaps only at times) as Fíriel, the farmer Maggot, Frodo or Looney:[12]

---

[12] The writer deals with the theme of immortality through the protagonists of his poems: "The Last Ship", "Frodo's Song", "The Sea Bell", "Looney". Many of the poems collected in *The Adventures of Tom Bombadil* end with a sense of emptiness or loss. See Shippey 2005, 396-397.

a mortal abandoned by the immortals and excluded from their company (cf. Shippey 2005, 398). He no longer believes he will be able to rejoin his creations after death, as Niggle does; he feels he has lost them, like the Silmarils. In any case, these later, gloomy reactions have no connection with *The Hobbit*, *The Lord of the Rings* or *The Silmarillion*, which preserve their purely literary justification: in them, the theory of "sub-creation" is unnecessary, even if in a letter the writer admits that he wrote the Ring epic to test his theory in the form of a long story.[13]

Tolkien himself discloses this on several occasions. In the documentary *Tolkien in Oxford* (1968), he says that "if you really come down to any large story that interests people – holds the attention for a considerable time [...] human stories are practically always about one thing, aren't they? Death."[14] On this subject, Tolkien quotes the French author Simone de Beauvoir:

> There is no such thing as a natural death. Nothing that happens to man is natural since his presence calls the whole world into question. All men must die, but for every man his own death is an accident, and even if he knows it and consents to it, an unjustifiable violation. (de Beauvoir 2001, 102)

Then he comments: "Well you may agree with these words or not, but those are the key-spring of *The Lord of the Rings*." This quotation is surprising and establishes a direct link between the two authors, above all as regards the theme of death. Simone de Beauvoir dealt thoroughly with the question in numerous books related to traumatic events in her life, like the death of her mother or that of her partner. Some scholars have even hypothesised her direct influence on the Oxford Professor,[15] considering for example, and not without good reason, "Athrabeth" as a critical comment on another book by Simone de Beauvoir: *All Men Are Mortal*.[16] I take the liberty of

---

13 *Letters* no. 328: "The book was written to please myself (at different levels), and as an experiment in the arts of long narrative, and of inducing 'Secondary Belief'. It was written slowly and with great care for detail, and finally emerged as a *Frameless Picture*: a searchlight, as it were, on a brief episode in History, and on a small part of our Middle-earth, surrounded by the glimmer of limitless extensions in time and space."
14 From the interview contained in Sibley 2001. See also Hammond & Scull 2006b, 611.
15 Galadriel's lament in *The Lord of the Rings* would echo a passage from *Le sang des autres* (*The Blood of Others*); a passage from the essay "On Fairy-Stories" would reflect the plot of *Tous les hommes sont mortels* (*All Men Are Mortal*). See Vink 2008, 121.
16 The book is dated 1946. See Vink 2008, 124.

adding that the quotation, mirroring Freud's thoughts, is the key to all of Tolkien's considerations regarding death, both his own and that of his loved ones, as can be seen from his works.

## 2.2 Death and the Desire for Immortality

Even if the present analysis is not centred on *The Lord of the Rings*, we must refer to what Tolkien writes in his letters regarding the concept of death in that work:[17] "I should say, if asked," the author writes, "the tale is not really about Power and Dominion: that only sets the wheels going; it is about Death and the desire for deathlessness. Which is hardly more than to say it is a tale written by a Man!" (*Letters* no. 203). Thus man and his desire to overcome his own limits. The author clarifies this point further, in another letter:

> Though it is only in reading the work myself (with criticisms in mind) that I become aware of the dominance of the theme of Death. (Not that there is any original 'message' in that: most of human art and thought is similarly preoccupied.) But certainly Death is not an Enemy! I said, or meant to say, that the 'message' was the hideous peril of confusing true 'immortality' with limitless serial longevity. Freedom from Time, and clinging to Time. The *confusion* is the work of the Enemy, and one of the chief causes of human disaster. Compare the death of Aragorn with a Ringwraith. The Elves call 'death' the Gift of God (to Men). Their temptation is different: towards a *fainéant* melancholy, burdened with Memory, leading to an attempt to halt Time. (*Letters* no. 208)

Man's art and thoughts are influenced by his confrontation with death. Time, its passing and the desire to halt it, is intimately linked to death.

The dimension of time is the logical necessity of death. The latter is the absence of time. On the other hand, its opposite, life, introduces time. The portrayal of death in the Hereafter is a portrayal of a life without time, as happens in fairy stories. The fairy story makes time eternal; it 'immortalises' it (from the Latin *immortalis*, 'not mortal', 'without death'), eluding death. Time is the essential element in the real order.

Tolkien thoroughly understands these concepts. He clarifies it once again in a passage explaining the ideas on which his work is based:

---

17 Regarding the psychological conditions of Frodo in the second half of *The Lord of the Rings*, see Livingston 2006 and more extensive studies like Petty 2003, 282, and Croft 2004, 133-138.

> I do not think that even Power or Domination is the real centre of my story. It provides the theme of a War, about something dark and threatening enough to seem at that time of supreme importance, but that is mainly 'a setting' for characters to show themselves. The real theme for me is about something much more permanent and difficult: Death and Immortality: the mystery of the love of the world in the hearts of a race 'doomed' to leave and seemingly lose it; the anguish in the hearts of a race 'doomed' not to leave it, until its whole evil-aroused story is complete. (*Letters* no. 186)

Death, immortality, anguish, and fate are therefore the themes underlying his story, embodied in a world of history, geography and, even more important, of time, because, as already stated, time depends on death and death on time. Without the death of every single instant, there is no space for the subsequent one and time cannot exist. One race "destined" to die and another one "destined" to live can have "something much more eternal and difficult" to teach each other regarding death and immortality and regarding time and its absence. Elves and men live in the world moving at different speeds, and the crossing of their paths must at some level shift from time to the absence of time. Tolkien carries out this passage, on the implicit level to establish a sense of 'other' time while remaining in the narrative present.

The central function of the relationship between mortals and immortals for Tolkien becomes even clearer if we read the *Silmarillion*. Even in the 'reduced' version published posthumously by his son Christopher as *The Silmarillion*, this work presents three great stories regarding mixed marriages between Elves and Men: the cycle of Beren and Lúthien, the Fall of Gondolin and the Story of Eärendil (respectively Beren and Lúthien, Tuor and Idril and the two half-elves Eärendil and Elwing). And a secondary plot of *The Lord of the Rings*, central to the story and also developed in the Appendices, is that of the marriage between Aragorn and Arwen, the last great marriage between Elves and Men.

Equally important is the meaning of 'other' time and how the contrast between Men and Elves develops this theme. The association Tolkien draws between both these races and death and immortality, and in turn with mystery, anguish and fate, appears simpler and clearer if examined more closely. The mystery of the love for the world existing in the hearts of Men "destined" to leave is quite easy to understand, as man has numerous experiences of love and loss. However, understanding the anguish in the hearts of the Elves "destined" not to leave the world, meaning not to die, is a little more difficult, given the fact that for most Men, death, although inevitable, is rarely seen as desirable. Tolkien gave some indication of this in "On Fairy-Stories", an essay we will return to later.

## 2.3 The Forest of Days

It is not difficult to understand why Tolkien, starting from his early writings, from 1917 on, was concerned with the theme of death and fleeing from it. When he writes "The Fall of Gondolin", the first leaf on the vast tree of his stories, Tolkien is an orphan: his mother died when he was twelve years old and he has no memory of his father, who died in South Africa when Tolkien was only four.

When his mother Mabel died, it was as if he had been mutilated. As Carpenter maintains, "the loss of his mother left a strong mark on Ronald's personality, making him a pessimist. Or, better, it highlighted two quite different aspects of his personality" (Carpenter 1977, 39). He goes on, describing Tolkien's two faces:

> He was by nature a pleasant, upright person, with a great love for life. [...] But after that event, his diaries and letters reveal a second side, more intimate but perhaps predominant. This part of his soul was capable of periods of profound desperation. More precisely, and above all in relation to his mother's death, when this trait prevailed in him, it conveyed to him an intimate awareness of the transience of things. Nothing could escape it, nothing would last forever, no battle would be won once and for all. (Carpenter 1977, 39)[18]

Carpenter also reports that, in addition to his mother's death, Tolkien was subject to attacks of profound melancholy, even desperation, although he kept them to himself. The new life that he slowly built for himself after that tragic event was threatened by World War I. At Oxford, he confided to a professor that the outbreak of the war was a severe blow for him, "the collapse of all my world," as he later defined it (*Letters* no. 306). And he was right: at the end of the conflict, as he himself recounts, many of his friends were dead, among them two members of his TCBS.[19] A whole generation perished in the trenches of France, under the bombs of heavy artillery and the bullets of machine-guns:

---

18 Verlyn Flieger also deals with this aspect. See Flieger 2007, 233.
19 It is the "Tea Club and Barrovian Society", the club of the writer's school friends, dedicated to discussion and intellectual debates. See Garth 2003 and 2008.

in the Battle of the Somme, there were more than 620,000 victims, 57,000 of them only on the first day.

One of the so-called "war poets",[20] Robert Graves, even described the death of *Faërie*, the fairy-tale kingdom.[21]

The fact that Tolkien dedicated his time to writing fantastic stories is a direct consequence of the war. "A real taste for fairy-stories was wakened by philology on the threshold of manhood," he later writes, "and quickened to full life by war."[22]

The thematic presence of death follows the vicissitudes of Tolkien's life and articulates his darkest moments. One example is the death of his friend C.S. Lewis. "So far I have felt the normal feelings of a man of my age – like an old tree that is losing all its leaves one by one," he writes in a letter. "This feels like an axe-blow near the roots. Very sad that we should have been so separated in the last years" (*Letters* no. 251).

In 1965, Tolkien writes: "I think of my mother's death […] worn out with persecution, poverty, and, largely consequent, disease" (*Letters* no. 267). In his later years, Tolkien thinks back even more to those he has lost. In 1972, he writes to his son Michael a few months after his wife's decease:

> But the feeling of insecurity is possibly (and I hope) due mainly to the maiming effect of the bereavement we have suffered. I do not feel quite 'real' or whole, and in a sense there is no one to talk to. […] suddenly I feel like a castaway left on a barren island under a heedless sky after the loss of a great ship. I remember trying to tell Marjorie Incledon this feeling, when I was not yet thirteen after the death of my mother (Nov. 9. 1904), and vainly waving a hand at the sky saying 'it is so empty and cold'. And again I remember after the death of Fr. Francis my 'second father' (at 77 in 1934), saying to C.S. Lewis: 'I feel like a lost survivor into a new alien world after the real world has passed away.' (*Letters* no. 332)

The death of his mother, the war, the loss of friends: all this leads Tolkien to frequently search himself regarding his desire to flee death, which he himself describes as "the oldest and deepest desire"[23] in "On Fairy-Stories", which is his essay containing these various considerations. According to the author, one of

---
20 For further information on the "war poets" see the essay by Simone Bonechi in this volume.
21 See the poem "Babylon", in the 1917 anthology *Fairies and Fusiliers*. See Garth 2003, 380.
22 Flieger & Anderson 2008, 56.
23 Flieger & Anderson 2008, 74.

Imagination's gifts is "Escape". He lists different types of the latter: flight to another world or flight from physical or moral pain. The latter are, however, only minor flights introducing the ultimate one, that of death.

## 3. The Heart of the Matter: Tree and Leaf

### 3.1 "On Fairy-Stories": the Great Flight

This essay was originally the text of a lecture in memory of Andrew Lang, held at the University of St. Andrews on March 8$^{th}$, 1939. It was revised and expanded to be included in the volume *Essays Presented to Charles Williams* and later published[24] along with "Leaf by Niggle" in *Tree and Leaf* in 1964; "Mythopoeia" and "The Homecoming of Beorhtnoth Beorhthelm's Son" were later added to the volume. It is precisely in this essay, as we have said, that we find the synthesis the Oxford writer devised to reconcile his need to write fantastic stories with the bitter reality of the war and the loss of his loved ones. It is for this purpose that Tolkien introduces the concept of "escapism". In the 1972 *Supplement to the Oxford English Dictionary* (*OED*), the term is defined for the first time: "The practice of searching for relief from what normally must be borne" (Shippey 2005, 449). The experience which more than any other "normally must be borne" is death. To this is added the fear of sterility, of not leaving descendants, who represent the most natural means of escaping death.

As a mortal being, man naturally wants to escape death and finds temporary escape in the happy ending of fairy stories. A large part of the essay is thus dedicated to defending the power of the literary art, ennobled by the term "sub-creation" (cf. Ferré 2001, 92-96): the merit of the persistent fascination of the fairy tales by the Brothers Grimm, the 'partial success' of *Macbeth*, the very existence of 'fantasy' as an art-form are all attributed to it. This same implication is concealed in the autobiographical phrase in which Tolkien reveals his love for dragons, a love arising from the fact that "Fantasy, the making or glimpsing of Other-worlds, was the heart of the desire of Faërie."[25] Tolkien expresses this

---

[24] The volume was incorporated into *The Tolkien Reader*, an anthology never published in Italy. Italian readers may find this essay in *Tree and Leaf*.
[25] Flieger & Anderson 2008, 55.

viewpoint with another neologism: "mythopoeia" (the art of inventing stories), which later became the title of a poem published in the most recent editions of *Tree and Leaf*, which will be discussed later (cf. chapter 3.5).

Once he has established this, Tolkien continues his essay by introducing another major type of escape. The writer maintains, in fact, that: "[t]he Human stories of the elves are doubtless full of the Escape from Deathlessness."[26] Elves and Men are two sides of the same coin: one embodies the profound yearning of the other. This is the heart of the mystery of Men and the anguish of the Elves. Each possesses what the other desires and desires what the other possesses. Just as Men dream of escaping from death, so the Elves dream of fleeing from immortality. One race is forced to abandon life and the world, while the other cannot avoid remaining alive and in the world.

Sub-creation is furthermore a way to overcome death: writing stories that others will read in the future, even if many centuries after the author's death, is yet another way man has found to overcome the limits of the human condition. Creating, inventing, writing stories is one of the activities Tolkien kept up throughout his long life. In his old age, when he was over seventy, the Professor lost the use of his right arm for several weeks, due to a shoulder problem. "I found not being able to use a pen or pencil," he writes to his editor on that occasion, "as defeating as the loss of her beak would be to a hen" (*Letters* no. 248). A large part of Tolkien's time was dedicated to the written word; this includes not only his books,[27] the considerable material connected to his academic work or the stories in his *Legendarium*,[28] much of which is still to be published.[29] There are also his letters. Many of them were written for business purposes, but in any case letter-writing was one of Tolkien's favourite pastimes, and an immense number of them has been preserved. By reading them, and by comparing

---

26 Flieger & Anderson 2008, 75.
27 In their *Bibliography*, Hammond and Anderson list thirty-nine "Books by J.R.R. Tolkien", thirty-six "Books edited or translated by or with contributions from" Tolkien, and thirty-nine "Contributions to periodicals", a list totalling 349 pages and which has subsequently been enlarged. See Hammond & Anderson 1993.
28 This was the name Tolkien gave to the monumental collection of his writings connected to Middle-earth. They comprise about 8100 pages and more than two million words. See Gilliver, Marshall & Weiner 2006, 153-154.
29 According to some studies, there are still about 5000 pages of original manuscripts to be published, mostly on linguistic or philological subjects, in addition to personal diaries. See Manni 2002, 22.

them to the drafts of his works we can understand much about the writer's attitude towards life and, consequently, towards death.

## 3.2 "On Fairy-Stories": the origins of his tales

While working on the Andrew Lang Lecture that gave rise to his essay, Tolkien considered the hypothesis of using some of Carl Gustav Jung's theories to explain the origin of fairy stories. This is clear from a note he made on the rough draft, referring to the psychology of the unconscious.[30] Verlyn Flieger is surprised by this, reporting the note and even a facsimile of the page.[31] As a matter of fact, in the essay, Tolkien quotes, even if only once, "archetypes".[32] He probably rejects its utilisation, giving the following justification: "I shall therefore pass lightly over the question of origins. I am too unlearned to deal with it in any other way."[33] The Professor must in any case have read something by Jung, as his knowledge is apparent when analysing the essay, but above all in consideration of the circles Tolkien frequented. The group of friends[34] to whom Tolkien read *The Lord of the Rings* for the first time, the so-called Inklings, were naturally inclined towards Jung, although their approach to him was a cautious one.[35]

According to Tolkien, one of the merits of fairy stories is "the satisfaction of certain primordial human desires,"[36] one of which is that "to survey the depths of space and time."[37] The Professor maintains: "Fairy-stories were plainly not

---

30 See Ms Tolkien 6, f. 3, in the Bodleian Library at Oxford.
31 See Flieger & Anderson 2008, 129, picture on p. 170.
32 Flieger & Anderson 2008, 42.
33 Flieger & Anderson 2008, 40.
34 "On Fairy-Stories" frequently refers to and is inspired by Owen Barfield, as for example in the passage on the invention of adjectives, the criticism of Max Müller (Flieger & Anderson 2008, 41) and the insistence on "participation" (*ibid.* 42-49). Some scholars assert a psychological and not a geographical dimension of Tolkien's "Perilous Realm": see Hiley 2008, 281. Ursula Le Guin even goes so far as to see Frodo, Sam, Sméagol and Gollum as four aspects of the same psyche: see Le Guin 1989.
35 C.S. Lewis confessed that he was "enchanted" by Jung, and, on some occasions, to have abandoned himself to Jungian-style critical writing (see Lewis 1969, 296-297). The writer also admitted that Maud Bodkin, the pioneer in literary criticism based on Jungian schemes, had considerably influenced him (see Lewis 2005, 105). Owen Barfield praised Jung for his understanding of the spiritual nature of the conscience and its evolutions: "The collective unconscious and its links to the myth are absolutely necessary antidotes to 20th-century materialism, which leads to the use of man himself as an object" (Barfield 1957, 133-134). On the other hand, Barfield criticised Jung's "spiritual hierarchies" as being too detached from the external world (see Barfield 1944, 193, 202).
36 Flieger & Anderson 2008, 35.
37 Flieger & Anderson 2008, 35.

primarily concerned with possibility, but with desirability."[38] Tolkien also speaks of the "the Cauldron of Story, waiting for the great figures of Myth and History, and for the yet nameless He or She."[39] All these elements are added like fresh branches to a woodpile that has accumulated from the origins of the desire to tell stories, which is the human mind itself. However, the Professor takes a clearer position when he has to give a definition of "Fantasy". After having revealed the inadequacy of the definitions in the *OED* and that of Samuel Taylor Coleridge, he states that by "fantasy" he means first of all "the Sub-creative Art in itself," but also "a quality of strangeness and wonder in the Expression, derived from the Image."[40] This phrase is fundamental as it implies the existence of the Image even before someone expresses it in any way. A diligent critic like Shippey goes so far as to define this phrase as one of the "most disconcerting statements" in "On Fairy-Stories" (2005, 87). In the essay "*Beowulf*. The Monsters and the Critics", Tolkien makes similar affirmations, particularly appreciating in the poem its balance and the "opposition of ends and beginnings. In its simplest terms it is a contrasted description of two moments in a great life, rising and setting; an elaboration of the ancient and intensely moving contrast between youth and age, first achievement and final death" (BMC 28).

Finally, Tolkien relates the fairy tale and the world of "Faërie" to dreams:

> It is true that Dream is not unconnected with Faërie. In dreams strange powers of the mind may be unlocked. In some of them a man may for a space wield the power of Faërie, that power which, even as it conceives the story, causes it to take living form and colour before the eyes. A real dream may indeed sometimes be a fairy-story of almost elvish ease and skill – while it is being dreamed. But if a waking writer tells you that his tale is only a thing imagined in his sleep, he cheats deliberately the primal desire at the heart of Faërie: the realization, independent of the conceiving mind, of imagined wonder.[41]

If the mechanism of dreams is reduced to actual human sleep, it would be seriously inadequate to justify the wonders appearing in those dreams, "like a good picture in a disfiguring frame," says Tolkien.[42] The above-quoted passage

---

38 Flieger & Anderson 2008, 55.
39 Flieger & Anderson 2008, 46.
40 Flieger & Anderson 2008, 59-60.
41 Flieger & Anderson 2008, 35.
42 Flieger & Anderson 2008, 35.

can be perfectly applied to Tolkien himself and to the fruit of a dream of his, a text inserted immediately after the essay "On Fairy-Stories" in *Tree and Leaf*.

## 3.3 "Leaf by Niggle": the Fairy Story within the Picture

The themes of sub-creation, escapism and the great flight from death, dealt with by the Oxford writer in his essay, are then literally put into practice in the fairy story in "Leaf by Niggle". While the writer admits that, from this point of view, *The Lord of the Rings* is a failure because "it was written slowly and with great care for detail, and finally emerged as a Frameless Picture" (*Letters* no. 328), the story of Niggle seems to be truly "a good picture in a good frame." The main reason might be that the story is the fruit of a dream, as we shall see shortly. Precisely of the type of dream discussed in the essay, the fruit of "unusual mental powers" and of which the writer should not doubt. And Tolkien admits that in this case he didn't "compose it in the ordinary sense."

In "Leaf by Niggle", the functions of Fantasy are illustrated by the sharp contrast between the real world, in which Niggle is immediately forgotten because he has not produced anything useful for society, and the world in which his sub-creation comes alive and plays a positive role. In this 'other' world, Tolkien illustrates the virtues of the secondary world of Faërie: the virtues of "Recovery, Escape and Consolation."[43] A further element for reflection is introduced in the story, the origin of which can be found in Tolkien's own problems with getting things done in time. Tolkien's greatest difficulty was in fact his meticulous perfectionism. In a letter dated 1938, while he was beginning to write the continuation of *The Hobbit*, the English writer admits: "They say it is the first step that costs the effort. I do not find it so. I am sure I could write unlimited 'first chapters'. I have indeed written many [...]" (*Letters* no. 23). It is not difficult to believe that the writer had numerous 'first chapters' in his desk drawers, but the problem was to finish those stories. He is aware of this when he begins to write "Leaf by Niggle". In the course of the years,

---

43 Flieger & Anderson 2008, 66. They are the virtues expressed in "On Fairy-Stories", from which comes the title of a chapter of the essay as well. See also Chance 2001b, 97. Bettelheim proposes adding a fifth one: a threat to the physical or moral existence of the hero. See Bettelheim 1990, 142.

the *Legendarium* had become a vast complex of stories, sagas, genealogies, grammars, dictionaries and philosophical essays.

Had it depended on him alone, it is probable that Tolkien would never have finished a single book in his entire life. What he needed was an editor's deadline and an impassioned audience. However, Tolkien was not yet aware of this and feared oblivion, gloomily imagining that his works would have survived, but was misunderstood and lacked readers (cf. *SD* 303, 308). In short, in 1944, Tolkien could surely gain the impression that "Leaf by Niggle" would have remained, along with *The Hobbit*, his only surviving work after thirty years of writing.

Shippey defines "Leaf by Niggle" as "quite clearly an autobiographical allegory in which Tolkien more or less directly comments on his purposes, his feelings and his career."[44] This brief story was first published in *The Dublin Review* in 1945. Carpenter suggests that the story was written just before the deadline, the product of Tolkien's "desperation" caused by his inability to complete his greatest work.[45] Reading his letters, it seems, however, that the story had been written in the winter of 1938-39, when only the first volume of *The Lord of the Rings* had been completed and Europe was threatened by war. In any case, this does not change the situation a great deal as in that period, too, the writer was suffering from anxiety and a creative crisis. It is probable that the story actually did arise from the writer's "concern" regarding *The Lord of the Rings* (*Letters* no. 199). In the course of time, Tolkien disclosed numerous details regarding its composition. From his letters, we deduce that:

- The story of Niggle derives from a dream, and Tolkien himself says he felt it was "derived": "I woke up one morning [...] with that odd thing virtually complete in my head. It took only a few hours to get down, and then copy out. I am not aware of ever 'thinking' of the story or composing it in the ordinary sense" (*Letters* no. 98).[46]

---

44 See Shippey 2005, 269 and Shippey 2007a, 355. As for Purtill he mentions three different possibilities of allegorical application: moral, aesthetic and religious. See Purtill 2003, 24f.
45 In that period, *The Lord of the Rings* was at a standstill, interrupted at the beginning of Book V: "I made an effort last year to finish it and failed," the author writes to Stanley Unwin, his editor, on March 18th, 1945 (*Letters* no. 98). More than a year later, once again to his editor and using almost the same words, he repeats the impossibility of continuing the story (cf. *Letters* no. 105).
46 The story was actually revised during these two initial phases, as revealed by the two typed copies (Ms Tolkien 6, ff. 23-40 and ff. 41-73) and, above all by the two manuscripts (Ms Tolkien 6, ff. 95-96

- It is one of the very few stories that is not 'absorbed' into the *Legendarium* of Middle-earth (*Letters* no. 131).
- In many senses, Niggle is Tolkien himself: his aspirations to have a "public pension" (*Letters* no. 98), his idling, his wasting time,[47] his worrying about his "interior tree", as *The Lord of the Rings* is defined (*Letters* no. 241).
- It is the only allegorical story that he wrote, even if this term does not always apply completely (cf. *Letters* no. 241).
- It reflects the writer's fear in 1943, under the bombs of World War II, in the midst of a creative crisis, certain that he will never manage to finish his novel (cf. *Letters* no. 241 and 199).
- Reading the story of Niggle still moves Tolkien (cf. *Letters* no. 241).
- Its initial title was "The Tree" (cf. *Letters* no. 99).[48]
- There are some biographical details: the poplar just outside his window, which his neighbour had "pruned and mutilated" without apparent reason; the name "Parish", deriving from that of a gardener he had really known (*Letters* no. 241).
- It was in any case written to be "universal" and confirm some of the theses in the essay "On Fairy-Stories". The passage explicitly quoted by the writer is the following: "It is easy for the student to feel that with all his labour he is collecting only a few leaves, many of them now torn or decayed, from the countless foliage of the Tree of Tales, with which the Forest of Days is carpeted" (*Letters* no. 248).

However, all these explanations on the origin of the story fail to include everything: "But none of that really illuminates 'Leaf by Niggle' much, does it? If it has any virtues, they remain as such, whether you know all this or do not" (*Letters* no. 241). The story in itself has value, and there is always something that escapes us: art is creativity and not meant to be explained.

Did Tolkien really dream the story? We do not know, but it appears to have arisen directly from his unconscious, as Steimel suggests (cf. 2008, 194). Once

---

and Ms Tolkien 14, ff. 2-22) in the Bodleian Library at Oxford.
47 "To niggle" in English means "to work giving too much attention to details, wasting time in frills or show." See also *Letters* no. 2.
48 The original title is present both in the manuscripts and in subsequent typed versions, even if corrected in pen. Note how from the initial totality of Niggle's project, the definitive title concentrates on the final result, the only leaf surviving the protagonist's death. Almost an irony, a *reductio ad minimum* announced from the very beginning of the story.

again in the "Introductory Note" to the 1964 edition of *Tree and Leaf*, the author confirms that he woke up one morning with the entire story "in mind", the product of a dream. Tolkien writes that the essay and the story are closely linked "by the symbols of Tree and Leaf, and by both touching in different ways on what is called in the essay 'sub-creation'" (Flieger & Anderson 2008, 147). Furthermore, in presenting the essay and the story as a homogeneous work, the writer emphasises the explicative nature of the story of Niggle.[49]

In any case, it is not difficult to find other, more personal sources[50] regarding the anxiety and worry that Carpenter discovers in the story and which the author himself mentions in his letters. Shippey maintains that, although as a whole it has religious implications,[51] "the story is simultaneously a personal apologia and self-criticism, expressed in the form of an allegory" (2000a, 267). Lodigiani reveals that, for Tolkien, "the Artist and his work are destined to perish and be forgotten, like all human things."[52]

The story has the power to console in various ways: it can console its sub-creator, who is afraid he will be completely forgotten after his death, with his works neglected; it can, if read as a 'purgatorial story', reduce the fear of death, depicting death itself and Purgatory as necessary steps leading to a final redemption (cf. Fornet-Ponse 2008, 157). Some scholars support an allegorical reading and interpret every detail as an autobiographical reference: Geier (2008, 213) goes so far as to find a direct correlation between Parish and the writer's wife, Edith. Others, on the other hand, maintain that creative art and the Great Flight are distractions rather than sources of consolation. Slack (2008, 271-272) suggests that the prefiguration of death actually intensified the protagonist's attachment to the real world. Kocher, however, asserts that the story may be seen as "Tolkien's attempt to find some meaning underlying all his work, if not in this life, at least in the next one" (2002, 161). Finally, Flieger renders

---

49 The text for the dust-jacket, which the writer sent to Allen & Unwin, states: "The second part contains what is a staging and a good illustration of the theories expressed in 'On Fairy-Stories' and one of the first short stories by Prof. Tolkien, 'Leaf by Niggle'. Like the later and vaster *The Lord of the Rings*, the story shows his mastery of the art of 'sub-creation', the power to give fantasy 'the consistency of reality'." See Ms Tolkien 6, f. 76, in the Bodleian Library at Oxford.
50 Priscilla Tolkien, the writer's daughter, maintains that "Leaf by Niggle" is "the most autobiographical" of her father's works. See Pearce 1998, 174.
51 It is interesting to note how in the essay "On Fairy-Stories", "religion" is equivalent to "myth" and to perceptible "representability". See also *Letters* no. 156.
52 Lodigiani 1982, 54. See also Shippey 2007b, 10.

the various interpretations compatible, saying that "both the allegorical and autobiographical viewpoints have a certain validity, and those who seek them can find elements supporting both in the story" (1997, 231).

From the very first lines, the story begins with the certainty of death: "There was once a little man called Niggle, who had a long journey to make" (*TL* 75). The reason for this journey is never explained, nor are we told how it is to be undertaken. The identification of the journey as death is confirmed at the end of the story,[53] but Shippey argues that it is already present in the very first sentence, a literal quotation of the Old English poem *Bede's Death-Song*: "Before that compelled journey ('*need-fare*') no man is wiser than he needs to be, in considering, before his departure, what will be judged to his soul after his death, good or evil."[54] Thus the long journey that the "little man" has to make (and that all men have to undertake) is surely death. If this were not the case, events would lack coherence on the secondary-world level as noted by Geier (2008, 227-228).

Like Tolkien, the painter Niggle begins to paint a tree, but then he loses his way in portraying the background behind it, the creatures living in its branches, the veins of its leaves and wood – from the universal to the detail and vice versa, the dreamer is led astray by the details of his creation, often losing sight of his ultimate goal totally wrapped up in the process of sub-creation. "It is a gift," exclaims Niggle when he contemplates his completed work. It is truly a gift, whether Niggle is referring to the painting or to the art of creating. The problem is that Niggle will never finish his painting. Like Tolkien, Niggle is a 'time-waster', a painter who is not very successful "in part because he had other things to do," that is, taking care of his garden, helping his neighbours, living and respecting the unwritten laws governing his small community: although reluctantly, in the end he always responds to the requests of others. Above all it is his duty to help his neighbour Parish, lame and very demanding, who continually interrupts his work.

In any case, the lack of time at the disposal of the creative artist is the dominant theme. Typical is the relationship with the other, a source of continual

---

53 It is revealed by Councillor Tompkins. See *TL* 93-94.
54 Shippey 2005, 43. See also Geier 2008, 227-228.

distraction. The neighbour, insistent and jealous of this "vital ecstasy" in which Niggle emerges himself every day, demands his attention. One could say that Parish kills Niggle, but this is not actually correct. Parish kills, takes away, the time Niggle has at his disposal (cf. Shippey 2000a, 273). For Kocher, the reason for the continual requests for time and energy on the part of the neighbour lies in the only contribution that he can make to Niggle's picture: no artist can sub-create successfully without having first understood the needs of the real world (cf. Kocher 2002, 166).

However, even his attacks of laziness, his continually-expanding project, his tendency to dwell on every tiny detail of every single leaf, contribute to the fact that Niggle cannot manage to finish his picture. The protagonist's experience becomes reality and gratification: those leaves drawn so precisely, to the point of becoming almost an obsession, are not simply a diversion, but his own existence put on canvas. It is quite obvious that the Tree is *The Lord of the Rings* (or perhaps a completely finished and integrated version of the entire story of Arda), Tolkien's way of working, not very systematic and with continuous delays, and that the greatly-feared journey is, as we have said, death. The problem of death is introduced along with time. The painter feels that his life will be fulfilled only when his painting is completed. For this reason, he has to bring his work (life) to completion (fullness) before his great journey (death). However, not everything can be completed. Paradoxically, it is necessary to know how to leave, to prepare oneself for departure, even if there are a thousand other things to do and to say, a thousand more leaves to paint.

## 3.4 "Leaf by Niggle": in the Hereafter of the Mind

Niggle's death is only part of the story. As a matter of fact, more than two-thirds of it takes place after the protagonist's departure. Niggle, who came down with a fever after going for an errand for Parish, has to depart suddenly, leaving his unfinished canvas, which is then requisitioned to repair some houses damaged in a flood. The Driver comes to fetch him; Niggle protests but does not rebel. There is no anguish, as would be natural for a man about to die. Niggle has no "anguish in his heart," as happens to the Elves in *The Lord of the Rings* and as

Tolkien explains in his letters (*Letters* no. 43). There is only astonishment on the part of the protagonist: when you least expect it, someone comes and tells you it is time to leave. The painter can take nothing with him, neither food nor clothes, except for a paint-box and a notebook for sketches.

The Hereafter, however, is represented as a continuous journey and is "the fulfilment of his dreams" (Kelly & Livingston 2009, 36). There are temporal and spatial elements. In the Hereafter, the painter is distracted by what interests him most: colours, plants, flowers, that is, the elements in his painting. Niggle finds himself in the "Workhouse infirmary", where he expiates his tendency to waste time, typical of his mortal life, by working hard, taking bitter medicines and meditating in the darkness. In the Hereafter, time is nearly devoid of all meaning: it expands, and centuries pass while Niggle labours. It is important to understand some nuances: "At first, during the first century or so (*I am merely giving his impressions*), he used to worry aimlessly about the past" (*TL* 83, italics are mine). The narrator himself intervenes to indicate that it is the protagonist who stresses the passing of time, or perhaps loses all sense of it. This is noteworthy if we realise that it is the writer himself who is underlining this aspect.

Time is the only thing regulating life. As long as Niggle is concerned about it, all he does is work hard and sleep in a dark place, where the sense of time cannot be deduced from any external element. Then Niggle loses even the desire for Time: "[…] in time he forgot what it was that he had wanted a week longer for" (*TL* 83); and only in the Hereafter does he finally succeed in regulating it, because precisely when he stops worrying about it, he becomes its master: "He was becoming master of his time" (*TL* 84). And Tolkien once again emphasises this point. Niggle now is concerned only with his duties in the Workhouse: he plans them carefully, calculating how much time he needs to make that board stop squeaking or to hang hinges on that door or repair the leg on that table. An attentive reader will also ask himself if he was not kept there to do these jobs precisely because he had become so good at them. The narrator again intervenes to clear up this potential doubt: "But that, of course, cannot have been the reason why they kept the poor little man so long" (*TL* 84). No, there is another reason: Niggle has to lose his sense of time. Tolkien notes: "He began to know just what he could do with it" (*TL* 84).

Hard work, the door knocker, the little cell, and the workhouse are the norm until Niggle reaches a point when he "never" has the sensation of being in a hurry. "He was quieter inside now, and at resting-time he could really rest" (*TL* 84). Freed from the worries of life, outside the bounds of earth, time no longer counts. Life no longer counts, and there is no longer any allusion to the distress suffered in life.

Niggle is describing the Hereafter of his imagination. "To ask what is the origin of stories," Tolkien explains in "On Fairy-Stories", "is to ask what is the origin of language and the mind."[55] As a matter of fact, in the story, the painter limits himself to what his mind is able to imagine: He speaks of colours, flowers and trees. The Hereafter he cannot imagine is at the edge of the picture, beyond the mountains. And when he leaves to go into and beyond those Mountains, the story ends. Death cannot be imagined. There is some indication of a religious dimension, but it is never explicit and must not let us forget that the story consists of and arises from a sense of earthly tragedy: failure, anxiety and frustration (cf. Shippey 2000a, 266-277). What Niggle finds is actually what he left behind in life. How the picture begins is important: "It had begun with a leaf caught in the wind, and it became a tree; and the tree grew, sending out innumerable branches, and thrusting out the most *fantastic* roots" (*TL* 76).

There are no well-defined places in the story: the Infirmary for the poor, the Workhouse. This is, however, as much as we are able to imagine about the Hereafter, as Freud had already said; in addition, there is always a Hereafter "beyond the Mountains." At the end, after the judgement of the two Voices that Rosebury considers the weakest part of the story,[56] the protagonist is invited to a place that has no name but takes that of those who created it, above all Niggle, the artist, the painter, but also Parish, the gardener: "Niggle's Parish", which can also be understood as "Niggle's parish",[57] just as in the real world there is "Niggle's garden"; the latter was greatly admired by his relatives but overly-neglected by its owner, to the extent that some visitors warned Niggle that he would find himself in trouble if he received "a visit from an Inspector" (*TL* 77).

---

55 Flieger & Anderson 2008, 38.
56 Cf. Rosebury 2003, 129.
57 It is a play on words with the literal meaning of the names of the two characters. It could be understood as "parish" in the sense of "Niggle's community".

"Niggle's Parish" is his painting, which had not previously existed and which now has a name: it is a land where "time is lost" (*TL* 94). It is a place which is useful "as a holiday, and a refreshment." "It is splendid for convalescence," the Voices say. "I am sending more and more [people] there. They seldom have to come back" (*TL* 95). Wasting time does not mean death: death is without time. Niggle's Parish is a place that did not exist before Niggle's arrival. If the Workhouse is Purgatory,[58] something is not right, as "Niggle's Parish" cannot be a second Purgatory. Another strange thing is the small bottle of tonic that Niggle and Parish have to take so they will not get overly tired while working together on the painting: if they feel the need to strengthen themselves with a tonic, then the story is not about life after death. Kelly and Livingston (2009, 34) note: "Such things would have no place in Paradise." The theological allegory functions only as "mere" inspiration: it initiates the story but does not continue to accompany all the elements in it (cf. Geier 2008, 230).

What is described thus seems to be the Hereafter in Niggle's mind, as it has been structured in his imagination. Alliot, indeed, interprets Parish as representing the needs of the body, as opposed to Niggle, who represents the needs of the mind.[59] Chance and Steimel are of the same opinion: "If Parish personifies the practical and economic needs of a geographical area, then "Niggle" personifies the earthly failure to supply those needs."[60] In the story, "Niggle's Parish" did not exist before his arrival – a clear sign of the sub-creative power of Fantasy, as described by Tolkien in "On Fairy-Stories"; in addition, the painting is given Niggle's name and, from that time on, becomes a useful place for the community (as, on the contrary, does not happen in the real world), in which others are sent "to waste time" or better, to lose the sensation of time, before going into the Mountains. In Tolkien's terminology, this is the final "eucatastrophe", and a psychological interpretation is fitting. For Shippey, their ultimate success depends on the cooperation between Niggle and Parish, seen as the two sides of the author's personality.[61]

---

[58] Numerous scholars confirm this. See Shippey 2005, 79.
[59] See Alliot 2008, 168-169; Geier 2008, 212.
[60] See Chance 2001b, 89 and Steimel 2008, 199.
[61] They are Tolkien's creative and practical sides. See Shippey 2000a, 274 and Ellison 1991, 30..

"The Tree was finished, though not finished with," thinks Niggle. "Just the other way about to what it used to be" (*TL* 90): in actual fact, it is Niggle's life that ends before coming to a close. Indeed, it is true that while he is alive, Niggle does not know how to finish his painting. Even if he still needs to complete "a number of inconclusive regions, that still needed work and thought," but now he knows how to do it: now "Niggle saw the point precisely, in each case" (*TL* 90). Having lost all sense of time, Niggle has died and can see his picture as he had imagined it in his dreams. When for the first time he entered the field he had painted, he seemed "to remember having seen or *dreamed* of that sweep of grass somewhere or other" (*TL* 88, italics mine). A little earlier he had contemplated the tree, "all the leaves he had ever laboured at were there, as *he had imagined them* rather than as he had made them" (*TL* 88, italics mine). That whole world thus derives from his mind; it is the fruit of his imagination, and it is as if his imagination visualises the Hereafter and what he wishes the tree had been like if he had finished it before dying.

Up to a certain point, the protagonist uses his imagination, and then there is always a Hereafter; it is the same thing as regards distances: "the Forest, of course, was a distant Forest, yet he could approach it, even enter it, without its losing that particular charm. He had never before been able to walk into the distance without turning it into mere surroundings" (*TL* 89). Tolkien plays on perspective and shows us the effect that would be produced if one lived inside a painting. Distances are actually minimal but the perspective and the dimensions in which they are painted render some places remote. Tolkien explicitly explains this: "as he walked, new distances opened out; so that you now had doubled, treble, and quadruple distances, doubly, trebly, and quadruply enchanting. You could go on and on, and have a whole country in a garden, or in a picture (if you preferred to call it that)" (*TL* 89).

We turn the pages of the calendar, time passes, day by day, sheet by sheet, leaf by leaf. However, the Mountains in the background mark the boundaries of existence, the limits of Niggle's imagination. Tolkien points out: "They did not seem to belong to the picture." The artist imagines a fantasy world, but in respect to the Hereafter, it is a preliminary, temporary stage: beyond the Mountains there is "something different, a further stage: another picture" (*TL* 89).

In the real world, however, the painting remains unfinished and is destroyed, with the exception of one leaf. The real world, the living one, rids itself of Niggle and forgets him. For Councillor Tompkins, the painter's art is useless: only "private day-dreaming" (*TL* 94).

## 3.5 "Mythopoeia": the Right to Dream

The reply to Councillor Tompkins, as well as to his friend C.S. Lewis, is "Mythopoeia". If in "Leaf by Niggle" the conflict between creativity, overcoming death and the recognition of the artist's worth while he is still alive is personified by Niggle and Parish, in this poem everything becomes more abstract and conceptualised, but more transparent. Before rendering it in prose, the concept had already been expressed in the form of poetry. The message is clear: dreaming is a right, a way of overcoming death and lifting oneself above the limits of existence, creating things that cannot be found in the interlacing of time, things that have their own validity, like Niggle's painting, in the real world itself. Or rather, the only things that last with the passing of time are precisely myths, the fruit of the artist's mind. The poem, dedicated by "Philomythus" to "Misomythus" (a "friend of myth" to an "enemy of myth"), is Tolkien's reply to C.S. Lewis's assertion that myths and fables are only fantasies, "lies [...] breathed through silver" (*TL* 97).

In this case as well the source can be traced to an episode in Tolkien's life, an impassioned night-time conversation on myths with Lewis and Hugo Dyson, which took place on 19 September 1931,[62] about seven years before the writing of "On Fairy-Stories". Surprisingly, the ideas are identical and already well-delineated, although in verse form. Like the story and essay before it, the poem shows that Tolkien obstinately believed that he would be able to put his creative vision into practice, despite the numerous difficulties linked to his disposition and the conditions of modern life; in spite of everything, he was determined to proceed, in the conviction that authentic sub-creation has spiritual value, although in the temporal world it may be defeated by circumstances or rejected by a hostile culture. "I bow not yet before the Iron

---

62 See Carpenter 1978, 42-45.

Crown, nor cast my own small golden sceptre down" (*TL* 100), the writer emphatically affirms towards the end of the poem.

The formal structure differs from that usually found in the writer's works. Clive Tolley presumes that the reason is due to the fact that Tolkien, in addition to replying to Lewis, wanted to criticise Alexander Pope and his "Essay on Criticism" and "Essay on Man", using the same literary form (cf. Tolley 2002, 82-84). According to Weinreich, "Mythopoeia" may be defined as "the creed of Tolkienian ontology" (2008, 325). In this case, too, the author rises questions about death and employs his favourite images: the tree, shade, the dream. The element of time, underscoring life, also reappears. Indeed, as in a book, people live and cross the stage:

> [...] as Time unrolls
> from dark beginnings to uncertain goals;
> and as on page o'er-written without clue,
> with script and limning packed of various hue,
> an endless multitude of forms appear. (*TL* 97)

Only poets, in the course of time, have known how to disclose their art, to give a name to "trees", in reply to "those that felt astir within by deep monition movements that were kin to life and death of trees, of beasts, of stars" (*TL* 98). Poets, who possess the gift of creativity, are the protagonists of poetry, able to overcome death.

> Great powers they slowly brought out of themselves
> and looking backward they beheld the elves
> that wrought on cunning forges in the mind,
> and light and dark on secret looms entwined. (*TL* 98)

It is the mind that allows poets to lift themselves above other men, as only for "man sub-creator" does light "from a single White to many hues, and endlessly combined in living shapes that move from mind to mind."(*TL* 99) These are the same arguments Tolkien uses in "On Fairy-Stories", when he deals with the birth of the adjective, which allows man to imagine a green sun and create a world in which a green sun is believable (cf. *BMC* 140). However, in the poem, unlike in the preceding prose passage, Tolkien stresses the right to sub-create, but to do it "by the law in which we're made" (*TL* 99). It is the heart of the poem, line 70, which closes stanza 5, which is the closest to "On

Fairy-Stories", similar to the point of constituting two aspects of the writer's vision of art (cf. Weinreich 2008, 337).

"Whence came the wish?", Tolkien asks himself:

> [...] and whence the power to dream,
> or some things fair and others ugly deem?
> All wishes are not idle, nor in vain
> fulfilment we devise – for pain is pain,
> not for itself to be desired, but ill. (*TL* 99)

The dream is the poet's shield. Artists "evil hate that quail in its shadow, and yet shut the gate," and they do not forget that night follows the day. "Blessed are the legend-makers with their rhyme of things not found within recorded time", the writer affirms. Because they are the ones who "have seen Death and ultimate defeat, and yet they would not in despair retreat" (*TL* 100). It is for this reason that Tolkien goes so far as to lay claim to the right to dream and, as already mentioned, will not bow before those not loving myths, forgoing the right to invent stories and breaking, like Prospero in *The Tempest*, his "little sceptre", his pen, his creative art.

All these considerations allow us to fully understand the words with which Tolkien, in a letter dated 1945, replies to his son Christopher, who had asked him what emotions *The Lord of the Rings* aroused in him. This work, in fact, incites in the author himself the "more customary" sensations of triumph, along with pathos and compassion for the tragedy of the characters; in addition, "one that moves me supremely and I find small difficulty in evoking: *the heart-racking sense of the vanished past*" (*Letters* no. 96, italics added). This laceration of the heart emerges in the book, expressed most efficaciously in the words of Gandalf regarding the Palantír[63] or, in a perspective closer to the themes we have been considering, in Sam's disquisition on the seamless web of history.[64]

---

[63] *LotR*, TT.III.11: "Even now my heart desires to test my will upon it, to see if I could not wrench it from him and turn it where I would – to look across the wide seas of water and of time to Tirion the Fair, and perceive the unimaginable hand and mind of Fëanor at their work, while both the White Tree and the Golden were in flower!"

[64] *LotR*, TT.IV.8: "'To think of it, we're in the same tale still! It's going on. Don't the great tales never end?' 'No, they never end as tales,' said Frodo. 'But the people in them come, and go when their part's ended. Our part will end later – or sooner.'"

Because, Tolkien writes, "[a] story must be told or there'll be no story, yet it is the untold stories that are most moving" (*Letters* no. 96). Because *The Lord of the Rings* and the references to *The Silmarillion* contained in it, along with "Leaf by Niggle" and its numerous allusions to what is "beyond the frame of the picture" provoke "a sudden sense of endless *untold* stories: mountains seen far away, never to be climbed, distant trees (like Niggle's) never to be approached" (*Letters* no. 96, author's italics). Because if the mountains were actually scaled, if the trees were reached, the writer concludes, they would only become 'near trees'.

# Lorenzo Gammarelli

## On the Edge of the Perilous Realm

> *Its author is still concerned primarily with man on earth, rehandling in a new perspective an ancient theme: that man, each man and all men, and all their works shall die.*
>
> (J.R.R. Tolkien, "*Beowulf*: The Monsters and the Critics")

The aim of this essay is to analyse Tolkien's shorter works, those short stories and poems that were published in less known or less widely distributed magazines, and are thus often difficult to access. Some of these works are set in Middle-earth, and may be more or less linked to the main *Legendarium* (analysed in Claudio A. Testi's essay), from which *The Lord of the Rings* and *The Silmarillion* sprung, even if this link is sometimes no more than a pseudo-erudite foreword, in which this Hobbit or that is recognised as author of a poem;[1] many other works have little or no connection to the body of texts constituting the *Legendarium*. All of them, however, fall into a common category, for all can be considered in some way to be fairy-tales, according to the definition given by Tolkien himself in his essay "On Fairy-Stories".

The selection of titles either by their length (or lack thereof) or their relevance to the subject of this book results inevitably in a heterogeneous essay. I hope, however, to be able to extract from most of these writings at least a relevant common theme: that is, the theme of loss, or bereavement.

I did not consider, for the purposes of this essay, the translations such as *Sir Gawain and the Green Knight*, *Pearl*, and *Sir Orfeo*.[2] For these works the theme of death and immortality is pivotal, and they are fully set inside the Perilous Realm, but they are the result of a transformation, and not of

---

1 See *ATB*, "Preface".
2 Tolkien's modern English translations of these works were published in 1975, edited by his son Christopher. They must not be confused with the critical editions of the same poems, to which Tolkien had also contributed.

sub-creation. Due to time constraints, I have not been able to consider the recently published *The Legend of Sigurd and Gudrún*. Lastly, I have not found any relevant elements in *Farmer Giles of Ham*.

## In Praise of Shortness

One point I would like to stress is the fact that although these works are short, they are not, and must not be considered, lesser ones. Their very shortness is what makes them even more interesting: as they are 'concentrated', they can show the author's thinking at a precise moment of his life, and thus contribute to the reconstruction of the evolution of his thought.

There exists little published criticism on these works,[3] for they are less widely known, and therefore less appealing both to readers and to critics. It may even be suspected that, being both 'simple' and short, they are not that accessible to multiple interpretations: a long work like *The Lord of the Rings* can be used (and has been used) to pursue an agenda, but with a short story it is much more difficult. Due to their shortness, these works tend to be more explicit in their content and messages (even to the point of being openly allegorical), so that it is much more difficult to exploit them for an interpretation that is not based on 'hard narrative facts'. In any case, because of their shortness and sometimes humorous tone, they are easily dismissed as lesser works.

There are noteworthy exceptions. Three major authors of Tolkien-related secondary literature devoted part of their studies to these works. Tom Shippey, in his seminal work *The Road to Middle-earth* presented a rather convincing allegorical-biographical interpretation, even if some of the reasoning may be a bit forced.[4] Paul Kocher had the advantage of writing when very little of the *Legendarium* was published, so that the scale and the depth of invention that went into the creation of Middle-earth and its universe were not fully known. Thus his study of Tolkien's main œuvre had to rely on the 'lesser works' in order to gain additional information. Verlyn Flieger deals

---

[3] For a full discussion of this point, see Hiley & Weinreich 2008b, i.
[4] His interpretation of *Smith of Wootton Major* as an allegory of the work of the philologist is not very convincing, especially in light of Verlyn Flieger's objections; Shippey later declared he is not completely satisfied with his own interpretation, see "Allegory versus Bounce" in Shippey 2007a.

extensively with *Smith of Wootton Major* in her new edition of the same tale. Furthermore, she has analysed the possible links between these poems and short stories and the themes prominent in the longer narratives in her two monographs *Splintered Light* and *A Question of Time*.

## The Perils of the Perilous Realm

The Perilous Realm of Faërie has, to paraphrase both the beginning of "On Fairy-Stories" and Boromir's words about the dangers of Lothlórien, an effect on the visitor: few come out who once go in, and of those few none is unchanged. The Perilous Realm is the place where fairy-tales are set, or, according to Tolkien's own definition, rather the place where those tales are set that tell stories not about Fairies, but about Faërie. However, most of the tales do not show any 'fairy beings', but tell of the adventures of mortal Men in the Perilous Realm or upon its shadowy marches (cf. OFS 16). Tolkien uses the adjective 'perilous' for two reasons: on the one hand, to stress the fact that fairy-tales, and their world, are not innocuous (and thus trivial), nor should they be exiled to the nursery room. On the other hand, Tolkien wished to point out the real and actual dangers of those places: the possibility to lose oneself and to pass in a different, maybe higher world. And the biggest peril of all: if one does not take in due consideration the prohibitions that traditionally follow any journey into the kingdom of the Elves, one risks the peril of being thoroughly excluded from Faërie itself.[5]

In his long essay "On Fairy-Stories", Tolkien stresses the difference between the Perilous Realm and the Land of Morpheus, the kingdom of dreams. He does not consider dreams to be true fairy-tales, so "any story that uses the machinery of Dream, the dreaming of actual human sleep, to explain the apparent occurrence of its marvels" (OFS 19) is not a fairy story proper. However, a few lines later he adds: "it is true that Dream is not unconnected with Faërie. In dreams [...] a man may for a space wield the power of Faërie" (OFS 19).

---

5 On the perils of the Perilous Realm, see Benvenuto 2008b, 251; Hiley 2008, 289-290 and Sternberg 2008, 312.

Tolkien is the first to violate this 'axiom' by connecting the land of the Elves to dreaming in his own mythology. There Lothlórien, as the name indicates, echoes Lórien, the garden and dwelling of Irmo, the Vala who presides over dreams and sleep. Or when he devises Olórë Mallë, the Path of Dreams that allows Men (according to different versions either artists or children) to come to Valinor by dreaming.

## The Homecoming of Beorhtnoth Beorhthelm's Son

The earliest drafts go back to the years 1931-33.[6] It was initially conceived as a poem only, but has been published in the scholarly journal *Essays & Studies by Members of the English Association* in 1953 with a foreword and an essay on the word *ofermod*. Inspired by an Old English heroic poem about the battle of Maldon, this alliterative poetic dialogue is at the same time both archaic and modern. Two servants of the Anglo-Saxon warrior Beorhtnoth are sent to recover the corpse of their lord who had fallen in the battle against the Viking raiders.

The dialogue between Torhthelm, young and inexperienced but with a mind full of songs and legends, and Tídwald, older and more down-to-earth, alludes several times to the theme of the accompanying essay, which contains a critique of heroism, seen as the pursuit of glory. The two characters show that a man has two options when facing death. Both of them are 'heroic', yet, at the same time, differ in certain points: the traditional northern-Germanic attitude looks towards death as a source of glory. It is based on a partial or negligible knowledge of the reality of things, is inspired by literature and epic poetry; then there is a more 'modern' attitude, based on a Christian view of the world. It sees death as a possibility not to be actively sought out, but rather to be avoided, and stresses the concept of responsibility: one who is responsible for the life and well-being of others must not put their – or his own – lives at risk unnecessarily.

---

6 See Honegger 2007 on the development of the drafts.

## Leaf by Niggle

This short story was written in 1942 and, according to Tolkien, in a sudden outburst of creativity without any previous planning or revision. It was then published in 1945 in the *Dublin Review*. The story is easy to read, but not that easy to summarize. It tells of a man called Niggle, an amateur painter, and of a journey he has to make. The journey is, of course, a metaphor for death, and Niggle at first arrives in a prison-hospital where he is forced to perform repetitive and boring tasks. He is later sent to a wonderful place where he comes across none other than the tree from his painting on which he had been working all his life.

Critical readings focused mainly on the allegorical-biographical dimension of the story, and on the themes relevant for creation and sub-creation,[7] neglecting the internal allegory[8] that identifies Niggle's journey with death.

Even when critics mention death, they do it often only in connection with Niggle as an alter-ego of Tolkien, or more generally as a representation of the creative artist. Thus, for example, they claim that the real meaning of the story is that the artist and his work are doomed to perish and to be forgotten, like all things human.

Other critics focus on the contrast between the 'real' world where the story begins, and the world of Niggle's picture, which, at first, is a world of imagination like Faërie, and later becomes the world of afterlife; in both cases, Niggle cannot see the connection between Faërie (his picture) and the real world, nor can he see the links between Faërie and the Great Escape (from death). This is why he fears the journey: he thinks that death will put an end to his endeavours to reach Faërie. Yet he, to his great surprise and delight, will find Faërie itself (his picture) at his journey's destination (cf. Slack 2008, 272).

---

7 This is probably because the story has been published for years together with "On Fairy-Stories" in a single volume, titled *Tree and Leaf*.
8 I hesitate to speak of allegory in this story, though it is doubtlessly the most openly allegorical among all the stories Tolkien wrote, because the relationship between the allegorical and the allegorized terms is explicit; not only in the text, but inside the story itself: the Journey, according to counsellor Tompkins, is not an allegory, but an euphemism. For Niggle, the real reality is the one of the journey: thus, it can be said that for him death is just an allegory of the journey. Tolkien wrote: "It is not really or properly an 'allegory' so much as 'mythical'" (*Letters* no. 163).

If we see not only the author-Niggle, but also the author-Tolkien, it is possible to claim that "Leaf by Niggle" served Tolkien the purpose to comfort himself and to exorcise some of his fears: a sub-creator, fearing to be forgotten after his death, and that his work will be considered irrelevant.[9]

## Poems of Death and Immortality

### The Lay of Aotrou and Itroun

The first version of this poem dates back to 1930, but the complete work was published only in 1945 in the *Welsh Review*. It is a poem inspired by a folk-tale motif that is cast in the form of a 12th-century Breton lay. Aotrou, a childless nobleman, obtains a magic potion from the Corrigan, a witch. He gives it to Itroun, his wife, and thus she is able to conceive and give birth to two children, a boy and a girl. In exchange for the potion, the witch had asked Aotrou for his love. He had rashly promised to grant her wish before knowing what this would entail. Now he prefers to keep his marital vows of fidelity and rather break his word to the witch and thus lose his knightly honour. He therefore refuses the witch and saves his soul from damnation. She, however, curses him, and after three days he dies, followed by Itroun, whose heart is broken. The story of Aotrou's refusal of the witch, the curse, and his death are derived directly from the folk tales that inspired Tolkien, but only in Tolkien is death deserved, or at least a direct consequence of Aotrou's attempt to rebel against Providence by using supernatural means, instead of meekly accepting his fate. Tolkien's moral is clear and unequivocal: Aotrou's fault lies not in submitting to the Corrigan, but in having any dealings with her at all (cf. Shippey 2000a, 294).

---

90 See Fornet-Ponse 2005, 157. The purgatorial nature of the story is mentioned by Tolkien (cf. *Letters* no. 153).

## Imram[10]

The first version of this poem dates back to 1945-46. It was inspired by the *Navigatio Sancti Brendani*, a text recounting the journey of the Irish saint Brendan, composed in the 10th century by an unknown author. The poem was published in 1955, in the magazine *Time and Tide*. The main protagonist is Saint Brendan, who on his deathbed tells a novice about his long sea-journey to unknown and wondrous lands – including some that we can identify as drowned Númenor and the shores of Valinor. The end of the journey is left open and the novice (and the reader), if he wishes to know more, would have to repeat the journey. The importance of this poem lies in the imagery it shares with Tolkien's mythology, such as the Straight Road towards the Blessed Realm:[11]

> where the round world plunges deeply down,
> but on the old road goes,
> as an unseen bridge that on arches runs
> to coast that no man knows

Moreover, this poem illustrates the possibility of incorporating the land of the Elves, and even Valinor, the home of the Valar (who therefore are not gods, nor demons, but angels) into a Christian world.

"The Lay of Aotrou and Itroun" and "Imram" have many points in common: both are written in verse, published in little-known magazines and have therefore been difficult to access for years. They are inspired by ancient poetic forms of Celtic origin (Breton and Irish, respectively), permeated by Christian spirituality but based on Pagan stories. Both poems make us feel as if we were reading something that belongs to an era long gone – a time when the boundaries between the land of the living and the land of the dead and of the Elves were not fixed and clear-cut. Finally, in "The Lay of Aotrou and Itroun" we find a rare (for Tolkien) example of death as punishment.

---

10 The title derives from Old Irish *immram*, which can be translated as "journey", and usually designates a story about the journey of a hero or a saint through afterlife. It often tells about the protagonist's visits to mysterious islands west of Ireland.

11 See Shippey 2000a, 288-289.

## The Adventures of Tom Bombadil

Published in 1962, this collection gathers poems written by Tolkien at different times. It sports a pseudo-scholarly preface that attributes the poems to various Hobbit authors. Tolkien was working by accretion, not unlike Niggle (cf. Turner 2008, 1-16). For this reason, far from being a mere *divertissement* of little to no interest, these poems are windows providing insight into the creative process and the thought of the author.[12]

### The Man in the Moon poems

"The Man in the Moon stayed up Too Late" and "The Man in the Moon came down Too Soon" are two poems for which Tom Shippey explores in depth the philological implications and their origin in traditional nursery rhymes.[13] More interesting, for our purpose, is the interpretation by Paul Kocher. He sees them as witnesses to the clash between Middle-earth (the Land of Men) and inhabitants of Faërie (cf. Kocher 2002, 212-213). Basically, the Man in the Moon is one of the characters forced to live between Faëry and the real world, in a constant condition of alienation and loneliness.

### The Stone Troll

A playful poem that provides some comic relief in *The Lord of the Rings* (where it was first published). Some lines are noteworthy here (16-18):

> But what be bones that lie in a hole?
> Thy nuncle was dead as a lump o'lead,
> Afore I found his shinbone.

---

12 It must be noted that the house of Tom Bombadil is itself part of the Perilous Realm; it is inside a forest and across a river, it is intimately connected to very dreamlike episodes (before being reached, with the sleepiness induced by Old Man Willow; during the stay, with the dreams of Frodo and the other Hobbits) and it is followed by a real descent into hell, with the adventure of the Barrow-wight. In the first draft Tom Bombadil's entire episode was to remain isolated from the chronology of events, even if later Tolkien chose to change this, as it would have caused too many problems with the chronology of his story. See Flieger 1997, 207-225, particularly for an analysis of Frodo's dreams.

13 See also Honegger 2005.

Obviously, a World War I veteran like Tolkien could not avoid feeling deeply about the problem of the burial of the fallen, and about the keeping of their remains.[14]

## The Mewlips

Even though the 'gothic' tone and atmosphere is suggestive of monsters worthy of Lovecraft's nightmares, or of Lord Dunsany's fantasy (cf. Nelson 2004, 177-181), reality is much more mundane – as can be seen by the original title of the poem: "Knocking at the Door: Lines Induced by Sensations When Waiting for an Answer at the Door of an Exalted Academical Person". The lugubrious imagery is merely the product of playing with sounds and associations.

## Shadow-bride

The basic structure is a paraphrase of Persephone's myth (cf. Kocher 2002, 218-219), where the concept of shadow replaces that of death.

## The Hoard

This poem, as the "Preface" points out (*ATB* 8), contains echoes of the story of Túrin and Mîm the Petty-dwarf, even if what this meant could fully be understood only a quarter of a century after the publication of the book, when *The Silmarillion* was finally released. Among all the poems of the collection, this is the one that stresses most the transience of human deeds, and death caused by greed. It may recall the "Pardoner's Tale" in Chaucer's *Canterbury Tales*, where three men go looking for Death, but find gold instead (without realizing that gold leads to death) (cf. Shippey 2007a, 342).

---

14 On this argument, see the essay by Simone Bonechi in this volume.

## The Sea-bell

W.H. Auden considered this poem one of Tolkien's finest poetic works (*Letters* no. 295); it is probably the most enigmatic, certainly the one that evokes a feeling of deep alienation typical for mortals who journey to Faërie, or have contact with the supernatural (which, once again, overlaps with the afterlife). The narrator, driven by the sea-sound heard in a shell, crosses the sea and arrives in the (seemingly deserted) realm of Faërie. Exasperated, he proclaims himself king of that land. Darkness falls on him and he is driven away. When he returns home, no one wants to talk or listen to him. The poem may be interpreted as an *imram* gone wrong, but the subtitle *Frodos dreme* leaves open a disturbing possibility: that it is the story of an alternate version of the end of *The Lord of the Rings*, one where Frodo, even after reaching Valinor, cannot find peace (cf. Shippey 2000a, 282).

## The Last Ship

The poem tells the story of Fíriel, a mortal maid who is offered a place on the ship by the last Elves leaving for the West. At first, she is tempted, but when taking a step towards the ship, she sinks into the mud of the river and realises that she is mortal, and thus cannot leave Middle-earth where she was born. Disconsolate, she returns home, where she is going to grow old and, in the end, die. The poem may be seen as a companion piece to the story of Beren and Lúthien. Here we see how things usually go: mortals remain mortal and cannot even leave to cross the sea with the Elves. The sense of bereavement, and of death, is inevitable in a story that tells of the failure of the "escape from death" (cf. Shippey 2000a, 281).

## Smith of Wootton Major

Tolkien started working on this story in 1964, and it was published in 1967. It is the last work of fiction published before his death in 1973. The story opens with the Feast of Good Children that is held every twenty-four years in the village of Wootton Major. The apprentice to the Master Cook puts a small fairy star into the cake, which is swallowed by the son of Smith, who later grows and becomes a skilful artisan. The star also gives him access to Faëry, the land of fairies, where he has many adventures and lastly meets the Queen and the King. When the time of the Feast of Good Children comes again, Smith leaves the star to Alf, who is now the Master Cook and who puts it in the new cake, so that another child will be able to know and explore the world of Faërie.

Critical reactions to *Smith of Wootton Major* differ. Some consider it "a minor work, late and summary, that shows no significant changes in comparison to previous works" (Palusci 1982, 127), others see it as "his best work, apart from *The Lord of the Rings*, and his more nearly perfect" (Rosebury 2003, 130). Something in this short story makes many readers suspect that there must be more to it, that there is a hidden meaning.

Many critics see it as "an autumnal farewell to art and imagination" (Lodigiani 1982, 37) in the tradition of Shakespeare's *The Tempest* (Kocher 2002, 201); or as an autobiographical allegory, showing the relationship between the work of an author and his sources of inspiration (cf. Shippey 2005, 380); or as an illustration of Tolkien's theory on Fantasy and Sub-creation as developed in "On Fairy-Stories".[15] It may also be relevant that the writing of the story followed briefly the death of C.S. Lewis in 1963 – a loss that may have strengthened the sense of bereavement (cf. Steimel 2008, 205).

Tolkien wrote an essay on the origin and potential meaning of the story, yet it was only published recently in the new edition of *Smith of Wootton Major*.[16] Tolkien, in his essay, comments on one of the main points of the story: what is the relationship between two races of intelligent beings, both capable of speech and free will, but divided by the fundamental difference that one is mortal, and the other immortal? What is the motivation of the members of one of the two races to have dealings with the members of the other? The conclusion of Tolkien's almost scientific reasoning is that the force that motivates Elves to take an interest in the fate of Men is the love that Elves bear for humanity.

---

15 Flieger points this out well: see *SWM* 50.
16 Verlyn Flieger published it in 2005 in *SWM*, 84-101.

In the succession of Master Cooks and the Fairy-Star-bearers, we can perceive a hint of the two different kinds of immortality: the one that makes us survive in memory, and the one that makes us survive in our children.

## Bilbo's Last Song

"Bilbo's Last Song" is a revision of a poem that Tolkien wrote in the twenties. He gave it to his assistant in 1970, to reward her for her help. This poem once again resumes the theme of bereavement and of weariness that seems to accompany those Hobbits who have been in contact with the Elves for some time. The imagery is decidedly crepuscular (lines 1-3).

> Day is ended, dim my eyes,
> but journey long before me lies.
> Farewell, friends! I hear the call

As for Niggle, journey and death are interwoven in a series of references that render the poem much more specific than a mere allegory:[17] it is not easy to understand which is the symbol and which the symbolized.

## Bereavement

Bereavement is a fundamental concept in Tolkien's works, both longer and shorter.[18] Bereavement is the sense of loss, the feeling or atmosphere that dominates in all the stories, particularly those where Elves are involved. It is, however, also a direct consequence of death: sadness and anxiety for the loss of someone dear who is no more. The same feeling, or one much alike, is noted when we come into contact with realms outside normal reality, such as the land of the Elves. Upon returning into our mundane world we are confronted with a lack of comprehension by all those people who have not shared our experience. Bereavement, therefore, is the link between the sensations we feel when we confront death and the sensations one feels when returning from Faëry. It is a bridge between death and immortality: this

---

[17] For an analysis of this theme in "Leaf by Niggle", see the essay by Roberto Arduini in this volume.
[18] For a review of the concept in Tolkien's longer works, *The Lord of the Rings* and *The Silmarillion*, see Senior 2000, 173-182 and Drout 2007, s.v. *Loss*.

is why it is the prevailing feeling in *Smith of Wootton Major*, the story that relies most prominently on the juxtaposition of the two worlds. It is also the reason why bereavement is so closely associated with the Elves in Tolkien's longer works, particularly *The Lord of the Rings*.

# Alberto Ladavas

## The Wrong Path of the Sub-creator: from the Fall to the Machine and the Escape from Mortality

> *Fear not death's decree for you;*
> *remember, it embraces those before you, and those after.*
> *Thus God has ordained for all flesh;*
> *why then should you reject the will of the Most High?*
> *Whether one has lived a thousand years, a hundred, or ten,*
> *in the nether world he has no claim on life.*
>
> (*Sirach* 41.3-4)

## 1. Fall, Mortality, and the Machine

In the letter dated 17th November, 1957 and addressed to Herbert Schiro, Tolkien wrote about *The Lord of the Rings* that "I should say, if asked, the tale is not really about Power and Dominion: that only sets the wheels going; it is about Death and the desire for deathlessness" (*Letters* no. 203). Although in this case the Professor was only referring to his most widely known work, it is evident to all readers of his books that death and immortality are central themes of his entire *Legendarium*,[1] as one can also deduce from another letter addressed to Milton Waldman and probably written at the end of 1951:

> all this stuff is mainly concerned with Fall, Mortality, and the Machine. With Fall inevitably, and that motive occurs in several modes. With Mortality, especially as it affects art and the creative (or as I should say, sub-creative) desire [...]. This desire is at once wedded to a passionate love of the real primary world, and hence filled with the sense of mortality, and yet unsatisfied by it. It has various opportunities of 'Fall'. It may become possessive, clinging to the things made as 'its own', the sub-creator wishes to be the Lord and God of his private creation. He will rebel against the laws of the Creator – especially against mortality. Both of these (alone or together) will lead to the desire for Power, for making the will more quickly effective, – and so to the Machine (or Magic). (*Letters* no. 131)

---

1 On the use of the word "*Legendarium*" by Tolkien, see Gilliver & Marshall & Weiner 2006, 153-154.

In this essay I will try to point out how this path of artistic achievement,[2] possessive attitude, wish for immortality in order to enjoy it as long as possible and the consequent rebellion against the divine laws, can be clearly seen in two well-known elements of Tolkien's sub-creation: the vicissitudes of the people of Númenor and the history of the Ringwraiths.

## 2. Númenor: Man in pursuit of immortality

In 1977, four years after Tolkien's death, Christopher Tolkien published *The Silmarillion*.[3] It contains legends, myths and historical accounts of the First Age of Middle-earth, accounts on how the Three Houses of Men helped the Elves and the Valar, the "angelic powers" (*Letters* no. 131) of Tolkien's cosmogony, to defeat Melkor, the Vala who during the creation had rebelled against the design of Eru Ilúvatar, the Creator God. Part of *The Silmarillion*, the "Akallabêth", is focused on the history of the descendants of these men, reporting that to "the Fathers of Men of the three faithful houses rich reward also was given. […] wisdom and power and life more enduring than any others of mortal race have possessed" (*S, Ak*), as well as a new abode, the island of Númenor, the westernmost among the lands inhabited by Men, and closest to Valinor. However, "they did not thus escape from the doom of death that Ilúvatar had set upon all Mankind, and they were mortal still, though their years were long […]. Therefore they grew wise and glorious, and in all things more like to the Firstborn than any other of the kindreds of Men" (*S, Ak*).

These rewards, however, also became the means of their temptation: the wisdom and knowledge so obtained allow the Númenóreans to create works of art of unsurpassed beauty, but their long life leads to an attitude of possessiveness towards these creations and to an increasing wish to have more and more time available to enjoy them. Since their most characteristic artistic expressions were the construction of ships and the art of sailing

---

2 See also Rialti 2004.
3 There exists no 'final' version of 'the Silmarillion' (i.e. the entire body of legends and tales, of which *The Silmarillion* offers a selection) – Tolkien worked on it for more than sixty years. For the historical development of Tolkien's mythology see: Flieger & Hostetter 2000; Whittingham 2007; Hammond & Scull 2006b, 906-917; Kane 2009.

> the Lords of Valinor forbade them to sail so far westward that the coasts of Númenor could no longer be seen; [...] But the design of Manwë was that the Númenóreans should not be tempted to seek the Blessed Realm, nor desire to overpass the limits set to their bliss, becoming enamoured of the immortality of the Valar and the Eldar and the lands where all things endure. (*S*, Ak)

Possessiveness may therefore lead Men to go beyond the limits of their happiness,[4] making them wish for a destiny that is not in their nature, that is against the divine law and that they could not endure: "each 'Kind' has a natural span, integral to its biological and spiritual nature. This cannot really be *increased* qualitatively or quantitatively; so that prolongation in time is like stretching a wire out ever tauter, or 'spreading butter ever thinner' – it becomes an intolerable torment" (*Letters* no. 131). This very image is drawn on in a very telling way by Bilbo, loaded with the burden of excessive longevity as a result of his possession of the Ring, shortly before his departure for Rivendell:

> I feel I need a holiday, a very long holiday, as I have told you before. Probably a permanent holiday: I don't expect I shall return. [...] I am old, Gandalf. I don't look it, but I am beginning to feel it in my heart of hearts. [...] I feel all thin, sort of *stretched*, if you know what I mean: like butter that has been scraped over too much bread. That can't be right. (*LotR*, FR.I.1)

Bilbo's words make us feel the burden of an excessively long life for a human being, and the consequent need of a refreshing 'eternal rest', as pointed out by Verlyn Flieger: "[Tolkien] makes a clear distinction between unending life, which he sees as bondage to the world without hope of renewal, and eternal life, which transcends death and leads to God" (Flieger 2002, 28). The Númenóreans, though, did not feel the same need as Bilbo but

> began to hunger for the undying city that they saw from afar, and the desire for an everlasting life, to escape from death and the ending of delight, grew strong upon them; [...] Thus it was that a shadow fell upon them: in which maybe the will of Morgoth was at work that still moved in the world. And the Númenóreans began to murmur, at first in their hearts, and then in open words, against the doom of Men, and most of all against the Ban which forbade them to sail into the West. (*S*, Ak)

So the fall of the Númenóreans starts with the rejection of their human nature and of their consequent mortality, identified with the prohibition to navigate towards Valinor and to set foot on the Blessed Realm, with the further ad-

---

4 On power in Tolkien's world see Chance 2001a.

dition of a strong desire for possession and a great arrogance, deriving from their increased power. In fact, they wonder:

> Why do the Lords of the West sit there in peace unending, while we must die and go we know not whither, leaving our home and all that we have made? [...] And since we have mastered all seas [...] why should we not go to Avallónë and greet there our friends? [...] Why should we not go even to Aman, and taste there, were it but for a day, the bliss of the Powers? (*S*, Ak)

It sounds like the same arrogance of the builders of the Tower of Babel who wanted to reach heaven[5] and, like the Biblical story, the divine punishment will also come for Númenor.

The Valar, through the Elves, get to know the intentions of the Númenóreans and, since they are very concerned about this development, they decide to send messengers to the King of Númenor to expound to him the fate and fashion of the world. These messengers of the Valar say that only the creator of the world and of all living beings can change their fate. It would thus be useless for the Númenóreans to go to the Blessed Realm, since it is not the land that causes the Valar to be immortal, but it is their very presence that blesses the land and immortality is part of their very nature. Furthermore, they point out that mortality is part of Men's nature as Eru created them, and that now the Númenóreans are claiming benefits of both Elves and Men: being allowed to visit the Valar but also to return to Middle-earth as they wish to enjoy its beauty; being immortal but still able to put an end to their life, should the burden of years become excessive. But this is clearly impossible, as the messengers explicitly say: "That cannot be. Nor can the Valar take away the gifts of Ilúvatar" (*S*, Ak). Finally, they remark how Men have been deceived about their fate: "And you are punished for the rebellion of Men, you say, in which you had small part, and so it is that you die. But that was not at first appointed for a punishment. Thus you escape, and leave the world, and are not bound to it, in hope or in weariness" (*S*, Ak).

Here lies the big mistake of man: the loss of a beloved person is a cause of grief, yet death is not a divine punishment, but a call to a higher fate outside the circles of the world. Man must recognize and accept this fate;

---

5 "Come, let us build ourselves a city and a tower with its top in the sky, and so make a name for ourselves; otherwise we shall be scattered all over the earth" (*Genesis* 11.4).

precisely as King Aragorn, the last descendant of the kings of Númenor in the Third Age, does so at the end of his life. He addresses Arwen, his queen, with the following words of consolation: "In sorrow we must go, but not in despair. Behold! we are not bound for ever to the circles of the world, and beyond them there is more than memory" (*LotR*, App. A.5).⁶ This Christian vision of death expresses a great faith in the fate God has allotted to man. In fact, as Tolkien noted, "the point of view of this mythology is that 'mortality' or a short span, and 'immortality' or an indefinite span was part of what we might call the biological and spiritual nature of the Children of God, Men and Elves (the firstborn) respectively, and could not be altered by anyone" (*Letters* no. 156).

However, the Númenóreans do not have the same faith as King Aragorn: "Why should we not envy the Valar [...]? For of us is required a blind trust, and a hope without assurance, knowing not what lies before us in a little while" (*S*, Ak).⁷ Yet, faith must be blind and hope without assurance,⁸ because Men cannot comprehend God's design; they can only give themselves up entirely to His will, accepting to act as His instruments and believing in what He communicates, as the messengers also point out:

> Indeed the mind of Ilúvatar concerning you is not known to the Valar, and he has not revealed all things that are to come. But this we hold to be true, that your home is not here, neither in the Land of Aman nor anywhere within the Circles of the World. [...] The love of Arda was set in your hearts by Ilúvatar, and he does not plant to no purpose. Nonetheless, many ages of Men unborn may pass ere that purpose is made known; and to you it will be revealed and not to the Valar. (*S*, Ak)

Many ages have passed since the time of the Númenóreans to the birth of Christ, the revelation of divine love to man.⁹

---

6 On this topic, see also the essay by Andrea Monda in this book.
7 About 'envy', see also the essays by Claudio A. Testi and Giampaolo Canzonieri in this book.
8 Tolkien states in letter no. 181 that in his works he is "only concerned with Death as part of the nature, physical and spiritual, of Man, and with Hope without guarantees" (*Letters* no. 181), the same with which Frodo faces the journey to Mount Doom in *The Lord of the Rings*.
9 It is important to remember that "Middle-earth is not an imaginary world. The name is the modern form (appearing in the 13th century and still in use) of *midden-erd* > *middel-erd*, an ancient name for the *oikoumenē*, the abiding place of Men, the objectively real world, in use specifically opposed to imaginary worlds (as Fairyland) or unseen worlds (as Heaven or Hell). The theatre of my tale is this earth, the one in which we now live, but the historical period is imaginary" (*Letters* no. 183).

Despite the good words of the Valar's messengers, the King of Númenor "was ill pleased with the counsel of the Messengers and gave little heed to it, and the greater part of his people followed him; for they wished still to escape death in their own day, not waiting upon hope" (S, Ak), i.e. the hope for a life after death.

But it is precisely during this time that a division occurs among the people of Númenor: a minority of them, although still loyal to the king, maintains the friendship and the relations with the Elves and accepts the counsel of the Valar. Still, even these Númenóreans, who call themselves the "Faithful" (i.e. those who keep the faith), "did not wholly escape from the affliction of their people, and they were troubled by the thought of death" (S, Ak), because man is constantly put to the test and always tempted to give in to despair.

Yet for the majority of Númenóreans "the fear of death grew ever darker upon them, and they delayed it by all means that they could; and they began to build great houses for their dead, while their wise men laboured unceasingly to discover if they might the secret of recalling life, or at the least of the prolonging of Men's days" (S, Ak). This means resorting to the Machine which leads to the Fall as discussed by Tolkien at the beginning of this essay; however, as the Valar's messengers have already made clear, the gift of Ilúvatar cannot be removed, Men's nature cannot be changed and, most of all, they do not have the power to create life according to their will, because the principle of creation belongs to God only.[10] In fact, even the wise men of Númenor "achieved only the art of preserving incorrupt the dead flesh of Men, and they filled all the land with silent tombs in which the thought of death was enshrined in the darkness" (S, Ak). Thus begins a pagan worship of the dead, which does not aim, as should be right, to preserve the memory of the deceased, but to try to extend their life by artificially preserving their physical body as a relic: "The

---

10 Brian Rosebury (2003, 180) notes that "[a]ccording to Christopher Tolkien, Tolkien several times expressly said that one of the underlying themes of *The Lord of the Rings* was 'the machine', a term which Tolkien used in an extended sense to signify the attempt to actualise our desires by coercing the world, and other wills, into satisfying them." Rosebury (2003, 180-181) goes on, "in Tolkien there is a more emphatic sense that the impropriety of the attempt to enforce one's will by means of the machine lies in the fact that it refuses submission to limitations that Nature (or the will of the Creator) imposes on human fulfilment. [...] God, it is implied, retains, and might exercise, the power to *realise* human, or mortal, imagination."

desire to escape death produced a cult of the dead, and they lavished wealth and art on tombs and memorials" (*Letters* no. 131).[11]

The power of Númenor reaches its apex during this period. Over the previous centuries its men sailed all the seas of the world and set foot on all known lands, being seen by the natives first as demigods and carriers of light and wisdom against Sauron's darkness, but then turning into tyrants and exploiters exactly like Sauron. He had been spreading his power to a large part of Middle-earth, and had himself venerated as a divinity by the subdued peoples. During the reign of the twenty-fourth King of Númenor, Ar-Pharazôn the Golden, Sauron becomes so bold as to attack the settlements established by the Númenóreans along the coasts of Middle-earth and, moreover, "he had taken now the title of King of Men, and declared his purpose to drive the Númenóreans into the sea, and destroy even Númenor, if that might be" (*S*, Ak). Ar-Pharazôn is furious and "his heart was filled with the desire for power unbounded and the sole dominion of his will. And he determined without counsel of the Valar, or the aid of any wisdom but his own, that the title of King of Men he would himself claim, and would compel Sauron to become his vassal and his servant" (*S*, Ak).

Ar-Pharazôn then orders to gather and equip a formidable army and, when everything is ready, wages war against Sauron. His reasons for doing so are misguided: inspired by great arrogance and by an insatiable thirst for power, he does not want to defeat Sauron to free the men suffering under his tyranny, but he just wants to replace him in order to have absolute power over the world.

Once Ar-Pharazôn arrives in Middle-earth, his army sets up camp and he sends heralds to Sauron in order to ask him to appear before him and pledge loyalty to him. Sauron, who had been abandoned by his servants, surpasses the king in cunningness. He judges correctly the military supremacy of the Númenóreans and humiliates himself before the King of Númenor "and men

---

11 It is interesting to note that this worship of the dead, with the embalmment of the bodies and the construction of large and rich funerary monuments, closely resembles that of the ancient Egyptians, as Tolkien himself remarks: "The Númenóreans of Gondor were proud, peculiar, and archaic, and I think are best pictured in (say) Egyptian terms. In many ways they resembled 'Egyptians' – the love of, and power to construct, the gigantic and massive. And in their great interest in ancestry and in tombs" (*Letters* no. 211). See Reynolds 2008 who compares the funerary practices of the primary world people with those of the peoples of Middle-earth.

wondered, for all that he said seemed fair and wise" (*S*, Ak).¹² It is interesting to note how, in *The Lord of the Rings*, the description of the Voice of Saruman, another 'fallen' Maia, is similar to Sauron's ability to enchant with words:

> Suddenly another voice spoke, low and melodious, its very sound an enchantment. Those who listened unwarily to that voice could seldom report the words that they heard; and if they did, they wondered, for little power remained in them. Mostly they remembered only that it was a delight to hear the voice speaking, all that it said seemed wise and reasonable, and desire awoke in them by swift agreement to seem wise themselves. When others spoke they seemed harsh and uncouth by contrast; and if they gainsaid the voice, anger was kindled in the hearts of those under the spell. For some the spell lasted only while the voice spoke to them, and when it spoke to another they smiled, as men do who see through a juggler's trick while others gape at it. For many the sound of the voice alone was enough to hold them enthralled; but for those whom it conquered the spell endured when they were far away. And ever they heard that soft voice whispering and urging them. But none were unmoved; none rejected its pleas and its commands without an effort of mind and will, so long as its master had control of it. (*LotR*, TT.III.10)

But Ar-Pharazôn's arrogance and thirst for power prevent him from having the necessary strength of will and spirit to detect the lies hidden in Sauron's words, so he ends up falling into the trap and does as Sauron had foreseen from the beginning. Ar-Pharazôn decides to take Sauron to Númenor as a hostage and a prisoner. Once on the island, Sauron's great knowledge and his cunning render him soon indispensable to the king and he seduces not only the king, but also the majority of the noblemen and the people. He claims that

> Darkness alone is worshipful, and the Lord thereof may yet make other worlds to be gifts to those that serve him, so that the increase of their power shall find no end. [...] for the Valar have deceived you concerning him, putting forward the name of Eru, a phantom devised in the folly of their hearts, seeking to enchain Men in servitude to themselves. For they are the oracle of this Eru, which speaks only what they will. But he that is their master shall yet prevail, and he will deliver you from this phantom; and his name is Melkor, Lord of All, Giver of Freedom, and he shall make you stronger than they. (*S*, Ak)

---

12 In the *Ósanwe-kenta*, the wise elf Pengoloð of Gondolin writes that "in time we discovered that [Melkor] had made a language for those who served him; and he has learned our tongue with ease. He has great skill in this matter. Beyond doubt he will master all tongues, even the fair speech of the Eldar. Therefore, if ever you should speak with him beware!" (*Ósanwe-kenta*, 27). It is quite plausible to assume that Sauron, Melkor's lieutenant during the First Age of Middle-earth, has learnt from his superior how to use the languages of Eru's Children to his own advantage in order deceive them successfully.

Sauron, by exploiting man's weakness (the desire for wealth, power and immortality), plays the role of the tempting devil. He utters the most terrible blasphemies, denies the existence of God, proclaims that the true creating divinity lives in the Darkness and not in the Light, and that he will finally prevail over the Light and will establish a never-ending eternal reign for its servants, and that the Ban of the Valar is just a shrewd lie to prevent Men from achieving eternal life and competing with them.

The Númenóreans, thus, abandon the worship of Eru completely and embrace a new religion worshipping Darkness and its lord Melkor, while the Faithful are openly persecuted and even sacrificed in the new temple that Sauron had built in the centre of the capital, "and in that temple, with spilling of blood and torment and great wickedness, men made sacrifice to Melkor that he should release them from Death" (S, Ak). But this obviously is not in his power, since he is not the creator, but only a great deceiver, and actually

> Death did not depart from the land, rather it came sooner and more often, and in many dreadful guises. For whereas aforetime men had grown slowly old, and had laid them down in the end to sleep, when they were weary at last of the world, now madness and sickness assailed them; and yet they were afraid to die and go out into the dark, the realm of the lord that they had taken; and they cursed themselves in their agony. (S, Ak)

So here we see again one of the key-elements of Tolkien's thought, as we have previously noted about Aragorn's death and as Fernando Castelli has pointed out: "Wishing for immortality 'within the life of the world' is an evil suggestion [...] The refusal of death and the claim to immortality 'within life' equals to the denial of one's nature to usurp a divine prerogative. Those who pursue this chimera give themselves up to the destructive forces of evil" (Castelli 2002, 442).

However, although the Númenóreans' happiness does not increase, their power and dominion extend more and more over Middle-earth, but "the years passed, and the King felt the shadow of death approach, as his days lengthened; and he was filled with fear and wrath" (S, Ak), and Sauron takes such an opportunity to spur him, now that he is at the summit of his power, to impose his will on everyone and to disregard any commandment or ban: "The Valar have possessed themselves of the land where there is no death; and they lie to you concerning it, hiding it as best they may, because of their avarice, and their fear lest the Kings of Men should wrest from them the deathless realm and rule the world in their stead" (*S*, Ak).

Ar-Pharazôn, by now advanced in age and close to dotage, is both frightened by death and extremely proud. He accepts Sauron's advice and orders to prepare the greatest army ever seen, and sets sail towards the Blessed Realm, breaking the ban of the Valar and making war against them in order to obtain immortality and the dominion of the world. Once in Aman, he claims that land for himself and encamps with his army right under the hill of Túna; at this point, "[f]aced by this rebellion, of appalling folly and blasphemy" (*Letters* no. 131), the Valar lay down their delegated power over the world and appeal to Eru, who intervenes by opening a deep chasm in the sea between the island of Númenor and the Blessed Realm. The Númenórean fleet is swallowed by the sea, which also devours the island of Númenor, while Ar-Pharazôn and his army are buried under the hill where they had made camp.

The divine intervention, though, is not only a punitive cataclysm, but causes also a physical and epochal change in the layout of the world. The Blessed Realm is removed from the world and placed where Men can no longer reach it, so that, no matter how far they push westwards, they cannot get there, but instead return eastwards, "for the world is round, and finite, and a circle inescapable – save by death" (*Letters* no. 131), as it must be according to God's will and man's nature and because, as Verlyn Flieger (2002, 28) has remarked, "Deathlessness is not true immortality, but simply prolongation of life. In Tolkien's view, the real escape from death is through death to eternal life."

The Second Age of Middle-earth so ends with an enormous catastrophe, but nine ships of the Faithful, led by Elendil and by his two sons, Isildur and Anárion, who have not listened to Sauron's lies and have kept their faith in Eru, "by grace of the Valar [...] were spared from the ruin of that day" (*S*, Ak) and reach the coasts of Middle-earth, where they establish new realms of Men that during the Third Age will oppose Sauron again; he, in fact, although sunk into the sea within his temple, "was not of mortal flesh, and though he was robbed now of that shape in which he had wrought so great an evil [...] yet his spirit arose out of the deep [...] and came back to Middle-earth" (*S*, Ak). Evil can be defeated, but will always rise again whenever man listens to it.

The Faithful of Elendil, however, are not the only Númenóreans surviving the catastrophe that strike their island. In fact, before Ar-Pharazôn waged war against Sauron, the latter had distributed the Nine Rings of Power that he had forged together with the Elves of Eregion to nine great men, "and it is said that among those whom he ensnared […] three were great lords of Númenórean race" (S, Ak). This is the rising of "the Úlairi […] that were the Ring-wraiths, his servants" (S, Ak), also known as Nazgûl in the Black Speech.

## 3. The Nazgûl: Man trying to escape death[13]

We do not have much information on the origins of the Ringwraiths, but the little we know follows a path of Fall, Death and Machine, very similar indeed to the one we have already seen concerning the people of Númenor: "Men proved easier to ensnare. Those who used the Nine Rings became mighty in their day, kings, sorcerers, and warriors of old. They obtained glory and great wealth, yet it turned to their undoing. They had, as it seemed, unending life, yet life became unendurable to them" (S, RiPo). These men, exactly like Ar-Pharazôn, are seduced by Sauron's lies, seeking immortality in order to enjoy forever the glory and wealth that the power of the Rings' magic has given them. But it is precisely this clinging to materiality that causes their damnation, first of all with such a long life that it becomes intolerable and then with a progressive consumption that perverts them, turning them into terrible creatures, and that takes them away from the light, hiding them from the sight of living beings. In fact, Faramir states: "It is said that [the Nazgûl] were men of Númenor who had fallen into dark wickedness; to them the Enemy had given rings of power, and he had devoured them: living ghosts they were become, terrible and evil" (*LotR,* TT.IV.6). The consumption process is slow and progressive, similar to the addiction to a drug:

> They could walk, if they would, unseen by all eyes in this world beneath the sun, and they could see things in worlds invisible to mortal men; but too often they beheld only the phantoms and delusions of Sauron. And one by one, sooner or later, according to their native strength and to the good or evil of their wills in the beginning, they fell under the thraldom of the ring that they bore and under the domination of the One, which was Sauron's. And they became for

---

13 On this topic see also Amy Amendt-Raduege 2010.

ever invisible save to him that wore the Ruling Ring, and they entered into the realm of shadows. (*S*, RiPo)

Using the Nine Rings, the Nazgûl then lose part of their human nature to become wraiths, shadows wandering in darkness. Gandalf explains to Frodo at the beginning of *The Lord of the Rings*: "A mortal [...] who keeps one of the Great Rings, does not die, but he does not grow or obtain more life, he merely continues, until at last every minute is a weariness. And if he often uses the Ring to make himself invisible, he *fades*: he becomes in the end invisible permanently, and walks in the twilight under the eye of the dark power that rules the Rings" (*LotR*, FR.I.1). Yet, invisibility is not only a change in their human nature but, as Emilia Lodigiani noted, "being invisible means not having an identity [and] renouncing one's name equals to accepting such a condition [...] the loss of the name is one more symbolic proof of the effects of evil" (Lodigiani 1982, 102). In fact none of the Ringwraiths is ever called by his former (human) name. But Lodigiani goes even beyond saying that "[i]nvisibility, in Tolkien's works, is the mortal disease of our century, a rust that mainly corrodes the most complex and tormented spirits, that end up judging the ethical behaviour, which by nature requires choices and sets boundaries, as spiritually too narrow" (Lodigiani 1982, 103).

As we have seen, the power of the Nine Rings keeps men's souls in their bodies and slows down – but cannot stop – the aging process. They grant an artificial life-extension, turning those who were men before into undead,[14] servants of the master that generated them. In this they are similar to the traditional vampire-figure. Aragorn's characterization of the wraiths points in this direction, too: "and at all times they smell the blood of living things, desiring and hating it" (*LotR*, FR.I.11). Furthermore, when Frodo wears the Ring he sees them in their 'true' form: "In their white faces burned keen and merciless eyes;

---

14 Paul Kocher (2002, 61), too, observes about the Nazgûl that "[n]ot only are they its slaves, no longer having any wills of their own, but through it they have suffered far-reaching physical changes. The process of lengthening life which has kept Bilbo and Frodo young for some scores of years has prolonged theirs for tens of centuries since the rings were forged in the Second Age. They seem never to have died in the usual sense. They still inhabit their original bodies, but these have faded and thinned in their component matter until they can no longer be said to exist in the dimension of the living." See also Amy Amendt-Raduege's (2010) discussion of the Ringwraiths.

under their mantles were long grey robes; upon their grey hairs were helms of silver; in their haggard hands were swords of steel" (*LotR*, FR.I.11).[15]

Thus, the Ringwraiths, although invisible in our world, still have their own form and appearance in the Invisible World – a sort of spiritual level that I already mentioned above, but that is never clearly explained by Tolkien in his works, and is only rarely mentioned, such as when Gandalf explains Glorfindel's apparition at the Ford of Bruinen: "the Elven-wise, lords of the Eldar from beyond the furthest seas [...] do not fear the Ringwraiths, for those who have dwelt in the Blessed Realm live at once in both worlds, and against both the Seen and the Unseen they have great power" (*LotR*, FR.II.1). One can note how Gandalf, the very wielder of the Flame of Anor and of Narya, the Ring of Fire – i.e. the good fire that gives warmth, life and hope – here expressly says that those who have seen the light of the Valar, and therefore of Eru/God, are not afraid to face darkness and its servants, because darkness is nothing but the absence of light and does not have an existence of its own. This is an idea very similar to the orthodox Christian vision of good and evil, firstly expounded by St. Augustine but then more clearly expressed by the philosopher Boethius in his treatise *De Consolatione Philosophiae*, according to which "there is no such thing as evil: [evil] is the absence of good",[16] which is in perfect accordance with the invisibility of the Nazgûl, with their non-existence or non-life.[17] The consequences of this idea are that evil alone cannot create,[18] that it has not been created but is the fruit of the voluntary exercise of free will by Satan/Melkor and man to move away from God and that at

---

15 About the analogies between the figure of the Nazgûl and that of the vampire see Benvenuto 2008a, 11-12.
16 See Shippey 2005, 159. Paul Kocher (2002, 68) furthermore notes that the "opposite view would be Manichaean, accepting the existence of a creative force in evil equal in power to that of the good. Tolkien firmly rejects it. When Sauron turns to evil he does so by choice, and is diminished in consequence."
17 Paul Kocher (2002, 75), instead, compares Tolkien's vision of good and evil to the "natural theology of Thomas Aquinas, whom it is reasonable to suppose that Tolkien, as a medievalist and a Catholic, knows well." Similarly to the process that leads the Nazgûl to a sort of non-existence, Kocher (2002, 76) remarks that "[a]fter a time [Sauron's] body became black and burning hot [...] This process describes not merely an almost Platonic loss of personal beauty but a diminution of physical existence. It is also a loss of normal intercourse with others, a retreat into a loneliness cut off from equals. Literally and figuratively, light is exchanged for darkness. [...] Aquinas would call them all losses of Being. Evil is not a thing in itself but a lessening of the Being inherent in the created order."
18 Frodo, in fact, says that "The Shadow [...] can only mock, it cannot make: not real new things of its own" (*LotR*, RK.VI.6).

the end of creation it will be cancelled, just as man's Fall has been redeemed by Christ's incarnation and death.[19]

Nevertheless, the Nazgûl are a real presence that must be faced and fought because, as Paul Kocher (2002, 54) noted, "the burden of *The Lord of the Rings* is that victory for the good is never automatic. It must be earned anew each time by every individual taking part." The main source of power for the Ringwraiths is not connected to their physical strength but, as Aragorn says, "their power is in terror" (*LotR*, FR.I.10),[20] and terror is obviously greater in those who are alone and remote from the light. In fact, in "dark and loneliness they are strongest; they will not openly attack a house where there are lights and many people – not until they are desperate" (*LotR*, FR.I.10); and what image does a house filled with light and people recall if not a church, the house of Christ?

Such an image, however, also recalls the legend of Thidhrandi (cf. Turville-Petre 1964, 222), a story set in Iceland shortly before the conversion to the Christian faith in the year 1000 A.D. The protagonists are the prophet Thorhall, who had converted to the new religion, and Thidhrandi, a pagan nobleman of irreproachable conduct. During a celebration in Thidhrandi's house, Thorhall warns the host and his family not to leave the house during the night or, should anyone knock, to open the door. When all the people who took part in the celebration fall asleep, someone is heard knocking hard on the door and Thidhrandi, heedless of the warning received, opens it and draws his sword. But he does not see anyone and so goes out to look around; he hears horses galloping from the North and notices nine women, clad in black with their swords unsheathed, coming towards him, while from the South he notices another group of nine women riding white horses and dressed in coloured clothes. Thidhrandi then tries to get back into the house, but the women in black reach him and, although he defends himself valiantly, they inflict a mortal wound upon him. He is then taken home, where the following morning, after telling this story, he dies.

---

19 On the Boethian concept of evil in Tolkien's works see Shippey 2005, 159-160; on Tolkien's idea of eschatology see Whittingham 2007, 170-200 and Franco Manni's essay in this book.
20 On terror as the main weapon of the Ringwraiths see Shippey 2000b.

The legend is a clear allegory of the advent of Christianity (the nine women on white horses) in Iceland, where the pagan religion (the nine women in black) requires one last sacrifice before disappearing: it is the noble Thidhrandi who, alone in the darkness of the night, far away from the light and warmth of his house and heedless of Thorhall's warning, and although fighting valiantly, finally succumbs. It is interesting to see how the legend also recalls the Nazgûl's attack against Frodo at the Ford of Bruinen, but with a different outcome: in this case the nine knights clad in black are scattered and routed by "a plumed cavalry of waves. White flames seemed to Frodo to flicker on their crests and he half fancied that he saw amid the water white riders upon white horses" (*LotR*, FR.I.2), a magnificent eucatastrophe in Tolkien's meaning of the word.

The Ringwraiths, as we have seen, may therefore be materially defeated and even destroyed, as happens to their leader during the Battle of the Pelennor Fields. Although protected by a "spell that knit his unseen sinews to his will" (*LotR*, RK.V.6), the blow inflicted by the sword of the Barrow-downs wielded by Merry, forged with Númenórean craft, breaks that spell, allowing Éowyn to stick "with her last strength [...] her sword between crown and mantle" (*LotR*, RK.V.6) of the invisible Lord of the Nazgûl, who thus dies falling to the ground, but "the mantle and hauberk were empty. Shapeless they lay now on the ground, torn and tumbled; and a cry went up into the shuddering air, and faded to a shrill wailing, passing with the wind, a voice bodiless and thin that died, and was swallowed up, and was never heard again in that age of this world" (*LotR*, RK.V.6).

In a very similar way the other Nazgûl disappear, too, when Gollum and the One Ring fall together into the lava of Mount Doom. With the destruction of the Ring, all the power that Sauron had poured into it fades away, and so does also the power that had unnaturally preserved the bodies of the Ringwraiths which, "with a cry that pierced all other sounds [...] came, shooting like flaming bolts, as caught in the fiery ruin of hill and sky they crackled, withered, and went out" (*LotR*, RK.V.3).

In conclusion, then, and in perfect accordance with the Boethian idea, once they are defeated all the Ringwraiths vanish into nothingness, they dissolve and disappear, finally completing the process of dissolution that the magic of Sauron and his Rings had postponed for too long; an absurd rejection of death that, in truth, is also a rejection of life, because, as Andrea Monda has underlined, "in order to live sensibly we need to learn to die, [since] death is that gift that sheds a light onto the mystery of life" (Monda 2008, 199). Death is Eru's gift to Men so that "history has a sense, there's Someone transmitting tension to men's vicissitudes, there's a design giving a direction to an otherwise empty and absurd story" (Monda 2008, 199).

# Simone Bonechi

## "In the Mounds of Mundburg": Death, War and Memory in Middle-earth

I will in this essay deal with the subject of death and immortality in Tolkien's works from the point of view of the funeral rites that he describes in his narratives, and will concentrate my analysis in particular on those concerning the war-dead. These funeral rites and the themes connected to burials will be linked, as far as possible, to the history of Britain from 1919 to 1945: the years during which Tolkien's Middle-earth works were being written. During this period, death in battle rose to such proportions as to involve British society as a whole. The consequent need to decide how to give a honourable burial to the fallen and how to remember and give sense to their death permeated the collective mentality as never before.

### 1. The historical context. The commemoration of the fallen in Britain 1919-1949

The United Kingdom of Great Britain and Ireland mobilized five million seven hundred thousand men to fight the Great War: seven hundred and twenty two thousand of these fell in battle. Upper and middle classes, accustomed to furnish practically the whole of the officers corps of the Regular Army and permeated by the public schools' ethic of service and patriotism, enthusiastically answered the call for volunteers. Oxford, Cambridge and dozens of other schools emptied and their alumni swelled the ranks of subalterns in the Army. The middle-class, the class from which Second Lieutenant John Ronald Reuel Tolkien and his closest friends came, was the one most affected by the war casualties: 29% of those serving in the war who matriculated at Oxford between 1910 and 1914 and 26% of those who matriculated at Cambridge in the same period lost their lives during the war, a percentage more than double than the national average of 12,8% of war fatalities.[1]

---

1 I take this data from Gregory 2008, 289-290. See also Stevenson 1990, 95-96 and Garth 2003, 8-9.

The war that Tolkien found himself fighting was different from those that had preceded it in British military history, not only because of the disproportionate vastness of the theatre of operation and scale of the forces involved, but also because, for the first time in its history, the Army that fought this war was formed for the greatest part by citizens in arms and for a large part by people who would be able to put their experience in writing.

In former wars, the need to provide an individual burial to privates soldiers (and often even to officers) was not an established concern: communal graves had accommodated the dead of the Napoleonic Wars, the Crimean War and the innumerable colonial campaigns. And only on very rare occasions had the civilian authorities ordered memorials to commemorate soldiers and officers killed in battle. We have to keep in mind that, until 1914, the British Army was composed entirely of professional volunteers and that to enlist as a soldier was considered a disgrace even by the lower classes. The sharp distinction between Army and society had, up to that moment, favored a detached social attitude towards the casualties suffered in war by the Armed Services. The South African War (1899-1902), with its massive influx of citizen volunteers to aid the regular Army and the unusual number of fatalities, had started to change this attitude. But nothing could have prepared British society for the shock of the Great War.

With casualties mounting at an appalling rate, public opinion began to demand insistently that something be done to record and preserve the tombs of the fallen. In February 1915 the Graves Registration Commission was officially given the task of finding and registering the graves of British officers and men in France, and to open negotiations with the French Government to acquire land in France for the building of war cemeteries. Exhumations and shipment of the bodies to Britain for burial were expressly forbidden in April 1915, not only due to reasons of hygiene, but also on account of the impossibility, had they been allowed, of treating impartially the claims by persons of different social status, on the principle of "equality in sacrifice".

On May 21$^{st}$ 1917 the Imperial War Graves Commission (IWGC) was instituted by Royal Charter, with the task of building and caring for war cemeteries and memorials that would celebrate the memory of the fallen. In its first meeting, the principle of "perpetuity in sepulture" together with that of "equality in sacrifice" for officers and soldiers alike was established. The fallen would receive the honour that had so far been reserved for the great figures of national history, and since it was not possible to bury them all "beneath the sacred shelter of existing monuments," structures at least as lasting had to be built in the far lands where they had been laid to rest.[2]

Sir Frederic Kenyon, director of the British Museum and adviser to the Commission on the architectural layout of war cemeteries, recommended a linear and clean plan, with rows of headstones, homogeneous in dimensions and design, laid out in plots of grass, separated by paths, with flowers, shrubs and trees arranged so as to give a general impression of peace and repose. War cemeteries had to confer something of the England the soldiers had died for: an idealized England, made of gardens and beautiful landscapes. The fusion between the classicism of architectural features and the picturesque horticultural arrangement was to create an atmosphere of natural peacefulness. Wherever possible, the graves had to look east (towards "the enemy") and somewhere in the cemetery a great altar stone would have to be placed, bearing some brief and apt inscription, and at some prominent point would rise a cross. The memorials eventually present would have to be characterized by sobriety and solemnity.

Kenyon suggested the names of renowned professionals like Edwin Lutyens, Herbert Baker and Reginald Blomfield as principal architects responsible for the design of cemeteries. Together with the planning of dozens of cemeteries and memorials, we owe to the former the Great War Stone, also known as the Stone of Remembrance, a great rectangular block of stone, a prominent element in every cemetery with more than four hundred graves. The stone bears the inscription "Their name liveth for evermore"[3] which was chosen by Rudyard Kipling, literary adviser to the IWGC. Blomfield designed the Cross of Sacrifice, erected in all the cemeteries: devoid of specific stylistic and historical connotations, it bears on one side a bronze sword, reversed, to symbolize the soldier's sacrifice.

---

2 Summers 2007, 12-17. See also Quinlan 2005, 69-89.
3 *Ecclesiasticus* 44, 14.

Alongside these enterprises by the established institutions, other forms of remembrance developed within British society. Rolls of Honour, street shrines (little, inexpensive shrines erected along the streets and bearing the names of the local people in active service and appropriate space for those killed) made their appearance in roads and churches, in public spaces, in the places of work of the enlisted men.[4]

The tenets of the IWGC were soon opposed by the religious authorities and the aristocracy. On May 4th, 1920, the issue was brought before the Parliament. The imposition of the principle of "equality in sacrifice and memory" was considered to clash with the right of the parents and families to care for the burial and commemoration of their dear ones according to their own wishes and religious faith. The weight of public opinion, the feelings of the ex-servicemen, and the flawed nature of the intrinsically discriminatory position of the opposing lobby, all played a part in the final victory of the principles of the IWGC, which were thus officially endorsed by the government.

The view of the soldiers on the proposed layout of war cemeteries was clearly expressed by an ex-officer in a letter that was read in the House of Commons during the debate:

> The uniformity of design was what appealed most strongly to all. That the fellowship of the War should be perpetuated in death by a true fellowship in memorial was the unanimous and emphatic desire of everyone, officer and man. Death, the great leveller of all rank, was very near to these men at the time (when the proposals of the IWGC were circulated), and their deliberate and expressed wish was that, as they fell, so they should lie, and their memory be perpetuated in like form throughout. Since the taking of that census of opinion many of those who voted have been laid to rest in France. They lie buried now on the field where they sealed their royal fellowship and sacrifice, and I for one feel that I shall betray their memory if I do not protest to the utmost of my power against any reversal of the decision they then gave. (Quinlan 2005, 82)[5]

For the hundreds of thousands of servicemen of whom all trace had been lost, the IWGC decided to commission special memorials, where the name of the missing would be engraved. The most famous and original of these was the Memorial to the Missing of the Somme, designed by Lutyens and inau-

---

4 This section is based mainly on the following texts: King 1998; Stamp 2007; Gregory 1994 and 2008; Winter 2004; Skelton & Gliddon 2008.
5 Concerning the opposition to the egalitarian principle, see Quinlan 2005, 80-83 and 263-272.

gurated in 1932 at Thiepval, in the very places where Tolkien had fought. It bears, together with 72,906 names, those of three of his fellow Exeter College students (cf. Garth 2008, 13-56).

While memorials and war cemeteries were being built on overseas battlefields, Britain was witnessing an intense phase of reconsideration and re-elaboration of the war experience and the meaning of victory. This 'remembrance boom' took the form of a formalization of the war experience in public ceremonies and memorials, on the one hand, and, on the other, of a burgeoning publication of war novels and memoirs.

The immediate issue these public and private expressions of concerns and desires addressed was that of giving a proper sense to the war and to the sacrifices it had imposed on everyone, and first and foremost to the greatest sacrifice of all: that of one's life.

The more common answer to this quest for meaning was to honour the fallen as individual heroes. They had faced evil embodied in form of Prussian militarism, strong with their faith in the principles of Liberty, Motherland and Religion. Steeped in a dogged spirit of service, to these high and noble ideals they had sacrificed their lives, winning victory and peace for Britain and the whole of Europe. Particular value was given to comradeship, to solidarity among fighting men, a collective virtue that went alongside the private one of self-sacrifice.

Even those that tried to give a less idealized and bowdlerized image of the war, testifying all its horror and brutality, were keen on saving the sacred value of comradeship: the fellowship of the trenches could redeem an otherwise devastating experience.

The debt of the nation towards the war dead was expressed all over the country with ceremonies and memorials. On November 11th, 1920 an "unknown soldier" was solemnly buried in Westminster Abbey beside the great figures of the nation. Meanwhile, in Whitehall, King George V unveiled the stone version of the provisional cenotaph (essentially a sarcophagus on top of a lofty pillar), realized by Edwyn Lutyens for the victory celebrations of 1919.

In every city and village in Great Britain the memory of the fallen was perpetuated through the institution of memorials, in the form of monuments (crosses, statues, columns, obelisks), memorial plaques and halls or more immaterial expressions, such as memorial funds named after those killed in battle and dedicated to relief activities. Monuments such as these, as well as the cenotaph for the whole nation, became the focus of the remembrance ceremonies held on November 11th every year from 1919 onward, preceded by the two-minutes Great Silence at eleven o'clock. Religious authorities usually gathered with local ones, also because many memorials were in churches or on church grounds. The rhetoric of sacrifice was thus intimately connected with Christian meaning right from the beginning.

And this rhetoric proclaimed, for the first time, a 'canonization of the common people': the war dead were not celebrated for accomplishing heroic deeds or actions beyond their simple duty as soldiers, but exactly for having done that duty to the bitter end, for their 'ordinariness'. Through them, the nation itself was celebrated.

Besides, the commemorative discourse as a whole tended to point out the ethical aspects of collective relationships, more than the personal and private dimension of mourning and consolation. The debt the living owed to the dead was thus translated, more often than not, in terms of the individual's responsibility to the community. Personal remembrance was restricted within the limits of family memory: in public commemoration the dead lost their individuality and were celebrated as a collective entity and in connection to the local community of which they had been a part:

> The idea of community was the basis on which a sense of validity, of meaning, for death in the war was constructed. Death could be made meaningful if it was seen as a service to the community, as protection of it, purification of it, a warning to it, or restoration of it to an older and better identity.
> (King 1998, 236)

War was thus interpreted as a harrowing and shocking experience, but also, through sorrow, as a spiritually beneficial, morally edifying one: the sacrifice of the fallen called all the survivors to the emulation of their virtues (comradeship, spirit of service, moral endurance, self-denial, faith in the justice of the cause) and to honour their memory by building a better world, a world where these virtues could flourish and be fully realized. This was the moral obligation that the living, ex-servicemen and civilians alike, had contracted with those that had made the Great Sacrifice.

With the passing of years the written contributions of ex-soldiers and civilians came to enrich collective perception of the conflict. Between the twenties and the thirties works were published that more than any others shaped the literary memory of the Great War in the years to come. Some of these works spoke the language of disillusion and anger. Robert Graves, Siegfried Sassoon, Wilfred Owen, Frederick Manning, Richard Aldington and others gave birth and gave strength to a new image of the war dead: a passive and terrified sufferer, crushed by the blind and brutal force of the war, a war seen as a purposeless, impersonal machine, abetted by "the old men" (generals and politicians), impassively grinding the lives and bodies of "the young", friends and foes alike.

Even if this is the picture that in the long run has shaped most of our contemporary perception of the Great War, it was not the most important one in the years we are examining, both in terms of percentage of the literary production and of impact on collective mentality. The majority of war novels, poetry and memoirs in this period were engaged not in launching invectives or in chanting the elegy for a world irreparably lost, but in the preservation and reaffirmation of what its authors thought was at the core of the "English culture".

These authors

> fashioned meaning out of change by describing the lessons learned in the ordeal of war, and by highlighting values which would reaffirm the strength and importance of links with the past. Morality, religion, tradition: such words made up a litany of appeals for post-war re-generation. [...] The use of elevated language and of spiritual images allowed the writers to portray the wounds etched in the memory of the survivors of the trenches while also offering the consolation of directions of meaning, in particular the absolute value of comradeship. These novels posited endurance, in spite of doubt and terror, as the way to renew the older conceptions of courage and heroism. [...] Tradition was both the highest expression of Englishness and the keystone of reconstruction. [...] It was contained in those values which were taken to be the underlying foundation for the whole of National life: religion, the country, England. The immutability of 'traditional values' was the most powerful myth asserted in these novels. (Bracco 1993, 197-198)

To represent death in battle as a sacrifice in the name of noble ideals, though, implied the engagement to act so as to give substance and reality to those ideals, under pain of showing the rhetoric of remembrance as hollow and inconsistent. But with the passing of time, peace and the better world for whom the soldiers were said to have died seemed to fade more and more in the distance on the European horizon. When the thirties came, the spreading and strengthening of totalitarian governments, the internal and external feebleness of the democracies, the hegemony of the "disillusionment school", made it clearer and clearer that, in spite of all sacrifices, patriotism and pacifism had failed.

The 1939 generation went to war with a more sober spirit and much less enthusiasm than the 1914 one: disenchantment and doggedness were its hallmarks. And soon new names came to be added to the rolls of 1914-1918 war dead. But after 1945, after Hiroshima and Auschwitz, it was much more difficult than in 1919 to revitalize the romantic and symbolic discourse of commemoration, and most of all that of optimism and faith in the possibility of realizing a better world from the sacrifice of battle.

## 2. From commemoration to sub-creation

It may appear risky, speaking of Tolkien, to try to determine how far and in which way external events may have influenced his literary work and the themes developed therein, given the unique nature of his work, so distant both from the patterns of the then budding modernism and from the style of the Victorian social novel. Nonetheless, comparing what we know of his ideas with the historical and cultural background of his epoch, we see how, once again, he emerges as a son of his time. His interest in the past, the value of memory, his love of England, the passion for social ties and relationships, the yearning to think and realize "great things": all these main traits of his character are shared not only by his closest friends, but also, in varying measure, by the great majority of the educated young people of his generation. The war and the loss of his friends would impart on this core of feelings an original and decisive impulse toward mythopoesis.

The language of commemoration must have touched deep and sensitive chords in Tolkien. Coming back to Oxford in 1919, he could not have avoided thinking of all the friends and acquaintances that had lost their lives on the battlefield.[6] Trying to make sense of the death of G.B. Smith and Rob Gilson replicated at a more intimate level the quest for meaning in which the entire British society was involved. On the same lines, the diffuse moral obligation felt by the living not to betray the ideals and purposes of the fallen, translated for Tolkien into the urge to let speak in his own works the now dead voices of his friends. The intellectual and emotional heritage of the T.C.B.S. was the baggage Tolkien brought back from the ruins of the pre-war world (cf. Garth 2003, 253-283).

It cannot be a surprise, then, that war, death and memory are at the centre of that sort of great *meditatio mortis* that is Tolkien's *Legendarium*, to quote the title of the first of Claudio A. Testi's essays in this volume. Death in battle is, Aragorn's and Denethor's cases excepted, practically the only type of death visually depicted in his works. As a matter of fact, Tolkien is interested in death as a consequence of a deliberate choice: whether direct consequence (as for Denethor and Aragorn), or indirect consequence (as for the soldier or warrior, who accepts the possibility of dying in battle or duel).

In Tolkien's works, death voluntarily accepted in the name of a cause acquires the value of a final meaningful event, it subsumes in itself both the conclusive word about the life just extinguished, and the memory that is left to future generations, carried on in stories and songs. To summarize, death is the occurrence that gives sense to all that comes before and after it. Funeral rites and burial customs come thus to be imbued with a strong symbolic value: they become the material form of the sense of the deceased's life.

Death as a biological event, the natural end to life, is instead taken for granted and totally excluded from the main narrative horizon, even in terms of remembrance and mourning: there are no cemeteries in Middle-earth. Royal necropolises like the Barrow Downs, the Barrowfield at Edoras, the Houses of

---

6 Of the 57 students that had matriculated at Exeter College the same year as Tolkien, 23 died as a result of the war. Their names are engraved on the memorial built in the college chapel, designed by Sir Reginald Blomfield, father of Tolkien's friend Austin, and one of the principal architects of IWGC. See Garth 2008, 48.

the Dead in Minas Tirith preserve not just the body and image of the dead, but also and more importantly, the historical memory of the nation.

The personal, intimate dimension of dying finds a place in Tolkien's stories only in the case of Aragorn. Voluntarily renouncing life before falling into dotage, he gives evidence that dying rests within the established order of things. He thus becomes the symbol of the right sense of life and of life's ending: not to cling to material things, but accept with tranquillity and confidence death as a 'natural' passage.[7]

But Aragorn's case is just an anticipation, a fleeting image from a golden age still far away in the future (or in an equally far away past). In time of crisis and upheavals the centre of the scene, in Middle-earth as in the Primary World, is occupied by death as a consequence of strife and struggle.

## 3. Funeral rites in Middle-earth: the fallen

Although *The Silmarillion* is interwoven with narratives of battles and assaults on fortified cities, the fate of the fallen is almost never depicted: the narrator hovers high above the battlefield and relates the events in outline, more as a chronicler than a reporter.

The one exception to this rule is the Battle of Unnumbered Tears. Tolkien dedicates a whole chapter to the catastrophic defeat of Elves and Men and, though keeping a 'high' tone, describes in detail the action of the armies and the deeds of champions of both sides, not sparing the reader the occasional macabre details, such as the pyramid raised by the orcs with the severed heads of the men of the House of Hador (cf. *S*, Qu.20).

After the battle, on the command of Morgoth, the orcs gather the corpses of their enemies so as to raise a great hill in the middle of the ashen plain of Anfauglith.

> *Haudh-en-Ndengin*, the Elves named it, the Hill of Slain, and *Haudh-en-Nirnaeth*, the Hill of Tears. But grass came there and grew again long and green

---

[7] For a careful investigation of the human dimension of death, see Roberto Arduini's essay in this volume.

upon that hill, alone in all the desert that Morgoth made; and no creature of Morgoth trod thereafter upon the earth beneath which the swords of the Eldar and the Edain crumbled into dust. (*S*, Qu.20)

It is, ironically, Morgoth who builds the first 'war memorial' of Middle-earth: because this actually is a memorial, being built for the purpose of conveying a specific message concerning war and fighting. The message of the Hill of Tears, as well as of the hideous trophy of severed heads, was to instill fear and terror in the hearts of Morgoth's foes. But Nature, acting according to a scheme that will be replicated several times in the tales of Middle-earth, intervened by covering with earth the mound of the slain and transforming it into a green hill in the middle of the desert, making it a symbol of grief, but also of unyielding hope.

All these meanings tied to the episode of the Hill of Slain are not a later elaboration of Tolkien's, but are present already in the earliest narratives of the First-Age *Legendarium*. They are to be found in the "Lay of the Children of Húrin", the poem in alliterative verse composed by Tolkien in Leeds between 1920 and 1925. The "Lay" relates how Túrin, travelling to Nargothrond after Beleg's killing, accompanied by the elf Flinding, finds himself journeying through Anfauglith by the moonlight and passing near the hill of the fallen, "bedewed as by drops of drooping tears." Having heard Flinding's words remembering the dead warriors, he shakes off his torpor and, turning his hand towards Thangorodrim, "thrice he cursed the maker of mourning, Morgoth Bauglir" (*LB* 58-59).

Remembrance, commemoration, awareness, stimulus to action: from the sight of the Hill of Tears spring all the elements that define the function of a memorial. From their grassy mound the anonymous dead of the Nirnaeth Arnoediad call the living to renew the struggle against "the maker of mourning" in which they gave their life.

In the cosmogonic epic of *The Silmarillion* there are no other episodes of this kind, but in *The Lord of the Rings*, where the dominant tone is that of romance, Tolkien more than once takes care to describe the fate of warriors killed in battle. But before showing us the fallen in the War of the Ring, he tells, in one of the more ambiguous episodes of the novel, of another, ancient 'war cemetery':

the burial ground of the warriors of Dagorlad, engulfed by the Dead Marshes by the time of Frodo's journey.

Tolkien brings the dead on the scene in a very unusual and disquieting way. First of all, Men, Elves and Orcs are united in death, one beside the other at the bottom of the pools: "grim faces and evil, and noble faces and sad" and "all foul, all rotting, all dead. A fell light is in them" (*LotR*, TT.IV.2). Is this an indirect rejection of the value of war as sacrifice in the name of a cause, to assert the absurdity of dividing the world in good guys and bad guys fighting each other, when war only serves to make plain, in the common destiny of death and decay, that equality we refused in life? As a matter of fact, the dead of the Dead Marshes trouble us in their anonymous desolation, in their utter lack of visibility, of hope, of justification.

Tolkien does not resolve the ambiguity of the episode, but points to a possible way out: as Sam says, the dead cannot be really there, after more than three thousand years; what we see are "phantoms," misleading and delusive images, like the "tricksy lights," the "candles of corpses" that light the marshes. It is probably "some devilry hatched in the Dark Land," with the purpose of sapping the morale of enemies that should venture there. But we do not know for certain, and the fallen of Dagorlad remain to warn us that "the wages of heroism is death," in all its loathsome physicality. They are, too, in their own way, a 'memorial' brutally laying bare the other face of glory.[8]

The corpses of the Dead Marshes have another peculiarity: they are the only ones to be laid to rest in graves, in the earth. In all other cases, the warriors fallen in the battles of the War of the Ring, like those of the Nirnaeth, are generally buried in mounds.

Mounds represent the more ancient burial form used in Great Britain: tombs of this kind are a feature of British landscape since the Neolithic Age and even the pagan Anglo-Saxons and the Vikings used this form of burial for their dead and dwelt on their magic and otherworldly powers in their mythologies. In Tolkien's

---

[8] On this episode, see Shippey 2000a, 216-218. See also Long 2005, 123-137. The quotation "the wages of heroism is death" is from *MC* 26.

Middle-earth, Men used mounds as main burial form since the remotest times (cf. *LotR*, App. A.1).

It is not by chance, then, that in *The Lord of the Rings* it is the Rohirrim who are shown as burying their dead in mounds, since the Riders of the Mark are in many ways similar to the ancient Anglo-Saxons. For the funeral rites of the Elves (they, too, bury their dead in mounds) we have to go back to *The Silmarillion*, while we know from the Appendices to *The Lord of the Rings* that Dwarves buried their dead in stone tombs, even if the only episode concerning their dead warriors is an exception to this rule: the fallen of Azanulbizar, too many to be buried according to custom, were burned on pyres. This, in any case, only heightens their importance: "but those who fell at Azanulbizar were honoured in memory, and to this day a Dwarf will say proudly of one of his sires: 'he was a burned Dwarf' and that is enough" (*LotR*, App. A.3 and n. 1).

Tolkien relates in detail the fate of the warriors killed in the battles in Rohan. After the victory of Helm's Deep, two mounds are raised and in these are buried the bodies of the men of West- and Eastfold. Below the dike, another mound contained the dead Dunlendings.[9] The corpses of the orcs were thrown in a deep pit, over which a hill of stones was raised, that was afterwards named the Death Down.

Only Háma, captain of the King's Guard, was buried in a grave at the foot of the Hornburg.

The fallen of the Battles of the Fords of Isen are likewise buried in a mound surrounded with stones and set about with many spears. Éomer feared that the bodies would be devoured by wolves and carrion fowls and is therefore positively surprised to see them honourably buried and utters an *impromptu* funeral oration: "Here let them rest! And when their spears have rotted and rusted, long still may their mound stand and guard the Fords of Isen!" (*LotR*, TT.III.8).

---

9 "But the men of Dunland were set apart in a mound below the Dike." This sentence has not been included in the English editions of *The Lord of the Rings* until 2004. Christopher Tolkien took notice of the omission and pointed it out in *WR* 40; Wayne G. Hammond and Christina Scull restored it to the text in the 50th anniversary editions (2004 and 2005).

And finally, the "Mounds of Mundburg" shelter the dead of the Pelennor. Their memorial, even more than the mounds themselves, is the lay of the anonymous Rohirrim bard that celebrates their deeds. After naming one by one the captains of the Mark and their "league-fellows" of Gondor who perished in the battlefield, he presents them all joined in the sleep of death: "Death in the morning and at day's ending / Lords took and lowly. Long now they sleep / under grass in Gondor by the Great River" (*LotR*, RK.V.6).

One of the first elements to emerge from these descriptions is the anonymity of the fallen. If the captains' names are recorded in epic songs, the burials have no sign that can reveal the single individuals resting therein. Even the sorrow and mourning of friends and relatives, in the very few instances in which Tolkien makes them plain (Rían dying of grief on the Hill of Slain, Théoden weeping for his dead captain), are relegated to the margins of the main narrative.

As I indicated above, speaking of the Great War dead, they lost their individuality, to be merged in and live on forever in the collective identity of the "fallen warriors". But while in post-war Britain the commemoration reached an equilibrium between the will to celebrate the dead collectively and the need to respect their individual identity, adopting a uniform headstone and engraving it with name and regiment of the fallen or remembering the names of the missing by writing them on special memorials, in Middle-earth we have the total identification of the fallen with his symbolic role, at least among Men and Elves. The name, so important to post-war mentality that it became the fusion point between public commemoration and private memory, loses its meaning in Middle-earth and merges in the communal identity (Eldar and Edain, Eorlingas, Riders of Théoden) and it is this latter that is celebrated and transmitted in the poetic memory, together with that of captains and sovereigns. Through the commemoration of the fallen it is one's loyalty to oaths and engagements that is acknowledged and honoured. In death, as in life, they exist in as much as they are members of a community:

> Now is the hour come, Riders of the Mark, sons of Eorl! Foes and fire are before you and your homes far behind. Yet, though you fight upon an alien field, the glory that you reap there shall be your own for ever. Oaths ye have take: now fulfil them all, to lord and land and league of friendship! (*LotR*, RK.V.5)

The soldier poet John McRae in one of the best know of Great War poems, "In Flanders Fields", says as much:

> [...]
> Take up our quarrel with the foe:
> to you from failing hands we throw
> the torch; be yours to hold it high.
> If ye break faith with us who die
> we shall not sleep, though poppies grow
> in Flanders Fields. (Davis 2005, 262)

Two further elements support and reinforce this 'communal' dimension of the fallen: the motivation behind the care given to the corpse and the choice of the burial place.

Why care for the dead body at all, in fact, since there is no religious prescription to do so in Middle-earth? The answer to this question lies in the solidarity between comrades, in that fellowship that, in the Primary World, is the only traditional value to come through unscathed from the crucible of the trenches. The comrades of the dead cannot allow their bodies to be devoured by carrion-beasts.[10]

Setting up a mound, besides showing respect and honour to the dead, creates a tangible and durable architectural 'mark', which serves as pivot for the transmission of future memory. Burial mounds become in this way milestones on the road of history, witness to a past that continues in the present; and they even become sometimes 'portals' that connect the world of the living with that of the dead, like the Great Barrow into which the hobbits are taken in "Fog on the Barrow-downs".[11]

And regarding the place of the burial: the battlefield of their last fight is always chosen as their resting place. Like their Great War counterparts, the dead warriors of Middle-earth remain on eternal watch over the fields on which they fought and fell. As the bard of "The Mounds of Mundburg" says, for them there is no coming home after death.

---

10 See *LotR*, TT.III.1: "'First we must tend the fallen' said Legolas. 'We cannot leave him lying like carrion among these foul Orcs'"; *LotR*, TT.III.8: "'Alas!' said Théoden. 'Must we pass this way, where the carrion-beasts devour so many good Riders of the Mark?'" and *LotR*, App. A.III n. 47: "To fire therefore they (the Dwarves) turned, rather than leave their kin to beast or bird or carrion-orc."
11 On the barrow episode see Flieger 2007, 99-112.

Avoiding the realism of a detailed personalization of the fallen and delegating the whole problem of their commemoration to the sole medium of bardic poetry, Tolkien kept his narrative of war events in an exclusively epic and timeless dimension and enhances thus the symbolic role of the burials. In them, the dead 'sleep' and speak to the living, recalling the fight and its price, the hard reality of life and the example of their sacrifice. They say to present and future generations: "We did our duty and fought in the 'good fight', keeping our oaths. Therefore we can rest in peace and live on in your memory, until the world be changed."

Tolkien's mythologizing of death runs contrary to what was happening in contemporary European culture, which was witnessing instead a 'return of the dead'. Sometimes this was to accuse the living, as in Abel Gance's film *J'accuse* (1918-1919), or to fight alongside them, as in Arthur Machen's tale "The Bowmen" (1914) and in the accounts of soldiers and civilian swearing to have seen angels fight against the Germans at Mons. In some other instances, the dead 'return' to give evidence of a continuing community between dead and living, as in the 'spirit photographs' that show Whitehall's cenotaph surrounded by the ghostly figures of the fallen. In Middle-earth, instead, the only 'returning dead', the only 'revenants', are exactly those that *have not* fought: the *Sleepless Dead* of Dunharrow, that broke their oath of allegiance to Isildur and would not fight against Sauron, and are as a consequence cursed and doomed to never find rest until their ancient pledge is fulfilled.

In representing the dead warriors of his wars, then, Tolkien rejected the idea of useless sacrifice, of futility, of disillusion. Though acknowledging the horror and cruelty of war, in his depiction of funeral rites he goes beyond these, underscoring the values that give, notwithstanding the weaknesses and wickedness that can and are found among the ranks of the "Just", sense and meaning to the death in battle: justice, loyalty, comradeship. The mounds of the fallen become thus monuments to the social virtues and death in battle the supreme act of citizenship.

## 4. "Their name liveth for evermore": eternal fame and hints of resurrection

Funeral rites and monuments on the one hand, epic poetry on the other are the practical forms of one of the two "escapes" from death that Tolkien puts at the core of his tale. The first escape is memory, the other is serial longevity (cf. *Letters* no. 211).[12] We have seen how 'memory', in Middle-earth, means 'fame', that is collective and, more importantly, poetic memory.

At the time of the events of *The Lord of the Rings*, as a matter of fact, rather than through Gondorian historiographical tradition, the memory of ancient heroes is perpetuated through poetic art, made and preserved by the Elves, who are themselves the 'living memory' of Middle-earth, and by the Rohirrim. This art performs an eminently commemorative task: the very characters of the novel acknowledge its eternalizing function, often expressing the hope of accomplishing deeds that will give "matter for mighty songs".

But Tolkien stresses more than once that this "immortality in fame" is, at best, just a temporary and inadequate escape: the *Púkel* of Dunharrow stand to show that, sooner or later, everything is destined to fall into oblivion: "Such was the dark Dunharrow, the work of long-forgotten men. Their name was lost and no song or legend remembered it." (*LotR*, RK.V.3)

Even the days of Arwen's life will be in the end forgotten and her tomb lost.

And still, the very barrows seem to hint at something more lasting than human memory: beyond their monumental function, in fact, the tombs in Middle-earth possess a sort of concrete 'vitality'.

We have seen how Nature, first of all, intervenes in the burial grounds, passing a distinct judgement on the bodies they shelter: the Hill of Slain of Nirnaeth Arnoediad is covered with grass; on the west side of the Kings' Barrows in Edoras the Everminds are in bloom; the grass grows high on Snowmane's mound. Moreover, the tombs of the heroes possess an aura that keeps the foes in awe and at a distance.[13]

---

12 Concerning the "escapes" see the contribution by Andrea Monda in this book.
13 See the description of the Hill of Tears and of the mounds of Fingolfin and Glorfindel of Gondolin

From the places defiled by the corpses of evil creatures, instead, Nature draws back: the spot where the Nazgûl's winged beast is buried remains forever barren, and the same happens to the Death Down, where the corpses of the orcs killed in the assault on Helm's Deep lie buried.

The presence or absence of vegetation (flowers, grass) in places where the dead lie (that brings to mind the garden-cemeteries of the Great War dead) gives an inkling that not all ends with death. As a matter of fact, tombs are always closely linked with the theme of 'rest', of 'sleep'. And one who sleeps and rests will sooner or later wake again.

It is in relationship with this 'life after death' that the Dúnedain, so far left in the background with respect to the Rohirrim, finally come to the fore. If it is the Rohirrim who officiate at the transformation of memory into 'fame', it is the descendants of Númenor that carry and bear witness to that unexpressed and still nebulous element that points and hints to a destiny transcending the earthly life of the body.

It is not by chance that there are no descriptions of burials for the Gondorian warriors fallen in the battles preceding the siege of Minas Tirith; indeed, the whole matter of funeral rites and of burials in Gondor is presented by Tolkien in a rather negative way, as the sign of an excessive clinging to life, the mark of a refusal of its natural ending:

> Death was ever present, because the Númenoreans still, as they had in their old kingdom, and so lost it, hungered after endless life unchanging. Kings made tombs more splendid than houses of the living and counted old names in the rolls of their descent dearer than the names of sons. (*LotR*, TT.IV.5)

Describing the greatest of the monument-building civilizations of Middle-earth,[14] Tolkien accomplishes and surpasses at the same time his own ideas about the value of 'memory' and begins to open the horizon of his sub-creation towards something that goes "beyond the circles of the world."[15]

---

in *The Silmarillion* (*S*, Qu.20, 18 and 23), and also those of the twins Fastred and Folcred, princes of Rohan fallen in a war against the Haradrim (*LotR*, RK.V.6).

14 On the Fall of Númenor and the connected problem of the "necessity of faith" see the essays by Alberto Ladavas and Giampaolo Canzonieri in this book.

15 For Tolkien's eschatology, see the masterful essay by Franco Manni in this volume.

In *The Lord of the Rings*, these themes are linked especially with the character of Faramir. It is in Faramir's refuge that Tolkien brings on stage the one 'religious' ceremony to be found in the entire long narrative: the silent grace before meals, facing west toward "Númenor that was, and beyond to Elvenhome that is, and to that which is beyond Elvenhome and will ever be" (*LotR*, TT.IV.5). It is Faramir who tells Frodo and Sam about the subdivision of Men according to how much their cultures still preserve "the old wisdom and beauty brought out of the West" (*LotR*, TT.IV.5). The whole chapter "The Window of the West" is embroidered with his reflections on the opposition between the thirst for martial glory as a value in itself and the capacity to see beyond that toward "true glory". The first term of this dialectic opposition is represented by Boromir,[16] "the proud and fearless, often rash, ever anxious for the victory of Minas Tirith (and his own glory therein)" (*LotR*, TT.IV.5) and by the Riders of the Mark, who love "war and valour as things good in themselves, both a sport and an end" (*LotR*, TT.IV.5); the second term of the opposition is represented by the Dúnedain of Gondor, the Middle Peoples, fascinated by martial glory but full of the "memory of other things", and particularly by Faramir himself, for whom true glory lies beyond the warrior's prowess, in that which this prowess defends: "the city of the Men of Númenor and […] her memory, her ancientry, her beauty and her present wisdom" (*LotR*, TT.IV.5).

In these "very sound reflections no doubt on martial glory and true glory" (*Letters* no. 66) the problem of the inadequacy of fame as an escape from death loses its sting and the final fall into oblivion its potential for anguish: true immortality lies not here, but in something that can be found beyond the world of living, something implicit in "the old wisdom and beauty brought out of the West."

It will be King Elessar, in whom has been re-established the full "splendour of the Kings of Men" of ancient Númenor before the fall, who will give with his death the more direct evidence of that which goes beyond the world and memory. In willingly laying aside his life and choosing the sleep of death, he comforts his queen saying: "In sorrow we must part, but not in despair. Behold!

---

16 On the evolution of Boromir from pagan hero to "Christian knight" see Forest-Hill 2008b, 73-97.

We are not bound forever to the circles of the world, and beyond them there is more than memory" (*LotR*, App. A.1).

To Aragorn, as well as to the warriors of the Pelennor, sleeping "under grass in Gondor by the Great River," and to the fallen that rest "In Flanders Fields", death is but a passage towards an otherworld still full of mystery, but also of hope. The tomb becomes thus for the dead a peaceful shelter, where they quietly wait "till the world is mended" (*LotR*, FR.I.8); for the living, a tangible sign of the mystery that awaits them at the end of earthly life (cf. Shippey 2000a, 177-178).

## 5. Conclusion: from the Shire to England

Tolkien scholars have often stressed the fact that the Shire and the Hobbits represent the link between the Primary World and Tolkien's sub-created world: their modernity mediates between the reader and the world of Middle-earth. Tolkien has made them at the same time a mirror and an idealization of the England of his youth, a sort of 'time bubble' in which the reader could more easily perceive the applicability of the tale to real history. Bucolic and low-mimetic as opposed to the epic-romantic world of Gondor and Rohan, the Shire too has to suffer the intrusion of the 'external world', with the coming of Saruman and his brigands and the return of Frodo, Sam, Merry and Pippin, now transformed and grown by their experience of "things deeper and higher" (*LotR*, RK.V.8).

The chapter in which the heroes raise a tamed and paralyzed Shire and use force to sweep away the oppression of Saruman's ruffians does nothing more than repeat at a more domestic level the message of the rest of the book: in this corrupt world fighting is an unavoidable consequence of the Fall, and it is necessary and rightful to engage in it; and if it is wrong to yield to the temptation of 'glory' and make it into a goal in itself, it is likewise wrong to give in to despair and defeatism. The 'war' of the Shire is led and won, in fact, by the two hobbits, Merry and Pippin who, fighting in the War of the Ring, have ennobled their rustic and parochial nature and have become true 'knights': "Deeper and higher things" have thus actually reached the Shire, bringing with them justice and the force to claim and defend it, even through violence and death, even unto the ultimate sacrifice. Fame so acquired is rightly deserved:

> The fallen Hobbits were laid together in a grave on the hill-side, where later a great stone was set up with a garden about it. So ended the Battle of Bywater [...]. In consequence, though it happily cost very few lives, it has a chapter to itself in the Red Book, and the names of all those who took part were made into a Roll, and learned by heart by Shire-historians. The very considerable rise in the fame and fortune of the Cottons dates from this time; but at the top of the Roll in all accounts stand the names of Captains Meriadoc and Peregrin. (*LotR*, RK.VI.8)

In a commemoration that replicates in almost every detail those of contemporary England (the great Stone of Remembrance set in a garden-cemetery, the inscription of the warriors' names in a Roll of Honour, the memory of the events and of the fallen perpetuated through history and tales), Tolkien re-establishes in that fictional England that is the Shire, the equilibrium between public commemoration and private memory that he had abandoned on the epic level: the names of those who took part in the battle, like those of the Great War dead, will "live for evermore."

But Tolkien also warns the reader: this is not the whole story. Beside the glory of living and dead there are the acts of unsung sacrifice and the incurable wounds of Frodo. And it is significant that Tolkien entrusts the representation of the human costs of the war to a 'non-combatant' like Frodo. In his mythological tales there is no trace of the feeling of guilt for the killing of a foe that permeates the work of Remarque or Owen. In the mythical wars of Middle-earth the enemy must first of all be fought, because this is the right and necessary thing to do. He can be the subject of empathy and compassion (see the episode of Sam and the Southron in *LotR*, TT.IV.4), but there can never be confusion as to who is the defender of a just cause and who fights to coerce and dominate: in Middle-earth the foe is never a *fellow-sufferer*.

Loading Frodo with the burden of the costs of victory, Tolkien preserves undimmed the glory of Merry and Pippin, as well as that of Théoden, Éomer, Aragorn and of the other Captains of the West; but at the same time, in the sacrifice of the little hobbit, he let the words of Gandalf echo: "victory cannot be achieved by arms" (*LotR*, RK.V.9). Weapons and war are the instruments of the Dark Lord and even if it is dutiful and praiseworthy to use them when compelled by the circumstances, it is not through them, through "military victory," that 'true', i.e. moral victory, can be achieved (cf. Dickerson 2004).

It is the endurance and sacrifice of Frodo, together with the hopefulness and devotion of Sam, that create the conditions for the final victory over Sauron. But not even these personal virtues, necessary addition to the social virtues of the warriors, are enough, by themselves, to guarantee the salvation of the Free Peoples. It needs the intervention of that unexpressed *quid* that permeates all the events of *The Lord of the Rings*: "Divine Providence" that has the pity of Bilbo and Frodo and Sam bring about Gollum's presence at the very end to assure the destruction of the Ring and to rescue the mission of the Ring-bearer from the most astounding failure.

And in this way Tolkien, through his master work that is also the most original and late fruit of the season of Great War literature, shows to himself and to England the road by which, having come out from the shadow of one war to enter that of another yet more terrible, they may find endurance and faith enough to suffer the loss of old and new friends, of old and new generations, going through the acceptance of the burden of sacrifice, past remembrance and glory, with eyes turned beyond "the circles of the world."

# Andrea Monda

## Death, Immortality and their Escapes: Memory and Longevity

### Foreword

The aim of this volume is to provide an answer to the easiest but at the same time most complex question the reader of a work of literature might ask himself: what is *The Lord of the Rings* about? At first sight it is the simplest of questions, typical of the younger readers, but it turns out to be – and especially in the case of a work of worth – the most difficult to answer. If a novel (and this is also true for a movie) is a good novel, the only way to answer the question would be to narrate its story. It is when the 'message' is too easily separated from the story that there is reason to worry. This could in fact be the sign of some kind of collateral frailty: if the message and the story can survive on their own, they can just as easily die on their own.

This perspective offers an additional confirmation of the quality of *The Lord of the Rings*: it is not easy to answer the question 'What is it about?'[1] As can be seen in other chapters of this book, it is Tolkien himself who formulates this question and answers it – on more than one occasion and more or less with the same words: "[o]ther than itself" (*Letters* no. 211) the narrative is about death and immortality. We can find reference to this in at least three of his letters:

1. To J. de Bortadano in April 1956:

    The real theme for me is about something much more permanent and difficult: Death and Immortality: the mystery of the love of the world in the hearts of a race 'doomed' to leave and seemingly lose it; the anguish in the hearts of a race 'doomed' not to leave it, until its whole evil-aroused story is complete. (*Letters* no. 186)

---

[1] See also the different views of Tolkienian criticism summarized in the essay by Franco Manni.

2. To H. Schiro on November 17th 1957:

> But I should say, if asked, the tale is not really about Power and Dominion: that only sets the wheels going; it is about Death and the desire for deathlessness. Which is hardly more than to say it is a tale written by a Man! (*Letters* no. 203)

3. To Rhona Beare on October 14th 1958:

> But I might say that if the tale is 'about' anything (other than itself), it is not as seems widely supposed about 'power'. Power-seeking is only the motive-power that sets events going, and is relatively unimportant, I think. It is mainly concerned with Death, and Immortality; and the 'escapes': serial longevity, and hoarding memory. (*Letters* no. 211)

My brief essay will be dedicated precisely to what the English author defines as "escapes": longevity and memory. For a better understanding of the meaning of this unusual expression it is once again necessary to refer to that precious and inexhaustible treasure represented by Tolkien's letters and especially the one which – if compared to the three letters previously mentioned – comes close to giving a synopsis and an explanation for them. I refer to the short letter of April 10th 1958 to the Dutch reader C. Ouboter to whom Tolkien reveals something about the 'message' of his tale:

> Though it is only in reading the work myself (with criticisms in mind) that I become aware of the dominance of the theme of Death. (Not that there is any original 'message' in that: most of human art and thought is similarly preoccupied.) But certainly Death is not an Enemy! I said, or meant to say, that the 'message' was the hideous peril of confusing true 'immortality' with limitless serial longevity. Freedom from Time, and clinging to Time. The *confusion* is the work of the Enemy, and one of the chief causes of human disaster. Compare the death of Aragorn with a Ringwraith. The Elves call 'death' the Gift of God (to Men). Their temptation is different: towards a fainéant melancholy, burdened with Memory, leading to an attempt to halt Time. (*Letters* no. 208)

This letter, keeping in mind Tolkien's other letters and literary texts, shows some important elements:

1. the tale is 'about itself';
2. besides this, death and immortality (and not power) are its central themes;
3. this is because of Tolkien's opinion that every work of art is connected to these themes;

4. confusion is the enemy, not death; or rather, the most important and soul-lacerating problem in human life is not death per se, but rather the agony of the heart which springs from that mysterious event which is death;
5. beyond the agony but connected to it, the main confusion originates from mistaking true immortality with unlimited longevity.

## 1. Longevity, or better *Longaevitas*

The first four points have already been examined in other essays in this anthology. We can therefore concentrate on the fifth point and talk briefly about longevity.

Longevity is an aspect which almost immediately catches the attention of Tolkien's readers who soon ask themselves how long the characters of his stories do actually live. All the characters in Middle-earth, no-one excluded, live longer than human beings. All of them – Man's progeny too and in particular the progeny of Gondor who are descendants of the ancient Númenóreans, the tiny Hobbits and the Dwarves – let alone the Elves, whose lives, only apparently endless, mislead the reader into "confusing true 'immortality' with limitless serial longevity." (For the time being I will omit the most extreme cases of 'hyper-long-lived' characters such as the Ents, the Nazgûl, Tom Bombadil etc.). They are all true *longaevi*, the use of the Latin word not being out of context: I am thinking in fact of the sixth chapter of C.S. Lewis's study on medieval philosophy and culture, *The Discarded Image*, entitled "The Longaevi" (Lewis 1990). I deem it inappropriate here and perhaps a little futile to underline the importance of philology and Tolkien's friendship with Lewis. However, it is a fact that this essay by Tolkien's friend and colleague proves to be extremely interesting and connects in a very stimulating way with the research carried out by Tolkien throughout his long years of teaching which finds its rich and accomplished expression in the essay "On Fairy-Stories".[2] The *longaevi* mentioned by Lewis are in fact the inhabitants of those 'fairy-stories'. They are the fairies but also the goblins, fauns, satyrs, sylvan elves, nymphs and so on; all creatures – here Lewis quotes Bernardus Silvestris – "as having a 'longer life' (than ours), though they are not immortal" (Lewis 1990, 122). Using words

---

2 For a more in-depth elaboration on this text, see Roberto Arduini's essay in this volume (pp. 69-101).

that Tolkien could have written himself, Lewis adds: "The alternative would have been to call them Fairies. But that word, tarnished by pantomime and bad children's books with worse illustrations, would have been dangerous as the title of a chapter" (Lewis 1990, 123). At the end of the chapter Lewis suggests four hypotheses on the origin and nature of the *longaevi* (rational beings other than Angels and Men; 'downgraded' Angels, fallen Angels, the Dead); but beyond any possible classification it is important to remark what Lewis states in the foreword on the existing relation between the medieval model of the Cosmos and these almost immortal creatures:

> They are marginal, fugitive creatures. They are perhaps the only creatures the Model does not assign, as it were, an official status. Herein lies their imaginative value. They soften the classic severity of the huge design. They intrude a welcome hint of wildness and uncertainty into a universe that is in danger of being a little too self-explanatory, too luminous." (Lewis 1990, 122)

Before closing this digression, characterized by an insidious philological twist, I would say that the whole of Tolkien's writings could be seen under the light of the *longaevitas* mentioned by Lewis. In fact, the Elves, the Dwarves, the Númenóreans and the Hobbits, too, may represent that "hint of wildness and uncertainty" that can soften the stiffness of the "cosmos", a Universe that is far "too self-explanatory, too luminous." These creatures, all of them long-lived, inhabit the world of the first three ages of Middle-earth, which is a world almost at its twilight, at an epochal moment, perhaps at the transition from the heathen era to the Christian era (cf. Shippey 2000a). In the last part of the novel we sense the same urge which was driving the Apostle Paul when warning the Corinthians that "time is running out" (I Cor 7, 29): with the impending arrival of the Fourth Age, the Age of Man (i.e. of the readers of Tolkien's books), life will become shorter and the *longaevi* will be destined to "fade".[3] In the long and by now famous letter written at the end of 1951 to Milton Waldman, Tolkien, describing his *longaevi* par excellence, the Elves, writes that their destiny

> is to be immortal, to love the beauty of the world, to bring it to full flower with their gifts of delicacy and perfection, to last while it lasts, never leaving it even when 'slain', but returning – and yet, when the Followers come, to teach

---

3 On the Elves' fading, see also Giampaolo Canzonieri's "A Misplaced Envy" and Claudio A. Testi's "Tolkien's *Legendarium* as a *meditatio mortis*" in this volume.

them, and make way for them, to 'fade' as the Followers grow and absorb the
life from which both proceed. (*Letters* no. 131)

Tolkien's story is a myth which takes place in our own world but at a different time. With respect to it, we men (meaning we men of the Western world with our industrialized societies strongly influenced by the development of technologies and the sciences) are the "Followers", those who have permanently taken over the *longaevi* of Middle-earth, a place which – it goes without saying – is placed 'in the middle', almost as a 'buffer' zone meant to soften the asperities inherent to all transitions of epochs. From this point of view the expression "escapes" – if connected to longevity and memory – may appear not entirely negative. One cannot but think of the "escapism" on which Tolkien dwells in the above mentioned "On Fairy-Stories" in order to define light and shadow of the matter.

## 2. Some *longaevi*: the Elves and the Hobbits

Nonetheless we are left with the impression of a negative nuance: *Longaevitas* and memory are still instances of "escapes" standing against the 'serious' themes of death and immortality, the central question pulsating at the core of Tolkien's literary production. Why is this so? We feel that Tolkien means that all living beings when facing death are confronted with the direst point of their existence and much depends on the way they tackle the crucial moment that leads them to the terrifying crossroads between death and immortality: one can face this fatal moment either by accepting the reality of death and going through it or by escaping, trying to avoid it, forging ways out and shortcuts which are, however, only illusions. In order to understand better such a complex subject the best method is perhaps to let oneself be guided by the Tolkienian *longaevi* themselves, by those characters who have to live and face death with its escapes.

We will therefore start with the *longaevi* par excellence: the Elves. We have already spoken about their destiny: to love the world, to protect its beauty and then fade. They bring the beauty of the world to completion – this is the feeling they convey to those who enter the hidden kingdoms of the Elves.

In his tale Tolkien dwells extensively on the account of the visit of the Fellowship of the Ring in Queen Galadriel's kingdom of Lothlórien, emphasizing the astonishment of its members. Sam, trying to explain to Frodo the feelings that left him speechless, exclaims: "but this is more elvish than anything I ever heard tell of. I feel as if I was inside a song. If you take my meaning" (*LotR*, FR.II.5). *Quendi*, the name given to the Elves by Tolkien, in fact refers to the Elves' skills not only in speech but also in singing, in enchanting, in creating poetry; they are the people of mythopoeia.

If we carefully observe how the wonderful wood of Lothlórien is described, we can guess how in this place the two instances of escapes from *longaevitas* and memory are intertwined. However, the intricacies of these tangles are not virtuous, but rather insidious, dangerous (and in fact the wood of Queen Galadriel is perceived with awe and suspicion in the rest of Middle-earth). Lothlórien, as the name already reveals, is a kingdom bearing close resemblance to the Homeric country of the Lotophagi, the eaters of the Lotus flower that causes men to lose their memory and induces in them a sweet and irresponsible oblivion. *Mutatis mutandis* is the destiny of the Elven kingdom of Lothlórien, with the difference that Elves, unlike the Lotophagi, do not live from oblivion but rather from memories. They are entrusted with the custody of the past, the protection of nature and beauty, of a world made of Nature, not of History. The result is therefore the same as in the heathen kingdom of the Lotophagi: to vegetate instead of living, to escape from reality, to refuse responsibility, to deny the passing of time.

In this 'fairy' place, cognition of time is lost and the confusion between true immortality and unlimited longevity, the danger mentioned by Tolkien in his letters, may become reality. This "confusion is work of the Enemy", and Tolkien warned more than once in his letters against the dangers of an elvish vision of life. The Elves, in fact, are preservers,[4] "embalmers," as Tolkien realistically defines them, criticizing them because they want

> to stop its change and history, stop its growth, keep it as a pleasaunce, even largely a desert, where they could be 'artists' – and they were overburdened with sadness and nostalgic regret. (*Letters* no. 154)

---

[4] Of all accusations against Tolkien, the one of being "conservative" is perhaps the most awkward, especially if seen in the light of his consideration of the Elves.

Here again we have the "hideous peril" Tolkien was talking about in his short letter of April 10th 1958: the elvish inability to obtain "freedom from time" clinging to time instead; the Elves fall prey to this danger and surrender to the temptation of "a fainéant melancholy, burdened with Memory, leading to an attempt to halt Time" (*Letters* no. 208).

They do not live but they remember, consumed by nostalgia, because a wrongful use of memory can transform it into a fatal rather than a vital gift: "idolatry" of memory leads to a suspension of life, to an existence merely natural and not historical, deprived of freedom which brings growth, development. Chesterton's pun on "intellectuals" springs to mind:

> What we call the intellectual world is divided into two types of people – those who worship the intellect and those who use it. There are exceptions; but, broadly speaking, they are never the same people. Those who use the intellect never worship it; they know too much about it. Those who worship the intellect never use it; as you can see by the things they say about it. (Chesterton 1994, 53-54)

The Elves, revering memory and the preservation of the beauty of nature, risk becoming the 'intellectuals' of Middle-earth. It is not by chance that Elves are totally unable to permanently defeat Sauron, the Dark Lord. On the contrary, there will even be a brief interlude of complicity between them (with reference to the creation of the magic rings) just as much as there will be between Sauron and the Númenóreans, the most 'Elven' men of Middle-earth. This might be the reason why the only Elf of the Fellowship of the Ring is Legolas. He is of royal birth (being the son of King Thranduil of Mirkwood) but not of the noblest lineage of the High Elves, meaning that he is somehow the least 'intellectual' (even if he, too, – as we shall soon see – suffers from the most intense of nostalgias). It is not by chance that the most decisive contribution to the victory over Sauron will be given by the least intellectual and most ordinary of beings conceivable, the Hobbits "who live in the holes."

It is interesting to remark how even the Hobbits, peaceful and tenacious as they can be, are not exempt from those same risks that lie in wait for the Elves. In other words, the terrible risk inherent in memory and longevity is a 'human' danger, universal and part of every being born on earth. Elves, in fact, are not the only creatures to live on "escapes"; neither are the Hobbits out of danger because they are also driven by their nature to "embalm" life, to live in the stillness of tradition. Their whole existence is marked by birthday parties accompanied by intricate genealogical trees and stuck in the cult of traditions (from the cultivation of pipe-weed to that of beer) and the (bad) habit of gossip. A peaceful village life where virtually nothing ever happens, where the most appetizing piece of 'news' is that of a bizarre Hobbit such as Bilbo who is getting closer and closer to the longevity record of the memorable Old Took.

Languid melancholy, a form of nostalgia with slightly different characteristics in the two races, is the 'sin' of both Elves and Hobbits. The Elves' melancholy, however, is much more romantic, almost existentialist and ontological. A much more insidious and fatal nostalgia then, as stressed by one of the most prominent Italian experts of Tolkien, the Franciscan friar Guglielmo Spirito in a long article of 1999 entitled "La Nostalgia di Legolas", later republished in the volume *Tra San Francesco e Tolkien*.[5] The author dwells in particular on the "heart-wrenching nostalgia" Elves feel for the sea:

> One thing is in fact Sam's nostalgia for the Shire in the most difficult moments of his journey, and another is the nostalgia that surfaces in Legolas when, hearing the sea-gulls singing, he is reminded of the sea. Sam's great nostalgia is for what he has left at home: his beautiful garden, the meetings with other hobbits always spent between a good meal and a relaxing smoke of good Westfarthing pipe-weed. The nostalgia for the simple small things that, if only for a moment, have the power of alleviating the 'real great nostalgia' that is inside us, and that is instead felt and expressed by the Elves in particular. (Spirito 2003, 86)

It is perhaps because of this concrete love for 'things' that the two Hobbits, Frodo and Sam, succeed in their mission and destroy the Ring, an endeavour that probably no Elf would have been able to accomplish. The tale in fact begins with the 'call', forcing the peaceful and predictable Hobbits to leave their home, their *habitat* and their mental *habitus*. The most difficult of challenges, Tolkien seems to suggest, is that of answering the call, coming out of one's own self, overcoming the nostalgia and languid melancholy that prey on the human heart.

---

5 Spirito 2003, 85-126.

## 3. A 'source' of longevity: the Ring

The 'call', or better, the cause for the call in Tolkien's tale takes the disquieting form of the Ring of Power. Perhaps the reason why the "escapes" of longevity and memory convey a negative feeling is linked precisely to the presence of the Ring, the first effect of which is in fact an insane longevity which will bring about serious consequences especially for Gollum and Bilbo, the two Hobbits who have borne the evil talisman longer than any other character of the novel. As Gandalf explains to Frodo at the beginning of the story:

> A mortal, Frodo, who keeps one of the Great Rings, does not die, but he does not grow or obtain more life, he merely continues, until at last every minute is a weariness. And if he often uses the Ring to make himself invisible, he fades: he becomes in the end invisible permanently, and walks in the twilight under the eye of the dark power that rules the Rings. (*LotR*, FR.I.2)

The "fading" caused by the Ring is very similar to the Elves' "fading": from this point of view we understand why the two-fold 'gift' of the Ring, longevity and invisibility, the two 'talents', are irrevocably connected to each other and to the unfortunate bearer who will be crushed by its power. Once again Tolkien, through the authoritative words of Gandalf the Wizard, sheds light on the core of the question between death and immortality. Not dying is equivalent to not living, to not growing and "enriching one's own life." The only way to live, paradoxically, is dying.[6] This explains why the Elves envy Men for being subject to death, "the gift of Ilúvatar."[7] This is why Gollum clings to the Ring as he would cling to time: to shun death. Gollum, and after him Bilbo and Frodo (and Sam too), are the Hobbits who bear the Ring, insidious source of longevity, and suffer the consequences. In the first chapter of *The Lord of the Rings*, Tolkien dwells on Bilbo and Frodo's "suspicious" longevity, "suspicious" even for the long-lived Hobbits. It is in fact Bilbo who, at the beginning of the story, explains to Gandalf his "fading" condition:

> 'I feel I need a holiday, a very long holiday, as I have told you before. Probably a permanent holiday: I don't expect I shall return. In fact, I don't mean to, and I have made all arrangements. I am old, Gandalf. I don't look it, but I am beginning to feel it in my heart of hearts. Well-preserved indeed!' he snorted.

---

6 Here the evangelical admonishment springs to mind: "For whoever wishes to save his life will lose it, but whoever loses his life for my sake will find it" (Mt 16, 25).
7 On the theme of envy, see Giampaolo Canzonieri's essay in this volume.

'Why, I feel all thin, sort of stretched, if you know what I mean: like butter that has been scraped over too much bread. That can't be right. I need a change, or something.' (*LotR*, FR.I.1)

Bilbo understands the importance of the change, of life going through death.

The Ring has the power to create 'confusion', the Enemy's doing. In other words, to confuse the hearts exactly on this fundamental point concerning how to face the ultimate transformation of death which, as Tolkien recalls, is not an enemy.

No matter where it happens to be, the presence of the Ring brings about the same upheaval, the same disturbances. We think of Gollum and before him of Isildur and then the nine Nazgûl, the Black Riders who are no longer among the living and have become Ringwraiths. It is no coincidence that Tolkien, in his letter to C. Ouboter, suggests that the Dutch reader compare Aragorn's death to that of a Ringwraith.

## 4. Aragorn and Arwen: the last of the *longaevi*

With Aragorn's death (which Tolkien, almost unwillingly, includes in the Appendices of the tale),[8] Tolkien's vision on the issue of death and immortality and its "escapes" takes on clearer and more defined outlines. Aragorn is in fact a Númenórean, a *longaevus*, who welcomes death confiding in immortality and refusing to live on memories alone. He is the last of the *longaevi* whose life unfolds at the moment of transition between the Third and the Fourth Age (the Age of Man) and with his behaviour he seems almost to prepare Middle-earth to this 'advent', to this new epoch when time will run faster.[9] Aragorn's life story could be interpreted as an atonement for the deeds of his ancestors; his arduous fight against Sauron's power (and the ensuing confu-

---

[8] Tolkien considers the episode of Aragorn's death as "the most important of the Appendices; it is part of the essential story, and is only placed so, because it could not be worked into the main narrative without destroying its structure: which is planned to be 'hobbito-centric', that is, primarily a study of the ennoblement (or sanctification) of the humble" (see *Letters* no. 181).

[9] It is natural to think of the 'hyper-long-lived' first men and biblical patriarchs whom we are told about in *Genesis* (and we find some of them again in Jesus's genealogies which open the gospels of Luke and Matthew). Here, too, time and life become shorter as the "fullness of time" and Christ's advent approach.

sion), without recurring to the 'short-cut' represented by the conquest of the Ring, has a redeeming effect:

- for the Númenóreans who 'flirted' with the Enemy;[10]
- for Isildur who failed at the most crucial moment;
- for the kings of Men who had fallen prey to the magic rings and had become the Ringwraiths;
- for the kings, the stewards and men of Gondor, reduced to "a withering people whose only 'hallows' were their tombs" (*Letters* no. 154).

Aragorn is therefore the Númenórean who acquits the Númenóreans: he truly is the descendant of Elendil the Faithful who, as is narrated in the "Akallabêth",[11] rejected the alliance with Sauron and did not sail to Valinor thus surviving the downfall of Númenor.

Aragorn is the descendant of Isildur and, unlike his ancestor, he escapes his "Bane", i.e. the power of the Ring, which ensnared Elendil's son at the most decisive moment of Sauron's defeat when he had the chance to destroy the terrifying talisman, as is narrated by Elrond at his Council:

> But Isildur would not listen to our counsel. 'This I will have as weregild for my father, and my brother', he said; and therefore whether we would or no, he took it to treasure it. But soon he was betrayed by it to his death; and so it is named in the North Isildur's Bane. (*LotR*, FR.II.2)

Memory, meant as "weregild", will once again prevent the happy ending of the story. It is a memory that takes on the shades of yearning and greed, the "hoarding memory" mentioned in the letter we quoted at the beginning of the essay.[12] The wounded stare, made blind and confused by grief of the newly-orphaned Isildur is completely turned towards the past. Pride, jealousy and possessiveness become his masters:[13] Isildur's destiny is sealed and atonement will only come through

---

10 I feel justified in using this unusual expression ("flirt with the Enemy") by Tolkien himself who uses the same words to explain that Elves "are *not* wholly good or in the right. Not so much because they had flirted with Sauron; as because with or without his assistance they were 'embalmers'" (*Letters* no. 154).
11 For a more exhaustive analysis of this text, see Alberto Ladavas's essay in this volume.
12 The original text of letter no. 208 to C. Ouboter talks about "serial longevity" and "hoarding memory", an "amassing" form of memory which brings to mind Gollum's "precioussss" and the Gospel verse which exhorts the accumulation of treasures in heaven, "for where your treasure is, there your heart will be also" (Mt 6,21).
13 Again, in the story contained in *The Silmarillion*, the aspect of Isildur's pride and greed for the Ring is

Aragorn who, although he had the chance, did not reach to take possession of the Ring. Aragorn, who, on his deathbed, although grieving the departing from the beloved Arwen, will take leave of her with these words: "In sorrow we must go, but not in despair. Behold! We are not bound for ever to the circles of the world, and beyond them is more than memory, Farewell!" (*LotR*, App. A.5). This is Aragorn's death which, in Tolkien's intentions, is to be compared to the non-death of the Ringwraiths. They too were powerful kings just as Aragorn was – but, instead, took hold of the talismans created by Sauron, and ended by refusing death and entered the Kingdom of Shadow, completely subjugated to the Enemy. In the moment of death Aragorn invites his wife Arwen to "look", not to turn her eyes towards the past but towards the future, towards something that is beyond the world and memory. If Aragorn is the last (and the redeemer) of the human *longaevi*, Arwen is the last (and the redeemer) of the elvish *longaevi*. She is in fact the Elven Lady, Galadriel's granddaughter, who was born and had lived for centuries in the atemporal gardens of Lothlórien, who, after defeating the tendency to confuse "true 'immortality' with limitless serial longevity," has chosen to live her life in love with the human Aragorn and die in Middle-earth long after her husband's death, giving up her privilege of sailing beyond the sea with the last ship in Frodo's favour who will leave with Bilbo in search of "healing". The long defeat[14] about which Galadriel was talking to Frodo under the trees of Lothlórien, is redeemed by the sacrifice of love made by her granddaughter Arwen who, grieving and at the same time hoping, accepts death for what it really is, the mysterious gift of Ilúvatar (God). Here we are at the heart of the tale, as pointed out by Father Ferdinando Castelli:

> The power of evil – Tolkien suggests – doesn't give life, but rather a purposeless and meaningless semblance of it which is more bitter than death itself. The wish for immortality "within the life of the world" is a suggestion that comes

---

highlighted: "And the Ring that he held seemed to him exceedingly fair to look on; and he would not suffer it to be destroyed. Taking it therefore he returned at first to Minas Anor, and there planted the White Tree in memory of his brother Anárion. But soon he departed, and after he had given counsel to Meneldil, his brother's son, and had committed to him the realm of the south, he bore away the Ring, to be an heirloom of his house, and marched north from Gondor by the way that Elendil had come [...]" (*S*, RiPo).

14 See *LotR*, FR.II.7: "long defeat" is the expression used by Queen Galadriel when she tells her own and her people's story to the members of the Fellowship of the Ring. The same expression is used by Tolkien in his letter from December 15th, 1956: "Actually I am a Christian, and indeed a Roman Catholic, so that I do not expect 'history' to be anything but a 'long defeat' – though it contains (and in a legend may contain more clearly and movingly) some samples or glimpses of final victory" (*Letters* no. 195).

from evil [...] The denial of death and the claim to immortality "within life" are equivalent to the denying of one's own nature to seize what is a divine prerogative. Those who follow this impossible dream abandon themselves to the destroying forces of evil. Wise and dignified, king Aragorn accepts death because he knows it is a law of nature. He closes the door of time, while opening the other one that leads beyond the boundaries of the world.
(Castelli 2002, 442)

We are at the core of the novel because it is about "other than itself", death and immortality and, in my opinion, the transition from the heathen to the Christian world as epitomized in the overcoming of the cyclical vision of time and life. There are no cycles in the 'Christian' Middle-earth. At the end of their stories the main characters must pass on the torch and clear the ground for those to come. Those who resist the passing of time risk the same end as the Elves of Lothlórien or the Ents of Fangorn or the oldest of Hobbits, Gollum: to be preserved and "fade" until they die of languor and idleness. The cycles are broken and dispersed by the wind of the Hobbits whose course allows Tolkien to affirm that history has a meaning, that there is someone (Providence, the hidden protagonist of the story) who imparts momentum to human events, that there is a divine plan which gives direction to history that would otherwise be empty and devoid of meaning (cf. Monda 2008).

## 5. Denethor and the 'memory-ill': Saruman, Treebeard and Tom Bombadil

### 5.1 Denethor

With his death Aragorn has redeemed the kings, the Stewards and Men of Gondor, whom Tolkien compares to the Elves because they too are affected by "sadness and nostalgic regrets", reduced to the rank of "a withering people whose only 'hallows' were their tombs" (*Letters* no. 154).

This characterisation of the men of Gondor is embodied in the person of Denethor, the last steward of Minas Tirith, the one who should have waited for the return of the king. For the noble and proud son of Ecthelion, however, the coming of Aragorn as king is not happy news. On the contrary it will be lethal although he will instinctively refuse to 'die' and try to survive through the Palantíri's short-cuts and the escape of memory. The Palantíri represent the escape provided by technology and magic: the illusion of defeating the Enemy on his own terrain. Whereas memory for Denethor is an authentic idol to which he is ready to sacrifice everything, even his own life and that of his son Faramir; the 'finale' of his story unfolds in the most sacred of places, the Rath Dínen, the cemetery where the tombs of the ancient kings and stewards of Gondor are located. Denethor is a man who, just like the Elves, is completely turned towards the past, and the custody of memory. It is not by accident that great stress is given to the fact that the Númenórean blood flows powerfully in his veins. His tragic figure is both the most heathen and the most Elven character ever created by Tolkien. In his lacerated soul we notice that "profound feeling of sadness, uneasiness and nostalgia" mentioned by Lasso de la Vega in his essay dedicated to the comparison of the Christian saint and the pagan hero (cf. Lasso de la Vega 1968).

## 5.2 Saruman

Saruman, too, is, in his own right, a guardian of memory, being the most knowledgeable repository of the history of the rings of power. He is an 'intellectual', somewhat aristocratic and snobbish, endowed with a machine-like brain but unable to recognise the signs of the new times changing the history of the world. The Hobbits are a true novelty but Saruman does not look into the future, he does not believe in these new, strange and apparently plain creatures. Instead he is completely turned to the past, trying to solve enigmas revolving around the story of the One Ring. The truth is that he is already under its spell, as is shown by his frequent turn towards the escape of technology and magic through the use of the Palantír (just as Denethor had done) and the 'creation' of the Uruk-hai. The one who is, however, ready to believe in the Hobbits, is his colleague Gandalf, who avoids both short-cuts (he almost never uses magic) and escapes, be they longevity (he accepts death at Balrog's hands) or memory (forgetful as he looks before the gates of Moria, where, we can bet, Saruman would have immediately recalled the magic word that was to open the enchanted threshold of the Dwarrowdelf).

## 5.3 Treebeard

Treebeard is also able to capture the sign of the approaching new era: although slowly and painstakingly, the oldest Ent will bow and take care of the Hobbits, thus altering the course of history. The effort required of him will be tremendous, because Treebeard is in reality a sort of embodiment of memories. He is the memory of Middle-earth, a self-moving memory box. Extremely long-lived, this chief of the shepherds of trees is a sort of registry of the flora and fauna of the universe created by Tolkien. We understand the affection felt by Tolkien towards this astonishing and touching character to whom, it seems, Tolkien gave manners of speech (or better: of mumbling) as borrowed from C.S. Lewis's peculiar manner of expression. Treebeard is in his own way a philologist, a cataloguer of all species in Middle-earth which "in order to exist" must be told, sung, included in poems and nursery rhymes, just as he will do with the Hobbits when he accepts Pippin's request: "'Why not make a new line?' said Pippin. 'Half-grown hobbits, the hole-dwellers'" (*LotR*, TT.III.4). The Hobbits are at the bottom of the ladder, but Treebeard is not a snob like Saruman and will humbly welcome them into "the poetic memory" of Middle-earth. Anything but snobbish, Treebeard and the Ents are hopelessly sad: they live essentially on memories and, of all memories, the most painful is that of the Entwives, by then lost together with the future of this most ancient progeny.

## 5.4 Tom Bombadil

The character of Tom Bombadil is in certain respects similar to that of Treebeard. He is another "shepherd of trees" but far more long-lived than an Ent. The Elves call him *Iarwain Ben-adar*, "the oldest and fatherless". At least this is the name Elrond gives him at his Council (*LotR*, FR.II.2). If Treebeard is rich in years and memories, so is Bombadil, but unlike the tree-man, the mysterious *genius loci* of the Old Forest is not sad but cheerful: for him the burden of age is neither heavy nor stifling. On the contrary, although extremely old, he always looks young, or better newly-born. A truly 'Franciscan' blithe spirit, Tom Bombadil walks through his woods with the gaiety and kindness of a man who discovers a new world and a new happiness at each step. He is as ancient as the first man; he is the first man on the first day of creation. The forgetfulness of old Tom is that of eternal youth and not the weariness of old Gandalf who takes upon himself the burden of the challenge of his times (the fight against Sauron, a challenge that Bombadil accepts on a completely different level, in fact he appears as if he is not at all involved in the war) and not even the obliviousness of old Gollum who has lost the memory of his roots, although, and this is paradoxical, he lives at the roots of the mountains. Sméagol-Gollum has forgotten his name, the light of the sun, the taste of almost all food, but most of all the taste of friendship. It is certain that not even he would have been able to open the magic door of Moria because he had forgotten the meaning of the old but ever new word: *mellon*, friend.

## 6. Conclusion

In Tolkien's opinion his narrative is essentially about "itself". He really means it when he says – one more time – to the Dutch reader C. Ouboter: "I was primarily writing an exciting story in an atmosphere and background such as I find personally attractive" (*Letters* no. 208). It is not (only) out of shyness or modesty that he states this; he is sincere, as is confirmed by the extraordinary world-wide success of his books. The main theme in this engrossing story is not power but the human theme par excellence: death and immortality. Faced with the dilemma, at the crossroads of death and immortality, Man is naturally and instinctively afraid and flees. All this is the consequence of the confusion created by the Enemy, of the Fall (another great theme underlying the whole of Tolkien's literary production). The direct reference here is that of the biblical narration and Catholic doctrine on which Tolkien draws liberally not only as a man in his private life but also and inevitably as a writer.

The "escapes" Tolkien is interested in are those of memory and longevity that he has represented not only through the enthralling plot of *The Lord of the Rings* but also through some of its characters, especially the Elves, Hobbits and Númenóreans. These all run the terrifying risk of confusing "true 'immortality' with limitless serial longevity."

In contrast, we have characters such as Aragorn, Arwen, Gandalf, and the Hobbits Bilbo and Frodo, who all succeed, often helped by the mysterious intervention of Providence, in resisting the temptation of the escapes. They face death, accepting it in self-denial because it is not the Enemy but a gift from God the Creator. In the end, the strength of these characters who face death and accept it lies in their weakness.

I would like to conclude this essay on Tolkien with an attempt to pay tribute to the writer-philologist who forged new words such as *eucatastrophe* and *sub-creator* by coining a new word myself: 'one-handedness'. With this new word (not a beautiful one, I admit) I would like to highlight Tolkien's poetic code and underline the most exquisitely Tolkienian concept of Tolkien's works. Tolkien is the singer of the one-handed Men. Being one-handed is a condition which often emerges in his stories, especially in those taken from *The Silmarillion*, where the main character is Beren the One-handed, but also in *The Lord of the Rings* where the main character Frodo loses, if not the whole hand, at least a finger ("Frodo of the Nine Fingers", as he is remembered in songs) and is also wounded, in all evidence, incurably. The Hobbits are one-handed par excellence: they are "the half-grown" as Treebeard calls them, the "halflings" as the Elves call them. The spiritual strength of this image, the power of this metaphor is evident: in the heart of the 20th century that begins with God's alleged death and the advent of the Super-Man foretold by Nietzsche, we have here an obscure writer-philologist from Oxford who chants the humble greatness of the Half-Man, the tiny Hobbits of Middle-earth who live in holes in the ground, because they possess the greatest virtue which is also the smallest: humility, from *humus*, ground. In Tolkien everything is made half, even Earth is Middle-earth, because nothing on Earth is yet accomplished. Fulfilment is still 'beyond', still about to come, an advent not yet materialized. This is the reason why there is no lasting space in Middle-earth for memory, for languorous melancholy and that longevity which is only a desperate clinging to time. Recognizing one's own one-handedness means avoiding easy ways out and escapes. Those who do not see their own one-handedness and perceive themselves as 'fulfilled' and 'all right', will inevitably be drawn to choose strength and become tyrannical over others and weak in themselves, trying for their own benefit to find shortcuts or escapes that will turn out to be just deviances from the true path and will only lead to perdition. With his engrossing story Tolkien says that whoever lingers on the escapes of longevity and memory and neglects turning towards the future with humble hope, whoever fails to apprehend the new elements that make their way into the history of mankind every day, is destined to live a life of nostalgic regrets and bitter despair.

It is not advisable to give a writer such a heavy and cumbersome label such as 'prophet'. Yet, at the close of this brief essay on death and immortality (and their escapes), a thought comes to my mind: some aspects of contemporary society have been unconsciously foreshadowed by the suggestions underlying Tolkien's stories, in particular those suggestions that are summarized under the name of 'bioethical issues'. If we ponder on the present condition of Man's biological life (in our developed western civilization), we can see that under several aspects our situation is similar to that of Middle-earth: thanks to the developments in medical science and technology, life expectancy is today longer than ever, diseases are almost defeated and pain reduced dramatically. These phenomena have brought about the repression of the last remaining taboos, pain and death, that are no longer part of our everyday inner 'landscape'. Up to Tolkien's time, wars, famines and epidemics caused death and suffering to be profusely present in the daily existence of families. Tolkien dies in 1973 and since then times have changed extremely fast. In order to be aware of this it is sufficient to think of the recent social, legal and ethical discussions about the concept of life and its end: euthanasia, biological will. The signs are different and sometimes contradicting: we go from a 'clinging to time' and a consequent denial of death (this is the case of therapeutic obstinacy to the eradication of the scandal of suffering and fear by means of euthanasia). We ask ourselves whether Tolkien – if faced with such phenomena only apparently opposed but in reality converging towards similar results – would have used the word 'escapes'. A society of the long-lived who deny death very much resembles the world described by Tolkien. A society highly influenced by means of mass communication such as television is more and more rooted in its memory and less and less open to new things which real life brings about. There is no doubt that television offers its audience a retrospective gaze on past events, as well as the countless self-referential programmes in which television looks only into itself, programmes which are only compilations aiming at celebrating the past of television (and I do not linger on the new social networks which closely remind us of the intriguing and insidious *palantíri*). Tolkien as a prophet of our times? Maybe. But this is not the appropriate time to discuss the subject. We just wanted to give a short and – I hope – reasoned outline of the main themes of the Tolkienian production: the relationship between Man and death and immortality. However, we chose an alternative approach to the ones seen before and as a counterweight we concentrated our attention on the escapes Man invents when faced with the decisive question, the escapes of memory and longevity.

# Claudio A. Testi

# Logic and Theology in Tolkien's Thanatology

## Preface

In my other essay presented in this volume I discussed the evolution of the concepts of death and immortality within Tolkien's *Legendarium* and came to the conclusion that Tolkien's meditation on these themes reached its apex in the years 1957-60. In Tolkien's writings there emerged a twofold movement based on an ongoing interplay between the presence of death and the hope for the future. The more death looms on the horizon of life the more we open our heart to bright hope; whereas the more we try to eliminate mortality from life by searching for a never-ending longevity the more we are overcome by dark despair.

In this further contribution of mine I would like to show the profound reasons for this "phenomenology" [1.1] by examining analytically the logical structure of the "Athrabeth Finrod ah Andreth" [1.2] and proposing a comparison between this thanatology [2.1] and the Catholic theology of death [2.3]. In this analysis I will also make reference to Tolkien's manuscripts and books which I had the chance to personally examine at the Bodleian Library and at the Oxford University English Faculty Library, and to an edition of the *Summa Theologica* by St. Thomas Aquinas owned by Tolkien himself [2.2].

## 1. On the harmony between Spirit (fëa) and Body (hröa)

### 1.1 Definition of the harmony between *fëa* & *hröa*

An essential concept which enables us to understand better the profound reasons for Tolkien's complex *meditatio mortis* is the harmony between *fëa* and *hröa* (spirit[1] and body), i.e. the bond that unites[2] spirit and body,[3] two different but matching entities[4] that fit one to the other.[5]

It is difficult to give a philosophical evaluation of this important concept which could be described as an Aristotelian element within a Platonic context.[6] Nevertheless it is exactly on this concept of harmony that both Tolkien's double definition of death (departure from Arda/severance of *fëa-hröa*), and the refusal of the theory that Elves reincarnate in their own children are based upon.

The concept of harmony between *fëa* and *hröa* is, as I am going to prove, also one of those fundamental principles which guide the important debate between Finrod and Andreth, which can be seen as an essay in natural theology. It demonstrates how, once given some preliminary remarks, certain conclusions follow necessarily. The dialogue, Tolkien explains, "is not presented as an argument of any cogency for Men in their present situation [...] though it may have some interest for Men who start with similar beliefs or assumptions to those held by the Elvish king Finrod" (*MR*, Commentary 329).

---

1 To render the elvish term *fëa* into English we will use the words 'spirit' and 'soul' without any further distinction (as Tolkien had it), even if 'technically' speaking the spirit is the deeper part of the human soul.
2 "The *Mirröanwi* [Incarnates] are made of a union of body and mind, of *hröa* and *fëa*, or as we say in picture the House and the Indweller" (*MR*, Athrabeth 316).
3 "For though by their prime nature, unmarred, they [the Elves] rightly dwell as spirit and body coherent, yet these are two things, not the same, and their severance (which is 'death') is a possibility inherent in their union" (*MR*, LawsA 244-245).
4 cf. *ibid*.
5 "But the body is not an inn to keep a traveller warm for a night, ere he goes on his way, and then to receive another. It is a house made for one dweller only, indeed not only house but raiment also; and it is not clear to me that we should in this case speak only for the raiment being fitted to the wearer rather than of the wearer being fitted to the raiment" (*MR*, Athrabeth 317).
6 According to Aristotle the soul is "the entelechy [form] of a natural body having life potentially within it" (*De Anima*, lib. II 412a 28). Therefore there is only one soul for one body and vice versa. According to Plato, however, the body is the "prison" of the soul (cf. *Phaedo* 62b). This expression in itself suggests a strong anthropologic dualism and hints at a soul that may reincarnate in different bodies (cf. the Myth of Er as narrated in Book X of the *Republic*). Tolkien again defines the body as "house for the soul" (cf. note 5). This image (the body as a building made for accommodating one spirit dweller only) seems to relate to a sort of Aristotelized Platonism. It must also be noticed that Tolkien's *fëa* is more equivalent to the Aristotelian rational soul that is not owned by plants or animals; although also the animals not endowed with a *fëa* can speak (*MR*, 410), the functions of thinking and inquiring are typical of Incarnates with a *fëa*/rational soul (*MR*, Athrabeth 349; cf. OK and *WJ* 405).

## 1.2 A brief analysis of the "Athrabeth Finrod Ah Andreth"[7]

### The "axioms"

Tolkien himself states in his commentary (*MR*, Commentary 330-331) that this dialogue is based on two basic facts accepted by everybody in Arda. The first being the existence of the Elves, the second being the existence of the Valar – and on seven axioms (which Finrod believes to be true because they are derived from one of these sources: his created nature, angelic instructions, thought or experience):

A. The existence of Eru;
B. The existence of two incarnate people (Men and Elves), exhibiting the union of *fëa* and *hröa* (soul and body);
C. The existing harmony between *fëa* and *hröa* as a mutual and perpetual bond;[8]
D. The separation of spirit (or soul) and body as being considered unnatural for Elves, (as a result of the "Marring of Arda" through the action of Melkor);[9]
E. Elvish immortality is seen as "serial longevity," bound to the History of Arda;
F. The possibility for a disembodied elvish *fëa* to return to an incarnate life (thanks to the power of the Valar);
G. The destiny of the human *fëa* is not connected with the duration of Arda.

Obviously, it is important to point out that these "axioms" are valid from the point of view of Elves and Men in Arda in an earlier age, and it does not necessarily correspond to what is true in our contemporary "primary" world.

### Opening of the dialogue and Finrod's opinion

After an introduction that sets their meeting at the time of the Long Peace, the period between the first appearance of the dragon Glaurung and the moment when the Siege of Angband was broken, the dialogue opens with Finrod considering, according to a firm belief among Elves, that Men have always had short lives and been destined to die; death here meant as a severance of *hröa*

---

[7] Tolkien studies scholars have begun to realize more and more the literary and philosophical value of the "Athrabeth"; cf. Birzer 2003, 57f.; Casey 2004; Flieger 2005a, 54f.; Wood 2003; Caldecott 2003; Wolf 2006; Agøy 1997; Vink 2004 and Fornet-Ponse 2005.
[8] "*Hröa* and *fëa* [...] are wholly distinct in kind, and not on the 'same plane of derivation from Eru', but were designed each for the other, to abide in perpetual harmony" (*MR*, Commentary 330).
[9] "The separation of *fëa* and *hröa* is 'unnatural', and proceeds not from the original design, but from the Marring of Arda, which is due to the operations of Melkor" (*MR*, Commentary 330-331).

and *fëa* (cf. *MR* 308-309). This beginning, from a logical point of view, corresponds to the classical part of dialectic (already extant in Plato's dialogues, assimilated within Aristotle's treatises on rhetoric, that reaches its climax with the *quaestiones* in the Middle Ages[10]), that is the part in which an authoritative and common opinion is quoted (in this case the Elvish point of view) but then prove to be false. Andreth immediately affirms angrily that this conception (which, after all, is Tolkien's 'old' idea of death as a gift, totally absent in the "Athrabeth") is false:

> 'Yet,' – asks Finrod – 'if we consider the briefness of life in all Middle-earth, must we not believe that your brevity is also part of your nature? Do not your own people believe this too? And yet from your words and their bitterness I guess that you think that we err.'
>
> 'I think that you err, and all who think likewise,' – answers Andreth – '[…] Men are not by nature short-lived.' (*MR* 308-309)

## Definition of the two meanings of 'death' and their origin

Finrod thus clarifies (cf. *MR* 309-311) the distinction between death as a severance of soul and body (which troubles all Incarnates) and death as a departure from the history of Arda (which affects only Men who, in contrast to the Elves, cannot come back to the world). But Andreth points out to him that for Elves the painful separation of spirit and body is not necessary and, even if it happens, the pain is mostly mitigated by their confidence in a likely redress in Arda (cf. *MR* 311). Andreth then explains that the fact that Men must die is not the result of the first fall of Melkor, which preceded the creation and, by marring all substance of Arda, made death possible (but not necessary) for the Elves. The unavoidable death for Men derives from the second malice of Melkor, by means of which he corrupted humanity (*MR* 312). Finrod nevertheless specifies that Melkor has not the power to change the nature of things, and Andreth accepts this specification (*MR* 313). Now, the Elvish king at first refers to the axiom of the harmony of *fëa* and *hröa* (axiom C: *MR* 314) and then 'demonstrates' axiom G: based on a keen psychological insight, he observes that Men

---

10 For a contemporary treatment of rhetoric see Perelman 1977. For some manual-like explanations about Thomistic and mediaeval logic, the correct meaning of rhetoric included, see Sanguineti 1988; Vernaux 1966; Schmidt 1966; Berselli & Testi 2005. For Tolkien's debt to the rhetoric of the Nordic sagas see Sullivan 2000.

"look at no thing for itself; that if they study it, it is to discover something else [...]"; therefore their *fëa* must be a 'guest' which is not intrinsically bound to Arda (*MR* 315-316).

## The first step of the demonstration: Andreth and the abandonment of the body

Andreth and Finrod develop a proper proof *ab absurdo*.[11] At first the wise woman comes to a necessarily logical consequence: if the body were destined to be abandoned in Arda by the *fëa* (hypothesis I) and thus the human soul untied from the history of Arda (axiom G), then would result disharmony between *fëa* and *hröa* (negation of the axiom C):

> For were it 'natural' for the body to be abandoned and die [hypothesis I], but 'natural' for the *fëa* to live on [axiom G], then there would indeed be disharmony in Man [negation of axiom C]. (*MR* 317)

Therefore, from I and G derives the negation of C; i.e., as Finrod will say, the separation of spirit and body entails pain and disharmony (not-C).

## Demonstration of the original assumption

Then Finrod 'uses' this 'result' of Andreth to demonstrate the necessary falseness of the abandonment of the body in Arda (hypothesis I):

> 'For if your claim is true, then lo!' – affirms Finrod – 'A *fëa* which is here but a traveller [axiom G] is wedded indissolubly to a *hröa* of Arda [axiom C]; to divide them is grievous hurt [from I and G derives the negation of C], and yet each must fulfil its right nature without tyranny of the other. Then this must surely follow: *the fëa when it departs must take with it the hröa* [negation of hypothesis I]. And what can this mean unless it be that the *fëa* shall have the power to uplift the *hröa*, as its eternal spouse and companion, into an endurance everlasting beyond Eä, and beyond Time?' (*MR* 317-318, italics added)

Therefore if from I and G leads to the negation of C (such as Andreth proved shortly before), and G and C are real axioms, then I must be false. This argument can be explained through the propositional logic:

$$[(I \wedge G \Rightarrow \text{not-}C) \wedge G \wedge C)] \Rightarrow \text{not } I^{12}$$

---

11 A proof *ab absurdo* assumes an hypothesis; in a next step it is shown that this leads to a contradiction; thus it is necessary to refute this hypothesis.

12 Symbol "∧" stands for the conjunction 'and', "⇒" refers to the (material) implication 'if... then...',

The falseness of I, i.e. the negation of the fact that the body is abandoned forever in Arda, is the first significant result obtained by Finrod, whose demonstration is based exactly on the harmony of body and soul (C); a truth that would be contradictorily denied if I (and G) were to be true. So, also the body must leave the Time of Arda to be reunited once more with the soul in everlasting harmony. This, however, can only happen by the Assumption of the body itself, as Tolkien himself states:

> Then basing his argument on the axiom that severance of *hröa* and *fëa* is unnatural and contrary to design, he comes (or if you like jumps) to the conclusion that the *fëa* of unfallen Man would have taken with it its *hröa* into the new mode of existence (free from Time). In other words, that 'assumption' was the natural end of each human life, though as far as we know it has been the end of the only 'unfallen' member of Mankind. (*MR*, Commentary 333)[13]

## Demonstration of a future healing

This Assumption does not occur at present since the body decays, but, being a proven truth, will occur some time in the future. From this we can also infer the necessary healing of the substance of Arda: therefore Finrod (in the final analysis still thanks to axiom C), "beheld as a vision Arda Remade" (*MR* 319)[14] and guesses at Eru's redemptive function assigned to Men (*MR* 319 and 322), and foresees that body and soul of the Incarnates will reunite in perpetual harmony.[15]

---

"not-" is used to express a negative statement. This formula is a logically true thesis from propositional calculus and can be easily verified through the truth tables. We used this marking (instead of the derivation notion "⊢") because it is more 'intuitive'. Besides, according to the deduction theorem, notations are equivalent inside the propositional logic. For an introduction to the symbolic logic see Rogers 1978 and Matteuzzi 1980.

13 Here Tolkien refers to the Virgin Mary (*MR* 357, note 6), since in *Letters* no. 212 dated 1958 he states that "The Assumption of Mary, the only unfallen person, may be regarded as in some ways a simple regaining of unfallen grace and liberty."

14 It is important to note that in the draft Athrabeth A, Arda Remade is presented first of all as a legend of Men and not as a 'deduction' by Finrod (cf. *MR*, AthrabethA 352).

15 "'Ah, wise lady!' said Finrod. 'I am an Elda, and again I was thinking of my own people. But nay, of all the Children of Eru, I was thinking that by the Second Children we might have been delivered from death. For ever as we spoke of death being a division of the united, I thought in my heart of a death that is not so: but the ending together of both. For that is what lies before us, so far as our reason could see: the completion of Arda and its end, and therefore also of us children of Arda; the end when all the long lives of the Elves shall be wholly in the past. And then suddenly I beheld as a vision Arda Remade; and there the Eldar completed but not ended could abide in the present for ever, and there walk, maybe, with the Children of Men, their deliverers, and sing to them such songs as, even in the Bliss beyond bliss, should make the green valleys ring and the everlasting mountain-tops to throb like harps'" (*MR* 319). And in his commentary Tolkien writes: "Since Finrod had already guessed that the redemptive function was originally specially assigned to Men, he probably proceeded to the

# Logic and Theology in Tolkien's Thanatology

Andreth confirms (*MR* 320) that there actually exists a tradition of lore mentioning this Old Hope, different from both *estel* (i.e. waiting for an uncertain good based on something certain) and from *amdir* (trust not derived from experience) (*MR* 320-322).

## Conclusion of the debate

The dialogue ends with the eschatological vision which is also meant to mitigate Andreth's anger and her envy of Elvish 'immortality' (serial longevity), mainly caused by her unrequited love for the Elf Aegnor (Finrod's brother) who left her because she was mortal (*MR* 323-326).

# 2. Tolkien's thanatology and Catholic theology

## 2.1 Tolkien's thanatology

The importance of this debate is really remarkable, not only from a literary point of view but also from a philosophical and theological one. It analyses with the unusual use of fiction the truest and unique problem of our being-in-the-world: thus it is worth analyzing in detail the majestic framework in which this subtle *meditatio mortis* is placed. First of all, in the "Athrabeth" and in other contemporary texts, we have three different scenes in the history of the created universe described:

i. Arda Unmarred, which inside Tolkien's world is a mere abstraction since Arda was tainted by evil from its very inception;[16]
ii. Arda Marred by the first malice of Melkor during the Music of the Ainur;
iii. Arda Marred after the second malice of Melkor, by means of which he provokes the Fall of Man.

With regard to his thanatology, Tolkien seems to be especially interested in two essential aspects of death: its being 'natural' and its 'conformity to

---

expectation that 'the coming of Eru', if it took place, would be specially and primarily concerned with Men: that is to an imaginative guess or vision that Eru would come incarnated in human form. This, however, does not appear in the Athrabeth" (*MR*, Commentary 335).
16 Cf. next note.

Eru's design'. Basing ourselves on Tolkien's texts we could define these two attributes in this way:

- 'natural' is an event 'inscribed' into the intrinsic structure of a being, and, as such, is also possible in a flawless world;[17]
- 'conform to the design' is an event that occurs in conformity with the creative design of God.[18]

Now, as regards these two 'values', what form should the mortality of Men and Elves, who are a union between body and soul, take?

First of all, it must be remembered that the existence of both people is (since the *Book of Lost Tales*) closely connected to Eru's mind which conceives them through a musical theme he created and which the Valar themselves do not have the capacity to understand. In particular, the *fëar* of these creatures are directly created by the One (cf. *MR*, Commentary 336). Yet, as regards death, the differences between the Children of Ilúvatar are big:

- The Elves are by nature bound to Arda (cf. supra, axiom E), therefore death as departure from Arda is evidently not natural and does not conform to the design. Death as a separation of spirit and body, however non-natural (axiom D), remains conform to the design since Eru created the Elves within a world already tainted by evil, thus making the painful separation of body and soul possible.[19]
- Men, on the other hand, are, since the very first versions of the Music of the Ainur in the *Book of Lost Tales*, detached from the story of Arda; hence their death as departure from Arda is natural and conform to the design. The "Athrabeth", in contrast to the previous concept of death as a gift, points out that the brevity of human life is due to the separation of *fëa* and *hröa* and is thus not natural nor does it conform to the design for Men, who have

---

17 "'Natural' can refer only to an ideal state, in which unmarred matter could for ever endure the indwelling of a perfectly adapted *fëa*" (*MR*, Athrabeth 342).
18 Cf. next note.
19 "We may say, therefore, that the Elves are destined to know 'death' in their mode, being sent into a world which contains 'death', and having a form for which 'death' is possible" (*MR*, LawsA 244-245). Likewise the fading of the Elves is not natural, but in conformity with the design, since Eru created them in a world where the substance of Arda's body was already marred by Melkor: "'Not natural', whether it is due wholly, as they earlier thought, to the weakening of the *hröa* (derived from the debility introduced by Melkor into the substance of Arda upon which it must feed), or partly to the inevitable working of a dominant *fëa* upon a material *hröa* through many ages" (*MR*, Commentary 342).

originally been destined to an Assumption that would have spared them the painful separation. This death that now afflicts them became a concrete possibility (and a necessity!) only as a result of the second malice of Melkor which put human beings in a condition of decay.

Undeniably the theory resulting from a fifty year long meditation transcends literature in its strictest sense and boldly takes it place alongside other great Western philosophical and religious reflections. A comparison with the Catholic tradition is therefore not only appropriate but necessary in order to fully understand Tolkien's multi-layered discourse.

## 2.2 Tolkien and Catholic theology

Tolkien was unquestionably a staunch "Roman Catholic" (*Letters* nos. 195, 213), he was deeply devotee to the Virgin Mary (*Letters* no. 142), considered his mother a martyr for her unbending faith (*Letters* nos. 142, 267), recommended to take the Holy Communion every day (*Letters* no. 250), believed in the Guardian Angel (*Letters* nos. 54, 89), considered the liberal sexual practices of the times as a sign of rampant concupiscence (*Letters* no. 43), viewed marriage as a mortification of the sexual instinct (*Letters* no. 43), was against divorce law (*Letters* no. 49) and used to go on pilgrimage to venerated places such as Lourdes (*Letters* no. 89).

Nevertheless, he carefully abstained from inserting references to Christianity in his works (*Letters* nos. 142, 211), an aspect that he always found fault with in the Arthurian cycle (*Letters* no. 131), and right from the start refused any allegorical or symbolic interpretation of his works (foreword to the second edition of *The Lord of the Rings*; *Letters* no. 131). Therefore his writings are loved and admired also by those who do not sympathize with any faith; a sign of the true greatness of his work, characteristic of a person dealing with real existential problems which concern every human being, regardless of religious creed.[20]

But it appears undeniable that Tolkien had well in mind the foundations of Christian theology, clearly a source of his mythopoeia. One needs only to refer to the theme of the Fall or the important role the humble plays within the his-

---

20 On the other hand 'catholic' in fact means 'universal', but this is not the place to examine such an important and wide theme.

tory of humanity (*Letters* no. 163). We come across this theological sensitivity in some of his letters where he talks about the sacraments (*Letters* no. 43), about the difference between Catholicism and Protestantism (*Letters* nos. 306, 83), about the Second Vatican Council and the reform of Pius X (*Letters* no. 250). However, he does not mention any Catholic theologian or authoritative source even in these cases, making it extremely difficult to reconstruct his doctrinal training.[21] On the other hand, Priscilla, Tolkien's fourth child, declared that he never read to his children any sort of "catechism", preferring religious narrations to any other form of dogmatic teaching.[22]

Nor did I, during my direct consultation of Tolkien's manuscripts preserved in the Oxford Bodleian Library, or of the collection of his books in the adjacent English Faculty Library (EFL), find any crucial element of interest. The EFL hosts the 'Tolkien's Celtic Library',[23] a collection of more than 300 volumes on language and literature owned by Tolkien and given to this library by Tolkien's family. These books, which are rich in comments and notes, mostly deal with philology and Anglo-Saxon literature. The most 'theological' books are the Latin text of the *Ancrene Riwle* (internal reference: VC 206) where on page 8 underlined in green we find the sentence "*Proverbiorum xviii: Mors et vitae in manibus linguae.*[24] *Proverbiorum [xiii] Qui custodit os suo custodit animam suam*"[25] and two collections of *Old English Homilies* (VC189, VC193), where, (on page 159 of the second volume) Tolkien wrote "*assumptio S. Mariae Virginis*". By examining the manuscripts of the essay "On Fairy-Stories" at the Bodleian Library,[26] I could find only a comment written in pencil on a page where Tolkien discusses the difference between miracles and magic. In this comment (which, as far as I know, no scholar has ever noticed) is stated that the distinction between magic and miracles was elaborated for the first time by Christian Theology (MS Tolkien 6, folio 6; cf. Flieger and Anderson 2008, 252-254). One of those Christian theologians who paid particular attention to this important distinction was

---

21 On this point see also to the initial part of the essay by Franco Manni in this volume.
22 Cf. Monda 2008, 31-32.
23 The name 'Tolkien's Celtic Library' is somewhat misleading since only about one third of the books are on Celtic studies topics. See Phelpstead (2011, 9-12 and 117-119).
24 "Death and life are in the power of the tongue" (*Proverbs* 18, 21).
25 "The one who guards his words guards his life" (*Proverbs* 13, 3).
26 Recently republished by Flieger and Anderson (2008) as *Tolkien On Fairy-stories*.

Saint Thomas Aquinas.[27] Now we must verify if and to which extent Tolkien had a chance to get first-hand knowledge of Aquinas's ideas.

In this endeavour I am somewhat assisted by the fact that I own an old edition of the *Summa Theologica*[28] which was part of Tolkien's private library. Each volume bears his signature ("John Reuel Tolkien" in the first three and "JRR Tolkien" in the fourth) which are, as can be proved by comparing the handwriting, identical to those which can be found in the books kept at the EFL. The signature in full "John Reuel Tolkien" on the first three books seems unfamiliar, but I could prove that it is more common for the years between 1922 and 1923. This leads us to think that Tolkien examined the *Summa* during that period. Some Tolkien experts have unofficially confirmed this to me. Mr. Zeally, person in charge of the St. Philip Bookshop in Oxford where I bought the volumes, pointed out to me[29] the opinion of Allison Milbank who is inclined to believe that both signatures and some comments are genuine (cf. Milbank 2009, 15; 27). Verlyn Flieger[30] and Carl Hostetter as well gave me their positive opinion on the authenticity of the signatures. Hostetter, through an acquaintance of his, told me that, according to the particular shape of the letter "J", they could be dated back exactly to the year 1923.[31] Thanks to him I obtained a confirmation from Christopher Tolkien that this same edition of the *Summa* is mentioned in a list, where his father had put down the books he had bought in the early 1920s. On this list (and in Tolkien's library) there seem to have been no other books by theologians or philosophers.[32]

Getting back to the *Summa*, it is of particular interest that it contains many notes; some of them being in pencil (grey, blue and red) and in purple ink. In

---

27 "Miracles are those things which are done outside the order of the whole created nature. But as we do not know all the power of created nature, it follows that when anything is done outside the order of created nature by a power unknown to us, it is called a miracle as regards ourselves. So when the demons do anything of their own natural power, these things are called "miracles" not in an absolute sense, but in reference to ourselves. In this way the magicians work miracles through the demons" (*Summa Theologica* I, q. 110, a. 4 ad 2; cp. *ibid*. q. 114 art. 4).
28 Printed in Venice in 1787, in four volumes.
29 Email messages from February 22nd to 26th, 2009.
30 Email message from August 22nd, 2009 and a brief examination of the item in Modena on May 22nd, 2010, during the conference "Tolkien and Philosophy".
31 Email message from May 10th, 2009.
32 Email messages from Hostetter of May 30th, 2009, reporting Christopher's opinion.

the books at the EFL I could find many marginal notes by Tolkien written with a pencil in the same colours.

Therefore we can maintain that Tolkien certainly owned and probably consulted this important theological text. This turns out to be important and highly significant for our topic since, as we will soon see, Tolkien's idea of an Assumption to an 'Edenic' state is present also in Saint Thomas Aquinas's work, which has always been a source of reference for Catholic theology. It is thus also important to make a comparison between the latter and the thanatology, which culminates in the "Athrabeth".

## 2.3 Comparison between Tolkien's thanatology and the Catholic theology concerning death

### Similarities

Both Catholic theology and Tolkien distinguish between various meanings of the term "death"[33] and different 'states of nature' which, in Catholicism, must be understood as "logical instruments drawn up by theology, not always with cleverness and sometimes with a little bit of confusion, in order to reach a better understanding of the one and only historical state, that is of the only human condition really existent" (Biffi 2004, 131). Restricting ourselves to the circumstances more connected to Tolkien's secondary world (Elves excluded, of course), there seem to be in Catholic theology three states of Humanity:

1. Pure nature: Man without sin and without special gifts (this is a mere concept that corresponds to the first scene of Arda's history in 2.1);
2. Complete and noble nature: Man in a state of innocence with preternatural and supernatural gifts[34] in an untainted world (the Earthly Paradise). This

---

[33] Besides death meant as an end of our permanence in this world or as a separation of body and soul, death assumes various other meanings: crucial moment of our existence, wicked estrangement from God and manifestation of the dying-together in Christ. On the different meanings of death in theology see Rahner 2008; Ladaria 2007, 217ff.; Bordoni 1979.

[34] Preternatural are those gifts that were not owned or requested by nature but which, being consistent with it, improve it (being natural in substance and supernatural in manner). These gifts are immortality, exemption from pain and the dominion over lust. Supernatural, on the other hand, are those gifts of a degree superior to nature, such as for example the friendship with God (supernatural both in manner and in substance). Both kinds of gifts were lost through the Original Sin. For a critical examination of these topics see Ladaria 2007, 213-225 and Biffi 2004, 133f.

state does not have a parallel in the *Legendarium*, according to which the world was created tainted by evil from its very inception (compare below);
3. Decayed nature: Man deprived of all gifts and corrupted by sin, which corresponds exactly to the third stage of Arda.[35]

## Identity

The most important case of identity between the two prospects is undoubtedly the existence of a Fall of humanity after which death enters history. Furthermore, both 'traditions' attribute the creation of the human soul directly to God/Eru.[36] For this reason the soul is not strictly bound to the history of the world. Death as a departure from the history of the world is thus natural in both cases and in conformity with the divine design for humanity. Along these lines the two courses of thought surprisingly converge with the thesis of the Assumption originally predicted for mankind prior to the Fall. On this point there are no 'dogmatic' pronouncements, although the two major Catholic *auctoritates*, Thomas Aquinas[37] and Augustine of Hippo,[38] both support this same thesis. As to the writings of Saint Thomas, we know for certain [2.2] that Tolkien read some passages from them, but we cannot tell whether and when Aquinas's ideas influenced the final result of the "Athrabeth".

---

35 Cf. Biffi 2004, 130. The author also mentions a nature redeemed at the beginning (Man to whom the redemption by Christ gave back the sanctifying grace) and a nature perfectly mended (which will be fulfilled only at the end of times. This is Tolkien's Arda Healed.)
36 Cf. Catechism of the Catholic Church, no. 382.
37 "Paradise was a fitting abode for Man as regards the incorruptibility of the primitive state. Now this incorruptibility was Man's, not by nature, but by a supernatural [preternatural in later theology] gift of God. Therefore that this might be attributed to God, and not to human nature, God made Man outside of paradise, and afterwards placed him there to live there during the whole of his animal life; and, having attained to the spiritual life, *to be transferred thence to heaven*" (*S.Th.*, I, q. 102, art. 4: my italics; cf. *De malo* q. 5 a. 5 ad 9). In the *Summa* examined in 2.2 there are no signs and annotations for this passage (nor for that one quoted in note 27). On Thomist doctrine regarding Edenic condition and Original Sin, also in connection with (possible) extraterrestrial creatures, see Strumia 2008.
38 "To clarify: if it had been necessary for parents to depart from this life and be succeeded by their children [...] how more rightly [as regards Enoch and Elijah, fallen men but nonetheless taken up into Heaven] thus and with how much higher likelihood the first men – who lived without any personal or parental sin – would have been allowed to be moved to a better life giving their place to their children" (*Supra Genesi ad Litteram* 9, 5, 6. 10-11). Also for Rahner the first man was destined (in case he did not commit sin) to go to that better life which now is expected for the whole of humanity at the end of times (Rahner 2008, 33).

## Differences

In my opinion, there are two main differences that must be pointed out in these thanatologies. The first one concerns the creation which, in the *Legendarium*, is tainted by evil from its very beginning (due to Melkor's "disharmonies" during the "Ainulindalë"); whereas in the Catholic Earthly Paradise evil does not exist.[39] It is important to remember that Tolkien was fully aware of this contrast.[40]

The other difference concerns the natural process of death as the separation of body and soul and its conformity to the grand design. According to Catholic theology, indeed, mortality is part of human nature. Its absence from the Earthly Paradise was due to a particular condition which went 'beyond' the strict natural order (original sanctity and justice[41]), giving Man immortality.[42] In these terms death is, from the Catholic point of view, natural[43] but does not

---

39 Of which it is, by the way, pointless to wonder how long it lasted or whether it even existed. Cf. Biffi 2004, 134; Ladaria 2007, 223.
40 "I suppose a difference between this Myth and what may be perhaps called Christian mythology is this. In the latter the Fall of Man is subsequent to and a consequence (though not a necessary consequence) of the 'Fall of the Angels' [...] In this Myth the rebellion of created free-will precedes creation of the World (Eä); and Eä has in it, sub-creatively introduced, evil, rebellions, discordant elements of its own nature already when the *Let it Be* was spoken" (*Letters* no. 212).
41 On the topic of the preternatural gifts and their value on the point of view of contemporary theology, see Ladaria 2007, 215f.; Biffi 2004, 133-134, De Lubac 1965.
42 "The Church, interpreting the symbolism of biblical language in an authentic way, in the light of the New Testament and Tradition, teaches that our first parents, Adam and Eve, were constituted in an original 'state of holiness and justice'" (Catechism of Catholic Church, no. 375). "By the radiance of this grace all dimensions of Man's life were confirmed. As long as he remained in the divine intimacy, Man would not have to suffer or die. The inner harmony of the human person, the harmony between man and woman, and finally the harmony between the first couple and all creation, comprised the state called 'original justice'" (Catechism of Catholic Church, no. 376). Beyond the topicality of the theology of the preternatural gifts (cf. note 41), "the fundamental feature of the 'original state' is undoubtedly the sanctity and justice that Man possessed before falling into sin; *these ones were not due to his nature*" (Ladaria 2007, 212). Likewise Rahner states that it "is – however – a true faith doctrine that death itself, seen in itself, is also a *natural event*, that is to say that it results from the physical-spiritual nature of Man" (Rahner 2008, 34). Regarding the theology of death see also Ratzinger 2008.
43 Here there are some pronunciations taken from Denzinger (1995; the second number refers to the 1950 edition), containing some errors not accepted by the Catholic Church:
a) "The *immortality* of the first man was not a benefit of grace, but a *natural condition*" (no. 1978/1078, Pius V, 1566-1572, *Errors* of Michael du Bay (Baii), Condemned in the Bull "Ex omnibus afflictionibus," Oct. 1, 1567, italics added).
b) "The proposition stated in these words: 'Taught by the Apostle, we regard death no longer as a natural condition of Man, but truly as a just penalty for original guilt,' since, under the deceitful mention of the name of the Apostle, it insinuates that death, which in the present state has been inflicted as a just punishment for sin by the just withdrawal of immortality, was not a natural condition of Man, as if immortality had not been a gratuitous gift, but a natural condition, – deceitful, rash, injurious to the Apostle, elsewhere condemned" (n. 2617/1517, Errors of the Synod of Pistoia, Condemned in the Constitution, "Auctorem fidei," Aug. 28, 1794).
c) For the Council of Trent, see next footnote.
d) For Saint Thomas Aquinas as well "death of Man is natural" (*S. Th.* II-II q. 164 a. 1 co; *In Johann*.

conform to the design. It came into the world when the Original Sin caused Man to lose the Edenic state forever and with it the gift of immortality.[44]

Tolkien reflected upon the naturalness of death for a long time, as becomes evident from the various texts I mentioned in my previous essay; thus we can state that:

- until 1958 Tolkien maintained tout court that human death was in fact natural[45] and in conformity with divine law;[46]
- from 1958 on [see the texts cited in my first essay in this volume in 2.3] he undergoes an important development which leads him to distinguish clearly between death as a severance of body and soul and death as a departure from Arda, and to regard death as separation as non-natural and not in conformity with the design, and death as a departure as natural and in conformity with the design [see 2.1 above].

Thus, Tolkien's thanatology differs from Catholic theology with its belief in death as the separation of body and soul at first in the point of being in conformity with the design, and from 1958 onwards in the aspect of non-naturality. The latter is certainly an important difference, of which, however, Tolkien was not aware. He wrongly[47] thought that according to the doctrine of the Catholic Church

---

ch. 10 lect. 4; see also *S.Th.* I-II q. 85 a. 5; *De Malo* q. 5 a. 5 co; *In Job* ch. 4; *Supra Epistolas ad Romanos* c. 5 lect. 3), since his body is made up of a material consisting of opposites which is, therefore, corruptible. For this reason he was subject to this corruption (In III *Sent.* d. 16 q. 1 a. 2 co) also inside the Earthly Paradise and without connection to the Original Sin. But God gave to Adam and Eve's souls a power to keep corporeity unimpaired and so to avoid the natural separation from their bodies (death) (cf. *ibid.*; *S.Th.* I. q. 97 a. 1; *S.Th.* I q. 102 a. 2). According to Saint Thomas the Original Sin deprived Man of this gift, so death was caused only indirectly, "per accidens" (*S.Th.* I-II. q. 85 a. 5). However, the human soul, thanks to its ability of performing an immaterial process (i.e. thinking), is immortal (comp. *Theol. L.* I c. 15). Therefore, a compound but incorruptible body would have been better in accordance with this aspect (cf. *S.Th.* I-II q. 85 a. 6 co). Nils Agøy, in a really important study (Agøy 1997, 21), wanted to demonstrate that for Saint Thomas death is not natural by quoting in the "sed contra" of this last article a thesis which, however, is "refuted" in the very same article.

44 "The Church's Magisterium, as authentic interpreter of the affirmations of Scripture and Tradition, teaches that death entered the world on account of Man's sin. Even though Man's nature is mortal God had destined him not to die. Death was therefore contrary to the plans of God the Creator and entered the world as a consequence of sin" (Catechism of Catholic Church, no. 1008). In the same way the Catechism of the Council of Trent (no. 33) affirms: "Adam had departed from the obedience due to God […] [H]e fell into the extreme misery of losing the sanctity and righteousness in which he was created; and of becoming subject to all those other evils, which are detailed more at large by the holy Council of Trent" (session V, can 1,2; session VI can. 1).

45 *Letters* nos. 131, 153 and 156; see also my first essay in this volume.
46 "He will rebel against the laws of the Creator – especially against mortality" (*Letters* no. 131).
47 On death as a gift or punishment see also Watkins 2008.

the death-separation was seen as being non-natural.[48] Thus, paradoxically, the theology of death as gift and natural for Man, instead of being bad theology (as Tolkien thought)[49] was, compared to the non-naturality asserted afterwards, closer to the original Catholic teachings.

However, it must be remembered that Tolkien never felt obliged to reiterate in his *Legendarium* the theology in force (*Letters* nos. 153, 263) with which there were, indeed, some parallels (*ibid.*). Nevertheless I hope that having shown these differences and similarities, as well as Tolkien's special attention towards the theme of death (and immortality) as being natural, I have contributed a topic of interest to the field of Tolkien studies.

The table below (where "N" stands for 'natural' and "C" for 'in conformity with the design') displays a summary of the conclusive points from this paragraph.

| Death as a Departure From Arda (World) | | | Death as a Separation of Body and Soul | | | | |
|---|---|---|---|---|---|---|---|
| *According to Tolkien* | *According to Catholic Theology* | | *According to Tolkien* | | | *According to Catholic Theology* | *According to Catholic Theology in Tolkien's opinion* |
| *Elf* | *Man* | *Man* | *Elf* | *Man before 1958* | *Man after 1958* | *Man* | *Man* |
| not-N not-C | N C | N C | not-N C | N C | not-N not-C | N not-C | not-N not-C |

---

48 It must be said that this separation always stays ambiguous in the *Legendarium*. He does not always make a clear distinction between separation as an act in which spirit and body are torn apart and separation as a state where the *fëa* lives far away from its *hröa*. This ambiguity may also be found in the "Athrabeth" where Tolkien talks about, apparently without distinguishing between them, "severing" (separation as an act, *MR* 316) and "severance" meant as state (*MR* 333). From the Tolkien texts I examined, however, it (cf. my first essay, 2.3) becomes very clear that both are not natural, whereas according to Catholic theology the first one is 'natural' and the second one 'unnatural' (according to the dogma of the resurrection of the body). On the relationship between resurrection and immortality see Cullman 1986

49 "Since 'mortality' is thus represented as a special gift of God to the Second Race of the Children (the *Eruhíni*, the Children of the One God) and not a punishment for a Fall, you may call that 'bad theology'. So it may be, in the primary world, but it is an imagination capable of elucidating truth, and a legitimate basis of legends" (*Letters* no. 153, in footnote).

## 3. Conclusion

Tolkien was neither a theologian nor a philosopher nor a logician. He was a philologist, a scholar and, above all, a man who, in his works, dealt with the great topics of human life, focusing most of all on the topic of death. He devoted his lifetime to his studies, changing and refining his attitudes by using not only narrative tools, but also philosophical, theological and logical ones, which reached a culmination point in the "Athrabeth Finrod ah Andreth"; a synthesis of profound literary and theoretical importance.

But death is not a problem exclusive to Tolkien – it is an issue concerning all of us. For this reason I hope that the essays in this volume can (even if only to a small degree) help present-day Man to reassess the topic. Although apparently overwhelming, this topic, as Tolkien shows us, can be fundamentally liberating and capable of letting us perceive better all that is really important in our existence.

# Giampaolo Canzonieri

## A Misplaced Envy
## Analogies and Differences between Elves and Men on the Idea of Pain

### Foreword[1]

Although this essay does not openly stray from the main subject of this anthology, the angle it focuses on is slightly different from the one naturally suggested by the shared subject. Rather than dwelling on the conflicting dualism between Death and Immortality, we intend to delve into the dualism between Death and Pain, aiming at evaluating how the latter is related to the former within the subject of the nature of the Elves and their relationship with Men. The essay is divided into two different sections, the first focused on inner pain and the second on physical pain. Each section, in its own turn, is structured as a support and a function of a specific question which this essay attempts to answer – if only hypothetically.[2]

## 1. On inner pain

### 1.1 Introduction

Let us tackle the subject beginning from the fundamental principles, which are, for as much as it is given us to know, the following:

---

[1] Note on the English translation: this essay was originally written in Italian and refers from time to time to the different connotation of correspondent Italian and English terms and to the overall difference between English and Italian. Since this is done from the point of view of an Italian, some sentences may sound a little 'odd' to an English speaking reader.
[2] As general reference to Tolkien's works the studies by Kocher 2002, Flieger 1997, Flieger 2002, Rosebury 2003 and Shippey 2005 were especially born in mind. As far as the concepts of death and immortality are concerned, the works by Davies 2003, Garbowski 2007 and Reynolds 2008 were particularly useful.

a. The death of the Elves is not caused by the passing of time,[3] which does not affect them except possibly on a temporal level of the same order as life of Arda itself;[4]
b. Elves can be slain;[5]
c. Elves – a far more interesting aspect – can die of grief;
d. Elves are not subject to diseases; therefore, their death is not caused by them;[6]

Intentionally leaving aside the first two statements, which – we are sure – have already been dealt with in depth in other essays of this anthology,[7] we will dwell mostly on the last two in order to underline some aspects which, in both cases and mostly in the last one, have possibly been less debated.

## 1.2 "Waste in Grief", or on why grief and pain are not exactly the same thing

That Elves can die of grief is a known fact, broadly discussed in countless fora including other essays of this collection, and stated with no possible ambiguity in *The Silmarillion*[8] where it has been codified by the well-known statement: "Elves die not till the world dies, unless they are slain or waste in grief" (*S*, Ainul).[9] Moreover, it is clearly documented in one episode of that same book, i.e. the death of Míriel, Fëanor's mother, whose destiny leaves no room for free interpretation of facts although – as it is in the Professor's style – it leaves space for speculations on its consequences and implications. Avoiding – for reasons already mentioned – further analysis of the Míriel episode *per se*,[10] let

---

3 See *Letters* no. 181: "They are therefore 'immortal'. *Not* 'eternally', but to endure with and within the created world, while its story lasts."
4 See *S*, Qu 1: "neither does age subdue their strength, unless one grow weary of ten thousand centuries." It may help to mention that in this essay the theme of Elves' fading has been intentionally omitted. Although elaborated at length by Tolkien, in fact, we find traces of it only in some of his posthumous writings. The reader will find reference to this subject in the essays by Claudio A. Testi and Andrea Monda in this volume.
5 See *Letters* no. 212 where, making reference to the Elves, Tolkien writes: "but they could be 'slain': that is their bodies could be destroyed, or mutilated so as to be unfit to sustain life."
6 See *Letters* no. 212: "The Elves were not subject to disease."
7 Please refer to the essays by Franco Manni and Roberto Arduini in this volume.
8 For the complexity of structure of *The Silmarillion* see Kilby 1977, Flieger and Hostetter 2000, Whittingham 2007 and Kane 2009.
9 See also *MR* 341: "Elves could die, and did die, by their will; as for example because of great grief."
10 For the importance of this character in Tolkien's *Legendarium* see Kane 2009.

us now underline some aspects which, as it has been pointed out, may open the way to less frequently debated subjects.

In a language such as English, based on a multiplicity of distinct, self-denoting nouns, "waste in grief" unequivocally identifies the intended sensation with a torment of an inner nature – one that, in Míriel's specific case, could be closely reminiscent of what we call today a *post partum* depression. English, in other words, does not need the additional information that is required in the "more evolved" – and therefore "less powerful" – Italian language, when a generic word such as "*dolore*" might mean, in lack of any adjective, both an inner and a physical pain. With our mind now irremediably focused on the power of this ominous word, "grief", we can't help, in an anthology that is supposed to be centred on Death being what most separates Men from Elves, to be led instead towards this element, grief, which they seem to have so strongly in common.

Although the Professor – speaking of himself – said: "I am in fact a Hobbit (in all but size)" (*Letters* no. 213), it is well-known that the people he had most at heart were the Elves, "Firstborn" not only in the Creator's majestic symphony, but also in the Sub-creator's humbler rhapsody.[11] The Elves are conceived by Tolkien as beings in all appearances destined to happiness: immortal, forever young, free from diseases, beautiful, of noble heart, brave, given to a deep sense of loyalty and honour, conceivers of language as means of communication and masters of word-craft as arcane instrument of power, in perfect communion with nature and in a direct dialogue with it, gifted by their own nature in the arts and crafts, which they unite into one whole, and also endowed with an inborn taste for beauty, its creation and appreciation. In other words, the perfect classical ideal of the Homeric καλὸς κἀγαθός, blended with the positive aspect of the Norse warlike ideal,[12] the most original shamanic (anti-)

---

11 The term "rhapsody" has not been chosen accidentally: the *Vocabolario Italiano Treccani*, which is for Italy what the *Oxford English Dictionary* is for England, defines it as follows: "In music, an instrumental composition, often in a solo form, in which more themes, almost always of popular origin, are developed in a free sequence of different variations endowed with epic meanings or ethnic and nationalistic exaltation." Although the term "exaltation" might not have been approved by Tolkien, we think he would have had no objections to the rest of the definition.

12 See *Letters* no. 45: "There is a great deal more force (and truth) than ignorant people imagine in the "Germanic" ideal. I was much attracted by it as an undergraduate (when Hitler was, I suppose, dabbling in paint, and had not heard of it), in reaction against the 'Classics'. You have to understand the good in things, to detect the real evil."

heroism of the Finnish tradition,[13] and the love for the countryside and the discreet cult for good taste typical of the well-born Englishman. In the Arda Unmarred of Eru's intentions a similar predisposition to bliss would without any doubt develop as a natural process into a condition of perpetual happiness. Eru himself testifies to this when he says: "But the Quendi shall be the fairest of all earthly creatures, and they shall have and shall conceive and bring forth more beauty than all my Children; and they shall have the greater bliss in this world" (S, Qu 1). By contrast, in the Arda Marred of the Elves' reality brought about by Melkor's discord,[14] happiness comes to take form in an early phase, but only to be soon overwhelmed by the destructive feelings, possessiveness and ambition *in primis*,[15] which, once again with the help of Melkor, surface among Elves and drive them to commit evil actions,[16] although still to a lesser degree than experienced by Men in later times. Although it is Melkor's doing – through the marring of Arda – which prevents the Elves from reaching the bliss they were meant for in Eru's original intentions, it is important to point out that his influence on the Elves' destiny has nothing to do with the Elves' nature, nor could it have for the well-known reason that Eru's Children and their nature were conceived by Eru alone.[17] Were this not enough, Evil, in Tolkien's vision, cannot create but can only corrupt and cannot therefore alter the intrinsic nature of any created being.

It furthers our purpose to quote a passage from *Morgoth's Ring* (*MR*), in which, by means of the literary artifice of, as it were, an 'ethical' debate among the Valar, Tolkien talks about the appearance of death and grief in Aman and of

---

[13] See Lord 1989, Foreword: "For the key to an understanding of the *Kalevala* is the power of the word, the power of incantation and of the story that brings power. Its heroes are word-masters and wonder-workers."

[14] As for the introduction of Evil in the Universe since its creation, the English scholar S. Caldecott, author of many essays on the influence of Tolkien's Catholic faith in his works, suggests that Tolkien intentionally exploits a detail that is not explicitly stated in the book of Genesis: "The Christian (and Jewish) tradition [...] never definitively established whether the angelic fall took place before or after the creation of matter. Lewis and Tolkien had therefore speculated that a prior, angelic fall would help to explain the great sufferings we observe in nature" (Caldecott 2003, 79).

[15] See *Letters* no. 131, where Tolkien states about the Elves that: "Their Fall is into possessiveness and (to a less degree) into perversion of their art to power."

[16] We should not think of Elves as always and necessarily 'good'. Tolkien himself leaves no doubt when he writes that "Elves themselves could do evil deeds" (*Letters* no. 212) and that "Elves are *not* wholly good or in the right" (*Letters* no. 154).

[17] See *S*, Qu 1: "For the Children of Ilúvatar were conceived by him alone; and they came with the third theme, and were not in the theme which Ilúvatar propounded at the beginning, and none of the Ainur had part in their making."

who is 'responsible' for them. Although grief emerges in the debate more as a consequence rather than the cause of death, the conclusions of the debate apply in full to the "waste in grief", all the more so when – as in this specific case – we are taking into consideration Míriel's death. Unprecedented as it is, Míriel's death takes the Valar aback, leaving them unable to understand its nature and implications and forcing them to ask themselves if it could have been one of those "new things" (*MR*, LawsA 244) that, proceeding directly from Eru, are necessarily good even if "not fully revealed to the Ainur" (*ibid.*), or if it could be, instead, another of the evil consequences of the marring action by Melkor.

The debate goes on in a circular form, with Manwë first expressing his own opinion, the other Valar supporting it or arguing against it, and then Manwë again, who, while maintaining his initial stance in its essence, adds new elements to it and integrates contributions by the other debaters. In the first passage we quote below, Ulmo maintains that death is an evil that can be ascribed to Melkor the Marrer:

> But Ulmo answered: "Nonetheless Míriel died. [...] And death is for the Eldar an evil, that is a thing unnatural in Arda Unmarred, which must proceed therefore from the marring. For if the death of Míriel was otherwise, and came from beyond Arda (as a new thing having no cause in the past) it would not bring grief or doubt. For Eru is Lord of All, and moveth all the devices of his creatures, even the malice of the Marrer, in his final purposes,[18] but he doth not of his prime motion impose grief upon them. But the death of Míriel has brought sorrow to Aman." (*MR,* LawsA 240-241)

Ulmo's thesis is therefore that Míriel's death, as a source of pain and doubt, never could 'by definition' derive from Eru, from whom evil could never be passed directly to his Children, and must as a consequence be ascribed to Melkor's marring action. Manwë, when closing the debate after the other Valar have expressed their opinions, declares that he agrees with Ulmo but also adds a crucial statement:

> We may say, therefore, that the Elves are destined to know "death" in their mode, being [...] sent into a world which contains "death", and having a form for which "death" is possible. For though by their prime nature, unmarred, they rightly dwell as spirit and body coherent, yet these are two things, not the

---

18 Ulmo reminds us here of Eru, when, in a passage of *The Silmarillion*, he tells Melkor: "And thou, Melkor, wilt discover all the secret thoughts of thy mind, and wilt perceive that they are but a part of the whole and tributary to its glory" (*S*, Ainul).

same, and their severance (which is "death") is a possibility inherent in their union. (*MR*, LawsA 244-245)

To sum up, Manwë adds that the possibility of death is not caused by Melkor, but is instead inherent to the Elves' "form" since the traumatic severance of body (*hröa*) from spirit (*fëa*), "which is death", is "a possibility inherent in their union."[19] This is not a statement to be underestimated. Manwë partially accepts Ulmo's thesis, which finds Melkor responsible for the Elves' death as a consequence of their presence in Arda Marred, where Melkor has created the conditions to make death possible by overturning the original concept. While doing so, however, he confirms that the possibility of death is an integral part of the Elves' nature and that Melkor's doing – evil as it may be – did not change their nature but 'only' created the conditions for an event to occur which – even though possible – should have never taken place in the original intentions. Therefore, death, and waste in grief as a specific aspect of it, exists *in posse* independently from Melkor, whose role – evil being unable to create – is that of allowing the waste in grief to come *in esse* through the marring of Arda, something that would have never been possible in Arda Unmarred. If Melkor is responsible for both the corruption of Arda and the disappearing, as it were, of the 'environmental' conditions which had been created to ensure the bliss of the Elves (Elves' destiny, as mentioned above), the change in conditions created by him does in no way affect their intrinsic characteristics, inevitably leading us to the conclusion that the possibility for Elves to die of grief was inborn with their nature since the moment of their creation.

Where is this long foreword leading us? If we accept the consequences of the principle that the possibility of death from grief is part of the Elves' nature, we are confronted with the question that we were urged to ask from the beginning: why was the possibility of death from grief introduced as being among the inborn characteristics of a people who, in their Creator's original intentions, should never have known grief?

The hypothesis we suggest is that the Sub-creator's intentions did not in this case coincide with those of the Creator's, and, in utmost humility, prevailed

---

19 For these themes, see Claudio A. Testi's essays and – regarding eschatology in Tolkien – see Franco Manni's essay.

over them. We think that the Elves' apparent predisposition to bliss was a mere literary device to give an even bigger emphasis to the true scenario in Tolkien's mind, a scenario in which not only the Elves were to know grief, but were to know it to an extent that they could die of it. Why then, we ask ourselves, such a persisting willingness to cause pain to a people Tolkien loved so much? There is an obvious answer to this question: writing stories about a happy people can only guarantee bland, unexciting results, whereas a truly enthralling narration needs to test the characters by putting them through situations in which pathos, in addition to giving the plot more engrossing elements, will allow the mechanism of catharsis to take place. It seems easy. Nevertheless, if we further evaluate the clear, explicit and minutely detailed representation of death from grief, in such evident contrast with Tolkien's usually preferred quasi-Michelangelesque *non-finito* style,[20] it seems to us that there should be a subtler answer, one that would remove any doubt that such a meaningful natural characteristic be the result of a simple and common narrative device, and prove instead that it originates from something deeper.

In a letter sent to his friend C.S. Lewis in 1948, Tolkien writes: "It is one of the mysteries of pain that it is, for the sufferer, an opportunity for good, a path of ascent however hard. But it remains an 'evil'" (*Letters* no. 113). This statement, even though confirming the negative nature of pain, confers to it (please note the quotes including the word "evil") the power to act as a catalyst to an inner growth which could give Good new opportunities, thus suggesting – if we look at it in this light – that the less obvious missing answer could be that a people who did not know pain would be excluded from a possible path towards Good, a path that, because of their fallible nature, they could sooner or later need to reach Salvation. Paradoxically, this condition would be a *diminutio* rather than a privilege,[21] and the possibility for Elves to know the suffering of the soul would then be part of the Elves' nature because suffering

---

20 See *Letters* no. 144: "I think it is good that there should be a lot of things unexplained (especially if an explanation actually exists); and I have perhaps from this point of view erred in trying to explain too much."
21 Even if from a slightly different perspective, this thesis is also sustained by Caldecott when he states that "the kind of creature that can only be perfected by its own choices (and so through Quest and trial) is more glorious than the kind that has only to be whatever it was made to be by another" (Caldecott 1998, as quoted in Pearce 1998, 107).

being possible, if not desirable or desired, it could serve as a key to Salvation.[22] Moreover, this knowledge would also move Elves closer to Men, who are so much more exposed to suffering, thus acting as an unifying factor between Firstborn and Secondborn, equals in the face of suffering before themselves and Eru and both united in that other passage of the aforementioned text where, making reference to all of Arda, not only to Elves, Manwë says that "Healing cometh only by suffering and patience" (*MR*, LawsA 239).

## 2. On physical pain

### 2.1 Introduction

After examining grief, that is inner pain, we will now take a deeper look at pain in the strictly physical sense. However, before analyzing the four points highlighted in the introduction of section 1.1, we would like to add two more elements which follow from point 'd' and are closely connected to the subject. To tell the truth, only one of these new elements can be considered 'canonically attested', whereas the other one – although generally accepted as being very likely – is to be considered (with a sole exception) only a hypothesis:

e. Elves can die as a consequence of natural agents such as hunger, thirst or cold;
f. Elves possess a resistance to natural agents at a much higher degree than Men.

Point 'e' being possibly considered 'obvious' by some, and point 'f' being – with a sole exception – only a hypothesis, we would like briefly to support both with some evidence. Analyzing them in the reverse order will help us to use point 'f' to show to what extent point 'e', despite appearances, is in the end much less 'obvious' than one might expect.

---

[22] See J. Pearce, who – when referring to the empathy of the Valië Nienna towards Arda's suffering (see *S*, Val) – affirms that "this suffering, properly understood and accepted, teaches both 'pity, and endurance in hope', as well as bringing 'strength to the spirit' and turning 'sorrow to wisdom'" (Pearce 1998, 149).

## 2.2 Elves and natural agents

A clear and explicit statement on the Elves' superior physical resistance to natural agents is given by Tolkien in *Morgoth's Ring* (Commentary to "Athrabeth" 341), where he makes reference to physical fatigue and writes that Elves "were thus capable of far greater and longer physical exertions (in pursuit of some dominant purpose of their minds) without weariness," thus providing a documentary basis to what the alert reader of *The Lord of the Rings* may have already been gathering from observing Legolas during the chase of the Uruk-hai, an episode which – quoting Aragorn himself – "shall be accounted a marvel among the Three Kindreds: Elves, Dwarves, and Men" (*LotR*, FR.III.1). In this episode we observe that the man and the dwarf show clear signs of progressive fatigue, whereas Legolas is totally at ease, able as he is to seriously consider continuing the chase overnight. The following morning he even outdoes Aragorn the Ranger who had been hardened by decades of life in the wilderness, and is the first to get up and wake the camp, brisk and alert "if indeed he had ever slept" (*LotR*, FR.III.2), ready for another day of chase during which he "stepped as lightly as ever" (*ibid.*) and one more night in which "Aragorn and Gimli slept fitfully, and whenever they awoke they saw Legolas standing beside them, or walking to and fro" (*ibid.*).

After this encouraging beginning, however, we have to acknowledge that no other explicit mention – at least for as much as we are allowed to know – is given in other passages which would support the thesis that the Elves' superior resistance to fatigue can also be extended to a resistance to the effects of other natural agents. As a consequence, the most natural, if not the only way to proceed is to make reference to those episodes which could, directly or indirectly, support or disprove our thesis. We will adopt this approach and draw a few examples directly from Tolkien's works:

- *The crossing of the Helcaraxë:* The passage in *The Silmarillion* in which the Noldor of Fingolfin and Finrod fly from Valinor and come to cross the Grinding Ice is highly enlightening. Elves travel up to lands where "the Valar only and Ungoliant" (*S*, Qu 9) had dared to go before, showing that, against all odds, they think they can accomplish the feat; they face the "desperate crossing" (*ibid.*) despite the presence of women and, most likely, of children in their ranks and, when at last they reach Middle-earth "with a lessened host" (*ibid.*), their losses can be presumed to have been somewhat limited if we consider that, at their arrival, "grievous as were their losses upon the road, the people of Fingolfin and of Finrod son of Finarfin were still more numerous than the followers of Fëanor" (*S*, Qu 13) who, in their turn, were powerful and numerous enough so that they had just overcome Morgoth's troops in the Dagor-nuin-Giliath. In addition, no explicit reference is made to deaths from cold. When talking about the fallen the text only says that they "perished" (*S*, Qu 9), providing no other details, and even when talking of Elenwë, Turgon's wife and Idril's mother, it only says that she "was lost" (*ibid.*). Drawing all this together, it is no wonder that we feel sure of the Elves' superior physical resistance or that, at the same time, we deem plausible that they be at least partially immune to the effects of cold.

- *Maedhros, Fingon, the Precipice and the Eagle:* again in *The Silmarillion*, in the chapter "Of the Return of the Noldor", we read that "Morgoth took Maedhros and hung him from the face of a precipice" (*S*, Qu 13) which – if we consider that the term "hung" unmistakably indicates that Maedhros is dangling in the void – is not an ideal condition in which to receive food and water let alone that the precipice is "upon Thangorodrim" (*ibid.*), that is in the icy North. Further, the Orcs – the only possible chance for the Elf to get food – "cowered still in the dark vaults beneath the earth" (*ibid.*) fearing the sun just arisen, so far from Maedhros that they could not hear Fingon locating him with his singing nor could they intervene during the difficult rescue of Fëanor's son; a rescue which was only possible thanks to the providential arrival of Thorondor, flying to the aid of the elf perhaps in the attempt to redeem the misdeed perpetrated by another eagle which, in another mythology, was tormenting another immortal hanging in chains from another precipice. If we consider that the duration of Maedhros's imprisonment is quite long, at least judging from what happens in Beleriand from the moment of his capture to the moment of his release, we can accept that the Elves' evident superior resistance to hunger and thirst might lead one to think that they hardly need food or water to survive.
- *Legolas on the Caradhras:* if we now consider *The Lord of the Rings*, a more meaningful example because it was directly published by Tolkien without his son Christopher's mediation, we cannot omit mentioning the episode in

which Legolas, on the icy-cold, snow-covered Caradhras, "had no boots, but wore only light shoes" (*LotR*, FR.II.3) during a storm which "had troubled him little" (*ibid.*). While in the case of the Helcaraxë we at least felt a sense of tragedy, we have here an elf who is going through hardships that have proved challenging even for such men as Aragon and Boromir – not to mention the poor hobbits – and despite them does not experience any fear as if cold could not affect him, rather being at ease like a child on a picnic and setting off on a reconnaissance tour bidding farewell to his exhausted fellows with a joyous and somewhat incongruous: "I go to find the Sun!" (*ibid.*).

The aforementioned episodes – albeit not unquestionably decisive – support the assumption that Elves are endowed with a higher resistance even to other natural agents besides the already proven resistance to physical exertion. Moreover, they show that their structure is by far stronger than Man's – or Dwarves', although this is at the moment not the focus of our concern – suggesting at the same time that point 'e' requires a certain degree of verification, even though one may well guess that, for people still endowed with vulnerable physical bodies, all sensations of them being invulnerable to natural agents must be necessarily deceitful. Only two examples will be used in this case, because we think both – and the first in particular – fully serve our purpose:

- *The abandonment of Eluréd and Elurín*: the few lines of *The Silmarillion* dedicated to what is probably the worst crime – at least in its nature if not in its magnitude – ascribable to the wicked zeal of Fëanor's sons even if in this case perpetrated by some no more closely identified "servants" (*S*, Qu 22), clearly say that, once the tragedy of the Ruin of Doriath was achieved, the young sons and heirs of Dior and Nimloth, Eluréd and Elurín, were abandoned "to starve in the forest" (*S*, Qu 22). Use of the word "starve" allows for no misinterpretation that their death was caused not only by lack of food but also from cold as it was meant in the past and probably by Tolkien who usually cherished archaic meanings. We can then accept this episode as decisive for our thesis, even though in this case, as for the Helcaraxë episode, Tolkien carefully avoids giving a definitive version by adding: "Of this Maedhros indeed repented, and sought for them long in the woods of Doriath; but his search was unavailing, and of the fate of Eluréd and Elurín no tale tells" (*S*, Qu 22).

- *Legolas during the chase of the Uruk-hai*: this episode, to which we have already made reference in order to confirm the Elves' documented resistance to fatigue, proves effective under two different aspects. The first being previously explained, we find clearly mentioned in *The Lord of the Rings* that "in the waybread of the Elves" Legolas "found all the sustenance that he needed" (*LotR*, TT.III.2) and this, although the Italian translation would appear a little contrived as against the subtler English text, leaves only slight room for doubt that the mentioned sustenance be of a material nature.

Now that we have examined and – when needed – supported our assumptions, i.e. the Elves' total immunity against diseases coupled with an attested vulnerability to natural agents although limited by their superior physical resistance, let us now go back to the main subject of this essay, which is centred on pain as a possible but neglected alternative to death as a source of resentment of Men against Elves.

## 3. Death and pain, or of the misplaced envy

Another suggestion that can be made from the use of a linguistic approach is that if Elves can waste in grief this does not necessarily imply that they can also "waste in pain", where "pain" – even though it is not always the case – is a term which primarily indicates a physical suffering and not an inner one. Obviously, it is not our intention to state that Elves are totally untouched by physical pain, but it is at the same time true that, once we exclude sickness and old age as a source of pain, there could be little doubt that the Elves' condition is once again markedly better than Man's. But there is more to it than that. If, as we have already seen, we have enough evidence to maintain that Elves be endowed with superior resistance to natural agents such as hunger, thirst and cold, let alone the already proven greater resistance to fatigue, this would somehow limit the sources of physical pain solely to wounds. In this case, too, however, Elves are more resistant than Men if we consider that it is explicitly stated that the latter "were more frail, more easily slain by weapon or mischance, and less easily healed" (*S*, Qu 12), whereas we find that the *fëar* of the Elves "far excelled the spirits of Men in power [...] protecting their bodies [...] and healing them swiftly of injuries, so that they recovered from wounds that would have proved fatal to Men" (*MR*, LawsB 218-219).

Where is all this leading us? The central point of our discussion can be summed up in the question: how is it possible that Man's resentment against Elves is so focussed on death, which has after all a limited influence on the overall quality of life, and is not – at least apparently – centred on physical pain, which afflicts the Secondborn so much more than death?

The question has its origin in a personal predicament: the writer of this essay finds it impossible to understand why Men envy Elves more for their freedom from death than for their freedom from pain. Why has an event such as death been creeping like a worm gnawing through the collective consciousness of Man deeper than the Elves' almost total freedom from physical pain, to which they are subject only when it is inflicted or is due to accidental traumas or totally exceptional environmental conditions? Death is certainly epochal, but it is mitigated by the promise of a continuity in a benign although unknown Beyond which nobody, in a Sub-creation apparently devoid of atheists, seems to question openly. Why ever should a Wise – and many among those who feel resentment against Elves are wise[23] – be so worried about a death which – if serenely accepted *à la* Aragorn – may even turn itself into a voluntary surrendering to the One? Why should he not rather feel much more deprived by the innumerable daily deaths caused by the pain ascribable to the other two more insidious Horsemen, that is Famine and Pestilence? To conclude, why this misplaced envy?

As often happens, we have no definite answers; however, were we to venture a guess, we might find one in another "problem" of Men's that Elves do not share, which we will from now on refer to as "necessity of faith." When confronted with death, we could say that Elves do not particularly need faith, they being – thanks to their history – endowed with solid and well-grounded certitudes. The Noldor had been living in Aman for ages and therefore know the Valar *de visu*. The Sindar have a Maia as their queen and are guided by Thingol, formerly Elwë, who had

---

23 The most meaningful example in this respect is Andreth, main character together with Finrod of the aforementioned "Athrabeth Finrod Ah Andreth". The text, of paramount importance but unfortunately never published in Italy, is in the form of a Platonic dialogue between Finrod, perhaps the most learned of the High Elves, and Andreth, a mortal woman counted among the Wise. They debate at length about the different meaning that death has for Elves and Men and the resentment of the latter against the immortality of the former; a resentment shared at least at the beginning by Andreth herself despite the deep bond – which is also of a personal nature – that exists between her and the Elves.

visited Aman and been in the presence of the Valar. Even the elusive and never clearly discernible Avari have known and listened to at least one Vala, Oromë, if only to refuse his summoning. Certainly, the Elves do not know what will become of them at the end of Arda.[24] Nonetheless, knowing all there is to know about the benign nature of the One, and having been direct witnesses to His communion with the Valar, they may well cherish with greater ease – although with some lingering traces of anxiety[25] – what they call *estel*, that is the ultimate trust that they will not be abandoned by Him.[26] Men, on the other hand, have no certitudes whatsoever. The acceptance of their destiny – as in the primary world – is to be based exclusively on faith with the sole exception, possibly, of whispered and surely not very comforting voices from a remote past when they had supposedly had – some doubt is legitimate – a direct contact with Eru just before rebelling against him and be punished for their rebellion.[27] Pain and death, if based on these assumptions, cannot be but the source of two different feelings in Men, fear and dread, similar but widely differing from each other, and it is well-known that dread, no matter in which universe or sub-universe, does have destructive effects of a far stronger magnitude.[28] In human experience, pain is something that is either present or not and, when it is present, it is also visible (and thus connected to fear) and as such it can be cured, endured, alleviated and in some cases even sublimated with some sort of self-gratification. Death, on the contrary, is absent and present at the same time, constantly incumbent and invisible (and thus connected to dread), and as such does not admit remedies or

---

24 See Finrod: "Now none of us know, though the Valar may know, the future of Arda, or how long it is ordained to endure. But it will not endure for ever. [...] You see us, the Quendi, still in the first ages of our being, and the end is far off. [...] But the end will come. That we all know. And then we must die" (*MR*, Athrabeth 311-312).
25 See Finrod: "We must perish utterly, it seems, for we belong to Arda (in *hröa* and *fëa*). And beyond that what? [...] Our hunter is slow-footed, but he never loses the trail. Beyond the day when he shall blow the mort, we have no certainty, no knowledge" (*MR*, Athrabeth 312).
26 See Finrod: "*Estel* we call it, that is "trust". [...] If we are indeed the Eruhin, the Children of the One, then He will not suffer Himself to be deprived of His own, not by any Enemy, not even by ourselves. This is the last foundation of *estel*, which we keep even when we contemplate the End: of all His designs the issue must be for His Children's joy" (*MR*, Athrabeth 320).
27 See *MR*, "The Tale of Adanel" 345.
28 An effective exemplification of this concept can be found in a work by C.S. Lewis specifically centred on the theme of pain: "Suppose you were told there was a tiger in the next room: you would know that you were in danger and would probably feel fear. But if you were told 'There is a ghost in the next room', and believed it, you would feel, indeed, what is often called fear, but of a different kind. It would not be based on the knowledge of danger, for no one is primarily afraid of what a ghost may do to him; but of the mere fact that it is a ghost. It is 'uncanny' rather than dangerous, and the special kind of fear it excites may be called Dread" (Lewis 1988, Chapter I, "Introductory").

bargaining but conjures up ghosts from the inner abyss that Man's mind is unable to control, thus inevitably leading him to the state that we have just mentioned that we called 'necessity of faith'. This is well witnessed in the "Akallabêth", in the answer given by the Númenóreans to the Valar's emissaries who are sent to try in vain to bring the Dúnedain to reason after they have shown the first signs of unrest: "Why should we not envy the Valar, or even the least of the Deathless? For of us is required a blind trust, and a hope without assurance, knowing not what lies before us in a little while"[29] (*S*, Ak).[30] Faith, as Tolkien was well aware, is not easy to build up or simple to maintain and the burden of its 'necessity' could then be the true if unconscious motivation for Man's inclination to focus their resentment on death, more dreaded and hated as an agent and bearer of the unknown than pain which is, on the contrary, real and visible. In support of this thesis we find the attitude of the Greats who – as Aragorn well reminds us – can distinguish between fear and dread and – being able to control both and bear the burden of the 'necessity of faith' – can accept death in its original nature of a gift by the One to Men thus transforming the Thief in the Night into a paternal call in the fullness of time and passing, serenely and willingly, to where there is "more than memory" (*LotR*, App. A.5).

It would be satisfactory to come to a close now with a pithy quotation, but we will shun the easy path for the sake of developing one more concept which has surfaced due to the reference to Aragorn and has been insistently preying on the mind. Arwen! What better example for behavioural analysis of the differences between Elves and Men than that of an elf become human? What better example than this one, for which "The Tale of Aragorn and Arwen" seems to have been written just to offer us elements of evaluation on this specific theme? None, we are tempted to say. It is then worth writing a few more lines attempting to employ Arwen's example as further support of our thesis. Before doing so, however, we may stress once again: Men's focussing on death, rather than on pain, is the key element that differentiates them and the Elves. This is due to the "necessity of faith" that death implies for Men. In this respect Arwen is a *unicum* in the Elvish world, being the only elf who is dramatically experiencing

---

29 Tolkien, as Verlyn Flieger puts it, offers us "no assurance of any future beyond death. The unknown must be accepted in faith. This is exactly the point. The ability to let go, to trust, is the ability to rely on faith. To cling to the known, the tangible [...] is to be bound" (Flieger 2002, 144).
30 For a detailed analysis of the fall of Númenor see the essay by Alberto Ladavas in this volume.

the passage from certitude to incertitude, from knowledge to the "necessity of faith." Even her great-great-grandmother Lúthien, who shared the same destiny, had in fact profited from greater certitudes thanks to her first experience of death when still an elf and the benign gift of a second life and a second death given to her by Eru himself, with Manwë as intermediary, in the only episode of the *Legendarium* which could possibly be judged a little overdone. On the contrary, when Arwen, urged by her love and just as Lúthien had done agrees to abandon the Elvish condition and be united to that of Man's, she does it without receiving any gift or special comfort. Unlike Lúthien, she acquires the 'necessity of faith' together with her mortality, exchanging a future of certitudes with the uncertain promise of an unknown gift. She is certainly no ordinary woman but, faced with such a burden, even she, the Evenstar, made wise by thousands of years spent in close contact with the greatest of the Noldor, Sindar and Men, falls under its weight. She wearily lives her last days, unable to accept the "bitter" (*LotR*, App. A.5) gift not even with the example and loving attentions of Aragorn, for the love of whom, trusting on whom, she had made the choice so many years before. Arwen resists for as long as Aragorn is in life but, after his death, when the prize of her choice is lost and only its price remains to be paid, she lives the rest of her life unhappily, imprisoned in a Middle-earth which her new nature prevents her to leave "whether I will or I nill" (*LotR*, App. A.5). Beyond the circles of the world there is more than memory but as always, as for everyone, even for Arwen Undómiel the misplaced envy is what she will be facing at the end of the path. The necessity of accepting the truth merely with the comfort of faith proves to be an unsustainable effort.

# Bibliography

## a) General

AGØY, Nils Ivar (1997), "The Fall and Man's Mortality. An Investigation in Some Theological Themes in J.R.R. Tolkien's 'Athrabeth Finrod ah Andreth'", In: *Arda Special* 1 (1997), pp. 16-27.

ALLIOT, Bertrand (2008), "The 'Meaning' of Leaf by Niggle", In: HILEY & WEINREICH, 2008a, pp. 165-190.

AMARANTH (2007), "Death in Tolkien's Legendarium", <<http://valarguild.org/varda/Tolkien/encyc/papers/Amaranth/DeathinTolkien.htm>> (14/11/2011).

AMENDT-RADUEGE, Amy (2010), "Better off Dead. The Lesson of the Ringwraiths", In: *Fastitocalon* 1, pp. 69-82.

ARIÈS, Philippe (1992), *L'uomo e la morte dal Medioevo a oggi*, Milan: Mondadori.

––– (2001), *Storia della morte in Occidente*, Milan: Rizzoli.

BACHMANN, Dieter and Thomas HONEGGER (2005), "Ein Mythos für das 20. Jahrhundert: Blut, Rasse und Erbgedächtnis bei Tolkien", In: *Hither Shore* 2, pp. 13-39.

BARFIELD, Owen (1944), *Romanticism Comes of Age*, Middletown, Connecticut: Wesleyan University Press.

––– (1957), *Saving the Appearances. A Study in Idolatry*, London: Faber Publishing.

BARONI, Pietro, Caterina ISOLDI, Edoardo RIALTI and Mattia ZUPO (2004), *Uno sguardo fino al mare*, Rimini: Il Cerchio.

BASSHAM, Gregory and Eric BRONSON, (2003), *"The Lord of the Rings" and Philosophy*, Chicago and Lasalle: Open Court.

BENVENUTO, Maria Raffaella (2008a), "From *Beowulf* to the Balrogs. The Roots of Fantastic Horror in *The Lord of the Rings*", In: FOREST-HILL 2008a, pp. 3-14.

––– (2008b), "Tolkien and the Perils of Faërie", In: HILEY & WEINREICH 2008a, pp. 251-262.

BERGSON, Henri (2002), *Saggio sui dati immediati della coscienza*, Milan: Raffaello Cortina Editore.

BERSELLI, Luigi and Claudio Antonio TESTI (2005), *Dimostrazione e induzione in Tommaso d'Aquino*, Modena: ETC.

BERTI, Enrico (1997), "Una metafisica problematica e dialettica", In: Francesco BARONE et al., *Metafisica. Il mondo nascosto*, Bari: Laterza, pp. 41-68.

BETTELHEIM, Bruno (1990), *Il mondo incantato. Uso, importanza e significati psico-analitici delle fiabe*, Milan: Feltrinelli.

BIFFI, Giacomo (2004), *Alla destra del Padre*, Milan: Jaca Book.

BIRZER, Bradley J. (2003), *John R.R. Tolkien's Sanctifying Myth. Understanding Middle-earth*, Intercollegiate Studies Institute: Wilmington.

––– (2007), "Aquinas", In: DROUT 2007, pp. 21-22.

BOBBIO, Norberto (1996), *De senectute e altri scritti autobiografici*, Torino: Einaudi.

BONCINELLI, Edoardo and Galeazzo SCIARRETTA (2005), *Verso l'immortalità*, Milan: Raffaello Cortina Editore.

BORDONI, Marcello (1979), "La morte nella teologia contemporanea", In: *Rivista del clero italiano* IX, pp. 848-855.

BORGES, Jorge Luis (1997a), "L' Aleph", In: *L'Aleph*, Milan: Feltrinelli.

––– (1997b), "L'Immortale", in *L'Aleph*, Milan: Feltrinelli.

BOSCO COLETSOS, Sandra and Marcella COSTA (eds.) (2005), *Fiaba, Märchen, Conte, Fairy Tale. Variazioni sul tema della metamorfosi*, Torino: Centro Scientifico Editore.

BRACCO, Rosa Maria (1993), *Merchants of Hope. British Middlebrow Writers and the First World War, 1919-1939*, London: Berg.

CALDECOTT, Stratford (1998), *Tolkien, Lewis, and Christian Myth*, manuscript cited in PEARCE 1999, pp. 61-62, 106.

––– (2003), *Secret Fire*, London: Longman and Todd Ltd.

––– and Thomas HONEGGER (eds.) (2008), *Tolkien's "The Lord of the Rings". Sources of Inspiration*, Zurich & Jena: Walking Tree Publishers.

CAMPBELL, Joseph (2008), *L'eroe dai mille volti*, Milan: Guanda.

CANONICI, Antonella and Gabriele ROSSI, (2007), *Semi-immortalità*, Milan: Lampi di Stampa.

CARPENTER, Humphrey (1977), *J.R.R. Tolkien. A Biography*, London: George Allen & Unwin.

––– (1978), *The Inklings. C.S. Lewis, J.R.R. Tolkien, Charles Williams and Their Friends*, London: George Allen & Unwin.

CASEY, Damien (2004), "The Gift of Ilùvatar", In: *The Australian Journal of Theology* 2 (February 2004), online, pages not numbered.

CASTELLI, Ferdinando (2002), "Tolkien, il signore della fantasia", In: *La Civiltà Cattolica* 3647 (June 1$^{st}$, 2002), pp. 432-444.

CHANCE, Jane (2001a), *"The Lord of the Rings". The Mythology of Power*, rev. ed., Lexington, Kentucky: The University Press of Kentucky.

––– (2001b), *Tolkien's Art. A Mythology for England*, rev. ed., Lexington, Kentucky: The University Press of Kentucky.

––– (ed.) (2003), *Tolkien the Medievalist*, New York & London: Routledge.

CHANCE, Jane and Alfred K. SIEVERS (eds.) (2005), *Tolkien's Modern Middle Ages*, London: Palgrave MacMillan.

CHESTERTON, Gilbert Keith (1994), *Perché sono cattolico*, Milan: Gribaudi.

CHISM, Christine (2003), "Myth and History in World War II", In: CHANCE 2003, pp. 63-92.

CHOAT, Alexander (2000), "Il desiderio di immortalità. Redenzione in un'era di caos", In: *Atti del convegno "J.R.R. Tolkien. Il viaggio della compagnia verso il Terzo Millennio"* (March 5$^{th}$, 2000), Rome: Azione Universitaria, pp. 28-32.

CLARK, George and Daniel TIMMONS (eds.) (2000), *J.R.R. Tolkien and his Literary Resonances*, Westport & London: Greenwood Press.

COLLINGWOOD, Robin G. (1946), *The Idea of History*, Oxford: Oxford University Press.

––– (2005), *Philosophy of Enchantment*, Oxford: Clarendon Press.

––– and J.N.L. MYRES, (1936), *Roman Britain and the English Settlements*, Oxford: Clarendon Press.

CRITCHLEY, Simon (2008), *The Book of the Dead Philosophers*, London: Granta Books.

CROCE, Benedetto (1915), *Zur Theorie und Geschichte der Historiographie*, Tübingen: Mohr.

––– (1922), *Frammenti di etica*, Bari: Laterza.

––– (1938), *La storia come pensiero e come azione*, Bari: Laterza.

CROFT, Janet Brennan (2004), *War and the Works of J.R.R. Tolkien*, Westport: Praeger.

CULLMAN, Oscar (1986), *Immortalità dell'anima o resurrezione dei morti?* Brescia: Paideia.

DAVIES, Bill (2003), "Choosing to Die. The Gift of Mortality in Middle-earth", In: BASSHAM & BRONSON 2003, pp. 123-136.

DAVIS, Robert (ed.) (2005), *Minds at War. Poetry and Experience of the First World War*, Burgess Hill: Saxon Books.

DE BEAUVOIR, Simone (2001), *Una morte dolcissima*, Torino: Einaudi.

DE KOSTER, Katie (ed.) (2000), *Readings on J.R.R. Tolkien*, San Diego: Greenhaven Press.

DE LUBAC, Henry (1965), *Le mystére du surnaturel*, Paris: Aubier.

DE MASI, Franco (2002), *I limiti dell'esistenza*, Torino: Bollati Boringhieri.

DENZINGER, Heinrich (1995), *Enchiridion symbolorum*, Bologna: EDB.

DEVAUX, Michael (2002), "'The Shadow of Death' in Tolkien", In: Ron PRISON (ed.) (2002), *A Tolkien Odyssey*, Leiden: De Tolkienwinkel, pp. 1-46.

––– (2008), "Itinerarium imaginationis ad Deum", In: *Communio* 218, pp. 30-40.

DICKERSON, Matthew (2004), *Following Gandalf*, Grand Rapids: Brazor Press.

DRAY, William H. (1995), *History as Re-enactment*, Oxford: Oxford University Press.

DROUT, Michael (ed.) (2007), *Tolkien Encyclopedia*, London: Routledge.

––– and Hilary Wynne (2000), "Tom Shippey's *J.R.R. Tolkien. Author of the Century* and a Look Back at Tolkien Criticism since 1982", In: *Envoi* 9.2 (autumn 2000), pp. 101-167.

DUNNE, John William (1984), *Esperimento con il tempo*, Milan: Longanesi.

DÜRRENMATT, Friedrich (1982), *Lo scrittore nel tempo*, Torino: Einaudi.

ELIAS, Norbert (1985), *La solitudine del morente*, Bologna: Il Mulino.

ELLISON, John A. (1991), "The 'Why' and the 'How'. Reflections on 'Leaf by Niggle'", in SHIPPEY 1991, pp. 23-32.

FERRÉ, Vincent (2001), *Tolkien. Sur le rivage de la Terre du Milieu*, Paris: Christian Bourgois Editeur.

FIMI, Dimitra (2009), *Tolkien, Race and Cultural History. From Fairies to Hobbits*, London: Palgrave Macmillan.

FISHER, Jason (ed.) (2011), *Tolkien and the Study of His Sources*, Jefferson, NC: McFarland.

FLIEGER, Verlyn (1995) "Tolkien's Experiment with Time", In: REYNOLDS & GOODKNIGHT 1995, pp. 39-44.

––– (1997), *A Question of Time*, Kent, Ohio: Kent State University Press.

––– (2002), *Splintered Light. Logos and Language in Tolkien's World*, Kent, Ohio: Kent State University Press.

––– (2005a), *Interrupted Music*, Kent, Ohio: Kent State University Press.

––– (2005b), "Afterword", In: *SWM*, pp. 59-68.

––– (2007), "The Curious Incident of the Dream at the Barrow. Memory and Reincarnation in Middle-earth", In: *Tolkien Studies* 4, pp. 99-112.

––– (2008), "Gilson, Smith and Baggins", In: CALDECOTT & HONEGGER 2008, pp. 85-95.

––– and Carl HOSTETTER (eds.) (2000), *Tolkien's Legendarium*, Westport & London: Greenwood Press.

––– and Douglas A. ANDERSON (eds.) (2008), *Tolkien On Fairy Stories*, London: HarperCollins.

FOREST-HILL, Lynn (ed.) (2008a), *The Mirror Crack'd. Fear and Horror in J.R.R. Tolkien's Major Works*, Newcastle upon Tyne: Cambridge Scholars Publishing.

––– (2008b), "Boromir, Byrhtnoth and Bayard. Finding a Language for Grief in J.R.R. Tolkien's *The Lord of the Rings*", *Tolkien Studies* 5, pp. 73-97.

FORNET-PONSE, Thomas (2005), "Tolkiens Theologie des Todes" In: *Hither Shore* 2, pp. 157-186.

––– (2006), "Freedom and Providence as Anti-Modern Elements?", In: WEINREICH & HONEGGER 2006, pp. 177-206.

––– (2008), "Theology and Fairy-Stories. A Theological Reading of Tolkien's Shorter Works?", In: HILEY & WEINREICH 2008a, pp. 135-164.

FRANCESCHETTI, Alberto (2006), "Morte e aldilà (punti di vista)", In: *Lo Specchio di Galadriel*, Rimini: Il Cerchio Iniziative Editoriali (fantàsia), pp. 147-164.

FREUD, Sigmund (1976a), "Il nostro modo di considerare la morte", In: *Considerazioni attuali sulla guerra e sulla morte*, part of: *Opere complete* VIII, Torino: Bollati Boringhieri.

––– (1976b), "Caducità", In: *Opere complete* VIII, Torino: Bollati Boringhieri.

FULTON, Robert and Robert BENDIKSEN (1994), *Death and Identity*, Philadelphia: The Charles Press Publishers.

FUSSELL, Paul (1975), *The Great War and Modern Memory*, Oxford: Oxford University Press.

GARBOWSKI, Christopher (2004), *Recovery and Transcendence for the Contemporary Mythmaker. The Spiritual Dimension in the Work of J.R.R. Tolkien*, Zurich and Berne: Walking Tree Publishers.

––– (2007), "Death", In: DROUT 2007, pp. 119-120.

GARTH, John (2003), *Tolkien and the Great War*, London: HarperCollins.

––– (2008), "Tolkien, Exeter College and the Great War", In: CALDECOTT & HONEGGER 2008, pp. 13-56.

Geier, Fabian (2008), "Leaf by Tolkien? Allegory and Biography in Tolkien's Literary Theory and Practice", In: Hiley & Weinreich 2008a, pp. 209-232.

Giaccherini, Enrico (1984), *Il cerchio magico*, Rome: Edizioni di Storia e Letteratura.

Gibelli, Antonio (2007), *L'officina della guerra*, Torino: Bollati Boringhieri.

Gilles, Donald and Giulio Giorello (eds.) (1998), *La filosofia della scienza nel XX secolo*, Bari: Laterza.

Gilliver, Peter, Jeremy Marshall and Edmund Weiner (2006), *The Ring of Words*, Oxford: Oxford University Press.

Grant, C. Sterling (1997), "'The Gift of Death'. Tolkien's Philosophy of Mortality", In: *Mythlore* 21.4, pp. 16-18, 38.

Greenwood, Linda (2005), "Love: The Gift of Death", In: *Tolkien Studies* 2, pp. 171-195.

Gregory, Adrian (1994), *The Silence of Memory. Armistice Day 1919-1939*, London: Berg.

--- (2008), *The Last Great War. British Society and the First World War*, Cambridge: Cambridge University Press.

Haecker, George (1934), *Virgil, Father of the West*, (transl. by Arthur Wesley Wheen), London: Sheed & Ward.

Hammond, Wayne G. and Douglas A. Anderson (1993), *J.R.R. Tolkien. A Descriptive Bibliography*, New Castle: Oak Knoll Books.

--- and Christina Scull (2006a), *The J.R.R. Tolkien Companion and Guide: Chronology*, London: HarperCollins.

--- and Christina Scull (2006b), *The J.R.R. Tolkien Companion and Guide: Reader's Guide*, London: HarperCollins.

--- and Christina Scull (eds.) (2006c), *The Lord of the Rings 1954-2004*, Milwaukee: Marquette University Press.

Heath, Iona (2009), *Modi di morire*, Torino: Bollati Boringhieri.

Hiley, Margaret (2008), "Journeys in the Dark", in Hiley & Weinreich 2008a, pp. 279-292.

--- and Frank Weinreich (eds.) (2008a), *Tolkien's Shorter Works*, Zurich & Jena: Walking Tree Publishers.

--- and Frank Weinreich (2008b), "Introduction", In: Hiley & Weinreich 2008a, pp. i-iv.

HONEGGER, Thomas (2005), "The Man in the Moon Poem" In: Thomas HONEGGER (ed.) (2005), *Root and Branch. Approaches Towards Understanding Tolkien*, (second edition; first edition 1999), Zurich and Berne: Walking Tree Publishers, pp. 9-70.

––– (2007), *"The Homecoming of Beorhtnoth*: Philology and the Literary Muse", In: *Tolkien Studies* 4, pp. 191-201.

––– (2011a), "The Rohirrim: 'Anglo-Saxons on Horseback?' An Inquiry into Tolkien's Use of Sources", In: FISHER 2011, pp. 116-132.

––– (2011b), "Time and Tide – Medieval Patterns of Interpreting the Passing of Time in Tolkien's Work", In: *Hither Shore* 8, pp. 86-99.

HOUGHTON, John William (2003), "Augustine in the Cottage of the Lost Play. The *Ainulindalë* as Asterisk Cosmogony", In: CHANCE 2003, pp. 171-182.

––– (2007), "Augustine of Hippo", In: DROUT 2007, pp. 43-44.

HUSSERL, Edmund (1935), *Die Philosophie in der Krisis der europäischen Menschheit (Philosophy and the Crisis of European Man)*, Wien, Vortrag.

INGLIS, Fred (2009), *History Man*, Princeton & Oxford: Princeton University Press.

JANKÉLÉVITCH, Vladimir (1977), *La Mort*, Paris: Flammarion.

––– (1995), *Pensare la Morte*, Milan: Raffaello Cortina Editore.

JOHNSON, Judith A. (1987), *J.R.R. Tolkien. Six Decades of Criticism*, Westport: Greenwood Press.

JONAS, Hans (1991), *Il diritto di morire*, Genoa: Il Melangolo.

KANE, Douglas Charles (2009), *Arda Reconstructed*, Bethlehem: Lehigh University Press.

KELLY, A. Keith and Michael LIVINGSTON (2009), "'A Far Green Country'. Tolkien, Paradise, and the End of All Things in Medieval Literature", In: *Mythlore* 27.3/4, no. 105/106, (Spring/Summer 2009), Mythopoetic Society: Altadena. Online edition.

KILBY, Clyde S. (1977), *Tolkien and the Silmarillion*, Wheaton: Harold Shaws Publishers.

KING, Alex (1998), *Memorials of the Great War in Britain. The Symbolism and Politics of Remembrance*, Oxford & New York, Berg.

KOCHER, Paul (2002), *Master of Middle-earth – The Fiction of J.R.R. Tolkien*, (first edition 1972), New York: Ballantine Books.

KREEFT, Peter (2005), *The Philosophy of Tolkien*, San Francisco: Ignatius Press.

LADARIA, Luis F. (2007), *Antropologia teologica*, Casale Monferrato: Piemme.

Lasso De La Vega, José S. (1968), *Eroe greco e santo cristiano*, Brescia: Paideia.

Leati, Alessandro (2004), "Il concetto di morte nell'opera di J.R.R. Tolkien", In: *Atti del 1° Convegno di Studi Parapsicologici* "Internet e la Vita oltre la Vita" (February 27th, 28th and 29th, 2004), Bologna: Klären Associazione Culturale e Filantropica, pp. 18-21.

Le Guin, Ursula (1989), "From Elfland to Poughkeepsie", In: *The Language of the Night*, London: The Women's Press, pp. 70-82.

Lewis, Alex (2009), "The Ogre in the Dungeon", *Mallorn* 47 (Spring 2009), pp. 15-18.

Lewis, Clive Staples (1969), "Psycho-Analysis and Literary Criticism", In: *Selected Literary Essays*, (edited by W. Hooper), Cambridge: Cambridge University Press, pp. 286-300.

--- (1988), *Il Problema della Sofferenza*, Chieti: Edizioni GBU.

--- (1990), *The Discarded Image*, (first edition 1964), Cambridge: Cambridge University Press.

--- (2005), *Come un fulmine a ciel sereno. Saggi letterari e recensioni*, (edited by E. Rialti), Genoa & Milan: Marietti 1820.

Lewis, Warren Hamilton (ed.) (1966), *Letters of C.S. Lewis*, London: Geoffrey Bles Publishing.

Livingston, Michael (2006), "The Shellshocked Hobbit. The First World War and Tolkien's Trauma of the Ring", In: *Mythlore* 25.1/2, no. 95/96, pp. 77-92.

Lodigiani, Emilia (1982), *Invito alla lettura di J.R.R. Tolkien*, Milan: Mursia.

Lombardi, Gabriel (2008), "Il maneggiamento del tempo", In: *Il tempo del soggetto dell'inconscio, Atti del V Incontro internazionale dei Forum-Scuola di Psicoanalisi dei Forum del Campo Lacaniano*, July 5th and 6th, 2008, San Paolo del Brasile.

Long, Rebecca (2005), "Fantastic Medievalism and the Great War in J.R.R. Tolkien's *The Lord of the Rings*", in Chance & sievers 2005, pp. 123-137.

Lord, Albert B. (1989), "Foreword to *The Kalevala*", In: Elias Lönnrot, *The Kalevala*, (translated by Keith Bosley), Oxford: Oxford University Press, pp. vii-x.

Lussu, Emilio (2005), *Un anno sull'altipiano*, Torino: Einaudi.

Manni, Franco (ed.) (2002), *Introduzione a Tolkien*, Milan: Simonelli Editore.

--- (ed.) (2005), *Mitopoiesi. Fantasia e Storia in Tolkien*, Brescia: Grafo Editore.

--- (2009), "Real and Imaginary History in *The Lord of the Rings*", In: *Mallorn* 47 (Spring 2009), pp. 28-37.

––– and Simone BONECHI (2008), "The Complexity of Tolkien's Attitude Towards the Second World War", in WELLS 2008, pp. 33-51.

MATHIE, Anne (2003), "Tolkien and the Gift of Mortality", <<http://www.firstthings.com/article/2007/01/tolkien-and-the-gift-of-mortality-17>> (14/11/2011).

MATTEUZZI, Maurizio (1980), *L'universo logico*, Faenza: Faenza Editrice.

MATTHEWS, Dorothy (2000), "Psychological Themes in *The Hobbit*", In: DE KOSTER 2000, pp. 61-70.

McRAE, John (1996), "In Flanders Field" (poem), In: ROBERTS 1996, p. 262.

MILBANK, Allison (2009), *Chesterton and Tolkien as Theologians*, London: T&G Clark.

MODELL, Arnold H. (1994), *Per una teoria del trattamento psicoanalitico*, Milan: Raffaello Cortina Editore.

MONDA, Andrea (2008), *L'anello e la Croce*, Catanzaro: Rubettino.

MORIN, Edgar (2002), *L'uomo e la morte*, Rome: Meltemi.

MORINI, Massimo (1999), *Le parole di Tolkien*, Faenza: Mobydick.

MORRIS, Richard (ed.) (1868), *Old English Homilies*, London: N. Trübner & Co.

NAGY, George (2007), "Plato", In: DROUT 2007, pp. 513-514.

NELSON, Charles (1998), "'The Halls of Waiting'. Death and Afterlife in Middle-earth", In: *Journal of the Fantastic in the Arts* 9, pp. 200-211.

NELSON, Dale G. (2004), "Possible Echoes of Blackwood and Dunsany in Tolkien's Fantasy", In: *Tolkien Studies* I, pp. 177-181.

NICOLINI, Fausto (1962), *Croce*, Torino: UTET.

NIETZSCHE, Friedrich (1873), *Unzeitgemässe Betrachtungen*, (Untimely Meditations) (1873-1876), <<http://gutenberg.spiegel.de/buch/3244/1>>.

OLMI, Antonio (ed.) (2008), *Il peccato originale tra teologia e scienza*, Bologna: Edizioni Studio Domenicano.

PAGGI, Marco (1990), *La spada e il labirinto*, Genoa: ECIG.

PALUSCI, Oriana (1982), *Tolkien*, Firenze: La Nuova Italia (Il Castoro 191).

PASCAL, Blaise (1967), *Pensieri*, Torino: Einaudi.

PASSARO, Errico and Marco RESPINTI, (2003), *Paganesimo e cristianesimo in Tolkien*, Rome: Il Minotauro.

PEARCE, Joseph (1998), *Tolkien. Man and Myth*, London: HarperCollins.

PERELMAN, Chaïm (1977), *Il dominio retorico. Retorica e argomentazione*, Torino: Einaudi.

PETTY, Anne C. (2003), *Tolkien in the Land of Heroes. Discovering the Human Spirit*, New York: Cold Spring Press.

PHELPSTEAD, Carl (2011), *Tolkien and Wales. Language, Literature and Identity*, Cardiff: University of Wales Press.

POPPER, Karl (1957), *The Poverty of Historicism*, London: Routledge and Kegan Paul. Ltd.

PURTILL, Richard L. (2003), *J.R.R. Tolkien. Myth, Morality and Religion*, (original edition 1984), San Francisco: Ignatius Press.

QUINLAN, Mark (2005), *Remembrance*, Hertford: Authors Online.

RAHNER, Karl (2008), *Sulla teologia della morte*, Brescia: Morcelliana.

RAK, Michele (2005), *Logica della fiaba*, Milan: Bruno Mondadori.

RATELIFF, John D. (2006), "'And all the Days of her Life are Forgotten'. *The Lord of the Rings* as Mythic Prehistory", In: HAMMOND & SCULL 2006c, pp. 67-100.

––– (2007), *The History of The Hobbit Part Two. Return to Bag-End*, London: HarperCollins.

RATZINGER, Joseph (2008), *Escatologia*, Assisi: Cittadella.

REYNOLDS, Patricia (2008), "Death and Funeral Practices in Middle-earth", <<http://www.tolkiensociety.org/ed/death.html>> (14/11/2011).

––– and Glen H. GOODNIGHT (eds.) (1995), *Proceedings of the J.R.R. Tolkien Centenary Conference*, Milton Keynes & Altadena: The Tolkien Society & The Mythopoeic Press.

REYNOLDS, Trevor (ed.) (1991), *Leaves From the Tree. J.R.R. Tolkien's Shorter Fiction*, London: The Tolkien Society,

RIALTI, Edoardo (2004), "Come oro cadono le foglie. La caduta, la morte, la macchina ne Il Signore degli Anelli", In: BARONI et al. 2004, pp. 83-92.

RICHTER, Dieter (2005), "La fiaba di Comare Morte e l'immagine della morte nella fiaba occidentale", In: BOSCO COLETSOS & COSTA 2005, pp. 159-167.

RICOEUR, Paul (1984), *Tempo e racconto*, Milan: Jaca Book.

ROBERTS, David (ed.) (1996), *Mind at War*, Burgess Hill: Saxon Books.

ROGERS, Robert (1978), *Logica matematica e teorie formalizzate*, Milan: Feltrinelli.

ROSEBURY, Brian (2003), *Tolkien. A Cultural Phenomenon*, Basingstoke: Palgrave Macmillan.

ROSENBERG, Alfred (1934), *Der Mythus des 20. Jahrhunderts*, (The Myth of the Twentieth Century), München: Hoheneichen Verlag.

RUIZ DE LA PEÑA, Juan (1981), *L'altra dimensione. Escatologia cristiana*, Rome: Borla.

SANGUINETI, Juan José (1988), *Logica e gnoseologia*, Rome: Urbaniana University Press.

SARAMAGO, José (2008), *Death with Interruptions*, London: Houghton Mifflin Harcourt.

SCHMIDT, Robert W. (1966), *The Domain of Logic According to St. Thomas Aquinas*, The Hague: Martinus Nijhoff.

SENARDI, Fulvio (ed.) (2008), *Scrittori in trincea. La letteratura e la grande guerra*, Rome: Carocci.

SENIOR, William A. (2000), "Loss Eternal in J.R.R. Tolkien's Middle-earth", In: CLARK & TIMMONS 2000, pp. 173-182.

SHIPPEY, Tom (2000a), *J.R.R. Tolkien. Author of the Century*, London: HarperCollins.

––– (2000b), "Orcs, Wrights and Wights", In: CLARK & TIMMONS 2000, pp. 183-198.

––– (2005), *The Road to Middle-earth*, London: HarperCollins.

––– (2007a), *Roots and Branches*, Zurich and Berne: Walking Tree Publishers.

––– (2007b), "Tolkien and the *Beowulf*-Poet", In: SHIPPEY 2007a, pp. 1-18.

––– (2008), "Introduction", In: *J.R.R. Tolkien: Tales from the Perilous Realm*, London: HarperCollins, pp. ix-xxviii.

SIBLEY, Brian (ed.) (2001), *J.R.R. Tolkien. An Audio Portrait*, BBC Audiobooks.

SIMONSON, Martin (2008), *The Lord of the Rings and the Western Narrative Tradition*, Zurich & Jena, Walking Tree Publishers.

SKELTON, Tim and Gerald GLIDDON (2008), *Lutyens and the Great War*, London: Frances Lincoln.

SLACK, Anna E. (2008), "A Star Above the Mast", in HILEY & WEINREICH 2008a, pp. 263-278.

SMITH, Ross (2007), *Inside Language. Linguistic and Aesthetic Theory in Tolkien*, (rev. edition 2011), Zurich and Jena: Walking Tree Publishers.

SPENGLER, Oscar (1918), *Der Untergang des Abendlandes*, (The Decline of the West), Wien: Braumüller.

SPENGLER (pseud.) (2003), "Tolkien's Ring. When Immortality Is Not Enough", *Asia Times Online*.

SPIRITO, Guglielmo ofm. (2003), *Tra San Francesco e Tolkien. Una lettura spirituale del Signore degli Anelli*, Rimini: Il Cerchio.

STAMP, Gavin (2007), *The Memorial to the Missing of the Somme*, London: Profile Books.

STEILA, Daniela (2009), *Vita/Morte*, Bologna: Il Mulino.

STEIMEL, Heidi (2008), "The Autobiographical Tolkien", In: HILEY & WEINREICH 2008a, pp. 191-208.

STERNBERG, Martin (2008), "'Smith of Wootton Major' Considered as a Religious Text", In: HILEY & WEINREICH 2008a, pp. 293-323.

STEVENSON, John (1990), *British Society 1914-1945*, London: Penguin.

STOKES, Geoffrey (2002), *Popper*, Bologna: Il Mulino.

STRUMIA, Alberto (2008), "Alcune riflessioni a partire dalla dottrina di S. Tommaso d'Aquino sul peccato originale", In: OLMI 2008, pp. 86-121.

SULLIVAN, Charles William III (2000), "Tolkien the Bard", In: CLARK & TIMMONS 2000, pp. 11-20.

SUMMERS, Jane (2007), *Remembered. The History of the Commonwealth War Graves Commission*, London and New York: Merrell.

TENENTI, Alberto (1989), *Il senso della morte e l'amore della vita nel Rinascimento*, Torino: Einaudi.

TOLKIEN, Christopher (1980), "*The Silmarillion* by J.R.R. Tolkien. A Brief Account of the Book and Its Making", In: *Mallorn* no. 14, pp. 3-8.

TOLLEY, Clive (2002), "Tolkien's 'Essay on Man'. A Look at Mythopoeia", In: *The Chesterton Review*. vol. XVIII, pp. 79-95.

TOYNBEE, Arnold (1934), *A Study of History*, Oxford: Oxford University Press,.

TURNER, Allan (2008), "Tom Bombadil. Poetry and Accretion", In: HILEY & WEINREICH 2008, pp. 1-16.

TURVILLE-PETRE, Edward Oswald Gabriel (1964), *Religione e miti del Nord*, Milan: Il Saggiatore.

VERNANT, Jean-Pierre (2007), *La Morte eroica nell'antica Grecia*, Genoa: Il Melangolo.

VERNAUX, Roger (1966), *Introduzione e Logica,* Brescia: Paideia.

VINK, Renée (2004),"The Wise Woman's Gospel", In: *Lembas Extra* 2004, pp. 15-40.

––– (2008), "Immortality and the Death of Love. J.R.R. Tolkien and Simone de Beauvoir", In: WELLS 2008, pp. 117-127.

VOVELLE, Michel (1990), *Ideologies and Mentalities*, Cambridge: Polity Press.

––– (2009), *La morte e l'Occidente*, Rome & Bari: Laterza.

WALKER, Steve (2009), *The Power of Tolkien's Prose*, New York: Palgrave Macmillan.

WATKINS, Zach (2008), "Mortality and Immortality. A Panel Discussion on 'Mortality and Immortality'", In: WELLS 2008, pp. 45-50.

WEINREICH, Frank (2008), "Metaphysics of Myth. The Platonic Ontology of Mythopoeia", In: HILEY & WEINREICH 2008, pp. 325-347.

––– and Thomas HONEGGER (eds.) (2006), *Tolkien and Modernity I*, Zurich and Berne: Walking Tree Publishers.

WELLS, Sarah (ed.) (2008), *Tolkien 2005. The Ring Goes Ever On. Proceedings*, Coventry: The Tolkien Society.

WEST, Richard C. (2006), "'Her Choice was made and her Doom was appointed'. Tragedy and Divine Comedy in the Tale of Aragorn and Arwen", In: HAMMOND & SCULL 2006c, pp. 317-329.

WHITTINGHAM, Elizabeth (2007), *The Evolution of Tolkien's Mythology*, Jefferson, NC: McFarland.

WILLIAMS, Bernard (1999), "The Makopulos Case. Reflecions on the Tedium of Immortality", In: Bernard WILLIAMS, *Problems of the Self*, Cambridge: Cambridge University Press, pp. 82-100.

WILLMOTT, Hedley Paul (2004), *La prima guerra mondiale*, Milan: Mondadori Electa.

WINTER, Jay (2004), *Sites of Memory, Sites of Mourning. The Great War in European Cultural History*, Cambridge: Cambridge University Press.

WOLF, Alexandra (2006): "Die 'Athrabeth Finrod ah Andreth' oder Das Menschenbild in Tolkiens Mythologie", In: *Hither Shore* 3, pp. 137-150.

WOOD, Ralph C. (2003), *The Gospel According to Tolkien. Visions of the Kingdom in Middle-earth*, Louisville: Westminster John Knox Press.

## b) Tolkien Studies Concerning Death and Immortality

Agøy, Nils Ivar (1997), "The Fall and Man's Mortality. An Investigation in Some Theological Themes in J.R.R.Tolkien's 'Athrabeth Finrod ah Andreth'", In: *Arda Special* 1 (1997), pp. 16-27.

Amaranth (2007), "Death in Tolkien's Legendarium", <<http://valarguild.org/varda/Tolkien/encyc/papers/Amaranth/DeathinTolkien.htm>> (14/11/2011).

Casey, Damien (2004), "The Gift of Ilúvatar", *The Australian Journal of Theology* 2 (February 2004), online.

Choat, Alexander (2000), "Il desiderio di immortalità: redenzione in un'era di caos", In: *Atti del convegno* "J.R.R. Tolkien. Il viaggio della compagnia verso il Terzo Millennio" (March 5th, 2000), Rome: Azione Universitaria, pp. 28-32.

Davies, Bill (2003), "Choosing to Die. The Gift of Mortality in Middle-earth", In: Bassham & Bronson 2003, pp. 123-136.

Devaux, Michael (2002), "'The Shadow of Death' in Tolkien", In: Ron Prison (ed.) (2002), *A Tolkien Odyssey*, Leiden: De Tolkienwinkel, pp. 1-46.

Ferré, Vincent (2001), *Tolkien. Sur le rivage de la Terre du Milieu*, Paris: Christian Bourgois Editeur.

Fornet-Ponse, Thomas (2005), "Tolkiens Theologie des Todes" In: *Hither Shore* 2, pp. 157-186.

Franceschetti, Alberto (2006), "Morte e aldilà (punti di vista)", In: *Lo Specchio di Galadriel*, Rimini: Il Cerchio Iniziative Editoriali (fantàsia), pp. 147-164.

Garbowski, Christopher (2007), "Death", In: Drout 2007, pp. 119-120.

Grant, C. Sterling (1997), "'The Gift of Death'. Tolkien's Philosophy of Mortality", In: *Mythlore* 21.4, pp. 16-18, 38.

Greenwood, Linda (2005), "Love: The Gift of Death", In: *Tolkien Studies* 2, pp. 171-195.

Kelly, A. Keith and Michael Livingston (2009), "'A Far Green Country'. Tolkien, Paradise, and the End of All Things in Medieval Literature", In: *Mythlore* 27.3/4, no. 105/106, (Spring/Summer 2009), Altadena: Mythopoetic Society.

Leati, Alessandro (2004), "Il concetto di morte nell'opera di J.R.R. Tolkien", In: *Atti del 1° Convegno di Studi Parapsicologici* "Internet e la Vita oltre la Vita" (February 27th, 28th and 29th, 2004), Bologna: Klären Associazione Culturale e Filantropica, pp. 18-21.

Mathie, Anne (2003), "Tolkien and the Gift of Mortality", <<http://www.firstthings.com/article/2007/01/tolkien-and-the-gift-of-mortality-17>> (14/11/2011).

NELSON, Charles (1998), "'The Halls of Waiting'. Death and Afterlife in Middle-earth", In: *Journal of the Fantastic in the Arts* 9, pp. 200-211.

REYNOLDS, Patricia (2008), "Death and Funeral Practices in Middle-earth", <<http://www.tolkiensociety.org/ed/death.html>> (14/11/2011).

RIALTI, Edoardo (2004), "Come oro cadono le foglie. La caduta, la morte, la macchina ne Il Signore degli Anelli", In: BARONI, ISOLDI, RIALTI & ZUPO 2004, pp. 83-92.

SENIOR, William A. (2000), "Loss Eternal in J.R.R. Tolkien's Middle-earth", In: CLARK & TIMMONS 2000, pp. 173-182.

SPENGLER (pseud.) (2003), "Tolkien's Ring. When Immortality Is Not Enough", *Asia Times Online*.

VINK, Renée (2004),"The Wise Woman's Gospel", In: *Lembas Extra* 2004, pp. 15-40.

––– (2008), "Immortality and the Death of Love. J.R.R. Tolkien and Simone de Beauvoir", In: WELLS 2008, pp. 117-127.

WATKINS, Zach (2008), "Mortality and Immortality. A Panel Discussion on 'Mortality and Immortality'", In: WELLS 2008, pp. 45-50.

WEST, Richard C. (2006), "Her Choice was made and her Doom was appointed", In: HAMMOND & SCULL 2006c, pp. 317-329.

WOLF, Alexandra (2006): "Die 'Athrabeth Finrod ah Andreth' oder Das Menschenbild in Tolkiens Mythologie", In: *Hither Shore* 3, pp. 137-150.

# Index

## A
Achilles 74
Adam 13, 188f.
Adûnâi 63
*The Adventures of Tom Bombadil (and Other Verses from the Red Book)* 69, 78, 103, 110f.
Aegnor 31, 61, 64, 181
*Aeneid* 28
aesthetic(s) 10, 25f., 35, 43, 89
afterlife 16, 51, 107, 109, 112
Age of Men, Fourth Age 28-30, 35, 158, 164
Agøy, Nils Ivar 189
"Ainulindalë"/Ainulindalë 31, 41, 52, 61f., 64f., 188, 194, 197
Ainur 32, 49f., 61, 181f., 196f.
"Akallabêth" 42, 118-127, 165, 207
Aldington, Richard 139
Alf 37, 113
Alfred 7
Alighieri, Dante 30
*All Men Are Mortal, Tous les hommes sont mortels* 79
*Alla destra del Padre* 186-188
allegory, allegorical, allegorize 37, 58f., 89-92, 96, 104, 107, 113f., 131, 183
"Allegory versus Bounce" 104
Alliot, Bertrand 96
*L'altra dimensione. Escatologia cristiana* 24
Aman/"Aman" 22, 31, 42f., 47, 52, 56, 59, 120f., 126, 196f., 205f.
"Amdir"/*amdir* 6, 181
Anárion 126, 166
*Ancrene Riwle* 184
*Ancrene Wisse* 37
Anderson, Douglas 25, 85
Andreth 6, 11f., 31f., 61, 63f., 67, 176, 178f., 181, 205
Andrew Lang Lecture 25, 86
*L'anello e la Croce* 132, 167, 184
Anfauglith 142f.
Anglo-Saxon 7, 11, 106, 144f., 184
angel, angelic 109, 118, 148, 158, 177, 183, 196
Annals 38, 41f.
"Annals of Aman" 41f., 44, 47, 52
"The Annals of Beleriand" 41, 62
"The Annals of Valinor" 41, 46
*Un anno sull'altipiano* 75
Anthony 28

anthropology, anthropologic(al) 5, 10-12, 15f., 176
Anticleia 73
*Antropologia teologica* 186, 188
Aotrou 108
Appendix to *The Lord of the Rings* 49, 60, 63, 65f., 121, 145, 147, 152, 166, 207f.
Aquinas, Thomas 5-7, 11, 17, 129, 175, 185-188
(King) Aragorn 8, 14, 16, 21, 26, 57f., 60, 66, 68, 74, 80f., 121, 125, 128, 130, 141f., 152f., 156, 164-167, 171, 201, 205, 207f.
Arda 12, 15, 17, 35, 42f., 45, 48-51, 53f., 56-61, 63, 66-68, 93, 121, 176-182, 186f., 189, 190, 194, 197f., 200, 206
Arda Marred 181, 196, 198
*Arda Reconstructed* 40, 118, 194
Arda Remade 60, 68, 180
Arda Unmarred 67, 181, 187, 196-198
Arduini, Roberto 13, 67, 69, 114, 142, 157, 194
Ariès, Philippe 39f.
Aristotle, Aristotelian 5, 11, 176, 178
Arnoediad 143, 149
Ar-Pharazôn 14, 123f., 126f.
art 69f., 77, 80, 84f., 87, 90-92, 98-100, 113, 117f., 122f., 149, 156, 196
artist, artistic 16, 35-37, 43, 70, 91, 93, 95, 97f., 100, 106f., 118, 160
Arwen (Undómiel) 20f., 26, 57f., 60, 63, 66, 81, 121, 149, 164, 166, 171, 207f.
Atani 6
ataraxia 19
*Athrabeth Finrod ah Andreth, The Debate of Finrod and Andreth* 5f., 11, 31f., 42, 45, 47f., 55, 60, 63, 67, 79, 175-178, 180-182, 186f., 190f., 201, 205f.
Atlantis 5, 7
"Auctorem fidei" 188
Auden, W.H. 9, 112
(Saint) Augustine of Hippo 5, 7, 9, 129, 187
Avalai 63
Avallónë 120
Avari 206
Ayer, A.J. 10
Azanulbizar 145

# B
"Babylon" 83
Bagshot Row 73
Baker, Herbert 135
Balrog 168
Bane 165
Barfield, Owen 86

Barrow Downs 131, 141, 147
Barrowfield 141
Barrow-wight 20, 110
Barth, Karl 9
Bassham, Gregory 7, 17, 28
Battle of Bywater 153
Battle of the Pelennor 131
Battle of Unnumbered Tears 142
Battles of the Fords of Isen 145
Bazell, Charles Ernest 5
Beare, Rhona 156
(Venerable) Bede 25, 28
*Bede's Death-Song* 92
Beleg 143
Beleriand 29, 202
Bëor the Old 62, 68
Beorhtnoth 106
*Beowulf* 7, 29, 37
"*Beowulf*. The Monster and the Critics" 87, 103
bereavement 83, 103, 112-115
Beren 26, 41, 45, 58f., 81, 112, 171
Bergson, Henri 5, 72f.
Berti, Enrico 34
Bettelheim, Bruno 72, 88
*Bible*, Biblical 13, 24, 36, 120, 164, 170, 188
Bilbo 14, 74, 119, 128, 154, 162-164, 171
"Bilbo's Last Song" 114
biography, biographical 25, 32, 70, 90
Black Men 73
Black Speech 127
Blessed Realm 53, 109, 119f. 126, 129
Bloch, Marc 35
Blomfield, Austin 141
Blomfield, Sir Reginald 135, 141
Bobbio, Norberto 19
Bodkin, Maud 86
Bodleian Library 10, 25, 86, 90f., 175, 184
body 11f., 39, 45-50, 52-58, 66f., 73, 77, 96, 122, 129, 142, 147, 150, 175-180, 182, 186, 188, 189-190, 197f.
Boethius, Boethian 5, 7, 129-131
Bombadil, Tom 110, 157, 167, 169
Bonechi, Simone 18, 75, 83, 111, 133
*The Book of the Dead Philosophers* 20

*The Book of Lost Tales* 41, 43-46, 49f., 59-61, 64, 68, 182
Borges, Jorge Luis 71, 74, 77
Boromir 14, 105, 151, 203
"The Bowmen" 148
Brendan 21, 109
Britain, British 25, 29, 133-137, 141, 144, 146
British Empire 29
*British Society 1914-1945* 133
Brothers Grimm 84

## C

Caesar 26
Caldecott, Stratford 196, 199
Cambridge 133
Cannistrà, Saverio 34
*Canterbury Tales* 111
Canzonieri, Giampaolo 14, 63, 121, 150, 158, 163, 193
Captains of the West 153
Caradhras 202f.
Carpenter, Humphrey 6, 8, 32, 35f., 82, 89, 91
Casey, Damien 11f., 21f.
Castelli, Fernando 125, 166
Catechism of Catholic Church 187-189
Catholicism, Catholic 24, 54, 58, 67, 129, 166, 170, 175, 181, 183f., 186-190, 196
Celeborn 31
Chance, Jane 96
Chaucer, Geoffrey 5, 7, 111
*Chaucer's Poetical Works* 7
*Chesterton and Tolkien as Theologians* 185
Chesterton, Gilbert Keith 161
Christianity, Christian 11-13, 16f., 20, 24, 27f., 58-60, 67f., 106, 109, 121, 129-131, 138, 151, 158, 166-168, 183f., 188, 196
Chronos 72
Churchill, Winston 28
Cleopatra 28
Coleridge, Samuel Taylor 87
Collingwood, Robin G. 25f.
Collingwood, W.G. 25
*Come un fulmine a ciel sereno* 86
commemoration 133, 136, 138, 140f., 143, 146, 148, 153
*Commentary* to "Athrabeth" 42, 45, 47-49, 54f., 67f., 176f., 180-182, 201
"Communion of the Saints" 24

Index                                                                 231

*Consolatio* 7
consolation 7, 88, 91, 121, 138f.
Contini, Gianfranco 34
*Contributo alla Critica di me stesso* 26
"Converse between Manwë and Eru" 42, 55
Corrigan 108
Councillor Tompkins 70, 92, 98
creation 12, 37f., 64, 77, 79, 92, 104, 107, 117f., 122, 130, 161, 168, 170, 178, 187f., 195f., 198
creativity, creative 7, 26, 37, 69f., 77, 89-91, 93, 96, 98-100, 107, 110, 117, 129, 182
Creator God 118
Critchley, Simon 19
*Critias* 7
Croce, Benedetto 5, 15, 18, 22, 25f.
Cross of Sacrifice 135
culture, cultural 19, 30f., 36, 39, 73, 98, 139f., 148, 151, 157
Curry, Patrick 10

# D
Dagorlad 144
Dagor-nuin-Giliath 202
Dante Alighieri 30
Dark Ages 36
Dark Land 144
Davis, Bill 19f., 57
Dawson, Christopher 28
*De Anima* 176
De Beauvoir, Simone 67, 79
De Bortadano, Joanna 155
*De Consolatione Philosophiae* 129
*De Malo* 187, 189
De Masi, Franco 13, 16, 75
*De senectute e altri scritti autobiografici* 19
Dead Marshes 20, 144
death 6, 10f., 13-24, 28f., 31-33, 35, 37, 39-45, 48-53, 55-88, 90-93, 95f., 98-100, 103, 106-109, 111-114, 117-123, 125-127, 130, 132f., 136, 138, 140-142, 144, 146-153, 155-157, 159, 163-168, 170-173, 175-178, 180-183, 186-190, 193-199, 202-208
*Death and Identity* 39
Death Down 145, 150
*Death with Interruptions* 77
deathless, deathlessness 16, 47, 62, 80, 85, 117, 126, 156, 207
Denethor 141, 167f.

Descartes, René 5
destiny 29, 31-33, 41, 43, 46-48, 50f., 53, 58-60, 64, 68, 73f., 119, 144, 150, 158-160, 165, 177, 194, 196, 198, 206, 208
Dewey, John 5
Dickerson, Matthew 31
*Dimostrazione e induzione in Tommaso d'Aquino* 178
Dior 203
*Il diritto di morire* 39
*The Discarded Image* 157f.
disenchantment 140
divine 7, 52, 66, 77, 118-121, 125f., 167, 187-189
Dolbear, Rupert 8
*The Domain of Logic According to St. Thomas Aquinas* 178
*Il dominio retorico. Retorica e argomentazione* 178
Doriath 29, 203
Dray, William H. 25
dream 6, , 28, 50, 69f., 72, 74, 85, 87-91, 94, 97-100, 105f., 167
Drout, Michael 7, 27
"The Drowning of Anadûnë" 41, 61, 63-65
Du Bay, Michael 188
*The Dublin Review* 89, 107
Dúnedain 150f., 207
Dunharrow 148f.
Dunland 145
Dunlendings 145
Dunne, J.W. 26, 50
dwarf 55, 145, 147, 157f., 201, 203
Dwarrowdelf 168
Dyson, Hugo 98

# E

Eä 49f., 54, 179, 188
Eärendil 81
*Ecclesiasticus* 135
Ecthelion 167
Edain 143, 146
Eddison, E.R. 8
Edoras 141, 149
English Faculty Library (EFL) 11, 175, 184-186
Elanor 21
Eldalië 59
Eldar 29, 50, 59, 62, 66, 119, 124, 129, 143, 146, 180, 197
Elendil (the Faithful) 28, 126f., 165f.

Elenwë 202
Elf, Elves, elvish 7, 11-17, 19f., 22f., 28, 30-35, 38, 40-59, 61-68, 80f., 85, 87, 94, 99, 105f., 109, 112-115, 118, 120-122, 124, 127, 142-146, 149, 156-163, 165-171, 176,-178, 180-182, 186, 190, 193-208
Elijah 187
Elrond 21, 31, 65f., 165, 169
Eluréd 203
Elurín 203
Elvenhome 151
Elwë 205
Elwing 81
*Enchiridion symbolorum* 188
*Encyclopaedia Britannica* 26
England, English 5, 25, 28f., 35, 46, 73, 75, 88, 90, 103, 106, 135, 139f., 145, 152-154, 156, 176, 193, 195f., 204
Enoch 187
ent 8, 29, 157, 167, 169
Éomer 145, 153
Eorl 146
Eorlingas 146
Éowyn 131
Eregion 127
*L'eroe dai mille volti* 74
*Eroe Greco e santo cristiano* 168
Eru 17, 49, 55, 62, 118, 120, 124-126, 129, 177, 180-182, 187, 196f., 200, 206, 208
Eruhin 6, 66, 206
escape, escapism 6f., 11f., 14f., 18 19, 21, 57, 62, 84f., 88, 107, 112, 117-120, 122f., 126f., 149, 151, 155f., 159-161, 163-165, 168, 170-173
*Escatologia* 188
*The Eschatological Nature of the Pilgrim Church* 24
eschatology, eschatological 5, 16, 24, 60, 130, 150, 181, 198
*Esperimento con il tempo* 50
*Essays & Studies by Members of the English Association* 106
"Essay on Criticism" 99
"Essay on Man" 99
*Essays Presented to Charles Williams* 84
Estel 6, 181, 206
ethics 9f.
eucatastrophe 14, 96, 131, 171
Europe, European 27-29, 38, 89, 137, 140, 148
Eve 188
Evermind 149
evil 129

*The Evolution of Tolkien's Mythology* 40, 60f., 118, 130, 194
"Ex omnibus afflictionibus" 188
Exeter College 137, 141
*An Experiment with Time* 26

# F

fable 37, 69, 71, 98
fade, fading 15, 28, 35, 41, 44-48, 50-54 56, 128, 131, 140, 158f., 163, 167, 182, 194
Faerie, Faërie, Faëry, Fairyland 37, 58, 83f., 87f., 105, 107, 110, 112-114, 121
*Fairies and Fusiliers* 83
fairy 105, 112, 160
fairy story, fairy tale 25, 62f., 65, 69, 71f., 80, 83f., 86-88, 103, 105, 157
faith 7, 58, 63, 68, 76, 121f., 126, 130, 136-138, 140, 147, 150, 154, 183, 188, 196, 205-208
Fall 15, 30, 34, 63, 65-67, 81, 117, 119, 122, 127, 130, 150-152, 170, 178, 181, 183, 187f., 190, 196
"The Fall of Gondolin" 81f.
Fall of Man 65, 181, 188
"The Fall of Númenor" 41f., 63-65, 150, 207
Fangorn (forest) 167
fantasy 20, 38, 76, 84, 87f., 91, 96f., 111, 113
Faramir 127, 151, 168
*Farmer Giles of Ham* 104
Fastred 150
fate 17, 19, 29, 32, 40f., 48, 59, 62, 64f., 68, 76, 81, 108, 113, 120f., 142f., 145, 203
fauns 157
*Faust* 29
*fëa* 47-49, 53-55, 68, 175-180, 182, 190, 198, 206
Fëanor 29, 31, 43, 46, 51-53, 100, 194, 202f.
Felagund 31
Fellowship of the Ring 23, 31, 160f., 166
*The Fellowship of the Ring* 19, 47, 54, 56, 119, 128-131, 152, 160, 163-166, 169, 201, 203
Ferré, Vincent 14, 24
fiction, fictional 7, 11, 15, 27, 29f., 32, 35f., 69, 77, 112, 153
Fimi, Dimitra 10, 25
Finarfin 31, 202
Fingolfin 31, 149, 201f.
Fingon 202
Finrod 6, 11, 48, 52, 61, 63f., 176-181, 201f., 205f.
Finwë 42, 52f., 57f.
Fíriel 78, 112

First Age 29, 31, 118, 124, 143
First World War, World War I, Great War 28f., 33, 75, 78, 82, 111, 133f., 139, 146f., 150, 153f.
Flame of Anor 129
Flieger, Verlyn 10, 26, 39, 50, 56, 82, 86, 91, 104f., 113, 119, 126, 185, 207
Flinding 143
Folcred 150
folk tales 46, 108
*Following Gandalf* 32, 64, 154
Ford of Bruinen 129, 131
Fords of Isen 145
*Frammenti di etica* 22, 26
France, French 9, 11, 34, 79, 82, 134, 136
Free Peoples 154
freedom 12, 14, 32, 44, 52, 56, 61, 64f., 80, 124, 156, 161, 205
Freud, Sigmund, Freudian 5, 13, 18f., 69, 73, 75-78, 80, 95
Frodo 14, 18, 20-24, 31, 78, 80, 86, 100, 110, 112, 121, 128f., 131, 144, 151-154, 160, 162f., 166, 171
"Frodo's Song" 78
Fui Nienna 59
Fussell, Paul 33

# G

Gaffer 73
(Queen) Galadriel 14, 29, 31,79, 160, 166
Gammarelli, Lorenzo 37, 103
Gance, Abel 148
Gandalf (the Wizard) 14, 20, 23, 31, 78, 100, 119, 128f., 153, 163, 168, 170f.
Garbowski, Christopher 13, 16, 31
Garth, John 10, 18
*Genesis* 120, 164, 196
Gentiles 27, 30
geography, geographic(al) 25, 31, 81, 86, 96
Germanic 34-36, 106, 195
Germany, German 5, 8f., 18, 35f., 148
Gift of Ilúvatar 31, 65-67, 122, 163, 166
Gift of God (to Men) 14, 62, 66, 80, 156, 187, 190
Gildor Inglorion 11
Gil-Galad 28
Gilson, Robert 22-24, 33, 141
Gimli 29, 201
Glaurung 177
Glorfindel/"Glorfindel" 55, 129, 149

goblins 157
God 7, 9, 11f., 21-23, 28, 33, 44, 51, 61-63, 66, 117, 119, 121f., 125f., 129, 166, 171, 182, 186f., 189f.
Goethe, Johann Wolfgang von 18, 29
Gollum 14, 24, 86, 131, 154, 163-165, 167, 170
Gondolin 29, 81, 124, 149
Gondor, Gondorian 74, 123, 146, 149-152, 157, 165-168
*The Gospel According to Tolkien. Visions of the Kingdom in Middle-earth* 11f., 177
grave 134f., 144f., 153
Graves, Robert 83, 139
Great Barrow 147
Great Britain 133, 138, 144
Great End 43, 60
Great Rings 128, 163
Great River 146, 152
Great Valar 49f.
*The Great War and Modern Memory* 33
Great War Stone 135
"The Grey Annals" 41f., 62, 68
Grey Havens 21, 31
grief 43, 45f., 48, 50-53, 56, 61f., 69, 75, 120, 143, 146, 165, 194-200, 204 168-170, 186
(Brothers) Grimm 84

# H

Hades 73
Haecker, Theodor 5
Halls of Mandos 51, 59
Háma 145
Hammond, Wayne G. 7, 85, 145
Haradrim 150
*Haudh-en-Ndengin*, Hill of Slain 142f., 146, 149
*Haudh-en-Nirnaeth*, Hill of Tears 142f., 149
heathen 158, 160, 167f.
Heaven 16, 18, 71, 120f., 165, 187
Hegel, Georg W. F., Hegelian, Hegelianism 5, 12, 27
Heidegger, Martin 34
Helcaraxë 201, 203
Hell 16, 18, 59, 110, 121
Helm's Deep 145, 150
High Elves 11, 23, 161, 205
historiography, historiographical 15, 25, 30, 149

history, historic(al) 5, 8-10, 12f., 16, 19, 23-31, 36f., 39f., 42f., 49, 54, 57-59, 68, 79, 81, 87, 100, 118, 121, 132-135, 140, 142, 147, 152f., 160f., 166-169, 172, 177-179, 181, 186f., 205
*History as Re-enactment* 25
*History Man* 25
*The History of Middle-earth* 13, 40
Hitler, Adolf, Hitlerian 28, 34, 195
"The Hoard" 111
hobbit 8, 11, 19, 21, 24, 42, 73, 75, 103, 110, 114, 147, 152f., 157-159, 161-163, 167-171, 195, 203
*The Hobbit* 41f., 69, 74f., 79, 88f.
"The Homecoming of Beorhtnoth Beorhthelm's Son" 84, 106
Homer, Homeric 74, 160, 195
Hornburg 145
Hostetter, Carl 6, 185
House of Hador 142
Houses of the Dead 141f.
*hröa* 47f., 55, 68, 175-180, 182, 190, 198, 206
humanity, human 12-14, 16f., 24, 30-32, 39, 42f., 45, 48f., 54-64, 66-68, 70-73, 75, 77-80, 85-87, 91, 105, 107, 111, 113, 119, 122, 128, 142, 149, 153, 156f., 161f., 166f., 170, 176-184, 186-189, 191, 206f.
Husserl, Edmund 5, 29

# I

Iceland 130f.
*The Idea of History* 25f.
*Ideologies and Mentalities* 31
Idril 81, 202
Ilúvatar 12, 15, 31, 59, 62, 64-66, 118, 120-122, 166, 182, 196
Imbar 54
"The Immortal" 77
*Immortalità dell'anima o resurrezione dei morti?* 190
immortality, immortal 14-17, 22-27, 29f., 32-35, 39-45, 47-50, 53f., 56-58, 61-68, 70f., 76-81, 85, 103, 108, 113f., 117-121, 125-127, 133, 149, 151, 155-160, 163f., 166f., 169f., 172f., 175, 177, 181, 186, 188-190, 193-195, 202, 205
Imperial War Graves Commission (IWGC) 134-136, 141
"Imram" 69, 109, 112
"In Flanders Fields" 147, 152
"In the Mounds of Mundburg" 133, 146f.
incarnation, incarnational 11, 28, 130
Incledon, Marjorie 83
*Iniziazione all'Estetica del Settecento* 26
Inklings 6, 9, 32, 36, 86,

*The Inklings. C.S. Lewis, J.R.R. Tolkien, Charles Williams and their Friends* 6, 9, 36, 98
inner pain 193, 200
*Inside Language. Linguistic and Aesthetic Theory in Tolkien* 10
*Interrupted Music* 42, 177
*Introduzione a Tolkien* 85
*Introduzione e Logica* 178
*Invito alla lettura di J.R.R. Tolkien* 91, 113, 128
Irmo 106
Isildur 28, 126, 148, 164f.
Italy, Italian 25, 34, 64, 66, 84, 162, 193, 195, 204f.
Itroun 108

## J

Jackson, Peter 21
Jankélévitch, Vladimir 40
*J'accuse* 148
Jesus Christ 13, 16, 20, 28, 121, 130, 164, 186f.
Jewish, Jews 12, 27, 30, 196
*Job* 189
*John* 21
journey 73-75, 77, 92-94, 105, 107, 109, 112, 114, 122, 144, 162
(Day of) Judgement 16, 18, 24, 58
Jung, Carl Gustav 8, 86

## K

"Kairos" 72
*Kalevala* 196
Kant, Immanuel 5
Kenyon, Frederic Sir 135
King Elessar 151
King George V 137
King(s) of Men 123, 126, 151, 165
King of Númenor 120, 122f.
King Thranduil of Mirkwood 161
Kingdom of Shadow 166
Kings' Barrows 149
Kipling, Rudyard 135
Kocher, Paul 91, 93, 104, 110
*Kortirion* 18
Kreeft, Peter 14

## L

Ladavas, Alberto 15, 60, 117, 150, 165, 207
Land of Morpheus 105
Lang, Andrew 84
Lasso de la Vega, José S. 168
*The Last Great War. British Society and the First World War* 133, 136
"The Last Ship" 78, 112
"The Later Quenta Silmarillion" 41f., 44, 46f., 51f., 60, 62, 68
Latin 5, 9, 11, 80, 158, 184
"The Laws and Customs among the Eldar" 11, 42, 47-49, 52f., 55, 57, 60, 176, 182, 197f., 200, 204
"The Lay of Aotrou and Itroun" 108f.
"The Lay of the Children of Húrin" 143
*The Lays of Beleriand* 52, 143
Le Guin, Ursula 86
*Leaf by Niggle* 14, 70, 84, 88-91, 93, 98, 101, 107f., 114
Leeds 143
legend 40, 67, 106, 118, 130f., 149, 166, 180, 190
*The Legend of Sigurd & Gudrún* 36, 104
Legendarium 11, 32, 39-43, 45, 54f., 58, 60, 62, 64f., 68f., 85, 89f., 103f., 117, 141, 143, 158, 175, 187f., 190, 194, 208
Legolas 29, 56, 147, 161, 163, 201-204
*The Letters of J. R. R. Tolkien* 5, 8, 11, 13-15, 17f., 20, 22f., 27-30, 32-37, 40, 42f., 45, 49, 54f., 57f., 61f., 66f., 69-72, 78-83, 85, 88-91, 94, 100f., 107f., 112, 117-119, 121, 123, 126, 149, 151, 155f., 159-161, 164-167, 170, 180, 183f. 188-190, 194-196, 199
Lewis, Clive Staples 6, 9f., 12, 33, 36, 83, 86, 98f., 113, 157f., 169, 196, 199, 206
*I limiti dell'esistenza* 13f., 16
Lingerers 52-54
literature, literary 5, 9, 18, 23, 25, 42, 56, 69f., 75, 77, 79, 84, 86, 99, 104, 106, 135, 139f., 154-156, 159, 170, 177, 181, 183f., 191, 196, 199
Lodigiani, Emilia 91, 128
logic, logical, logician 14, 70-72, 80, 175, 178- 180, 186, 191
*Logica della fiaba* 72f.
*Logica e gnoseologia* 178
*Logica matematica e teorie formalizzate* 180
Long Peace 177
"The Longaevi" 157
*longaevitas, longaevi, longaevus* 157-160, 164, 166
(serial) longevity 14-16, 34f., 49f., 57f., 63, 66, 68, 80, 119, 149, 155-157, 159-163, 165f., 168, 170-173, 175, 177, 181
Looney 78
"Looney" 78

Lord Dunsany 111
Lord of the Darkness 67
Lord of the Nazgûl, Lord of the Ringwraiths 20, 131
*The Lord of the Rings* 8f., 14, 18, 20-24, 28, 32f., 35-37, 40-42, 47, 54, 56f., 63, 65, 69, 72, 74, 79-81, 86, 88-91, 93f., 100, 102, 104, 110, 112-115, 117, 121f., 124, 128, 130, 143, 145, 149, 151, 154f., 163, 170f., 183, 201f., 204
*The Lord of the Rings and the Western Narrative Tradition* 42
"The Lord of the Rings". *The Mythology of Power* 119
loss 10, 13, 29, 48, 78, 81-85, 103, 113f., 120, 128f., 140, 154, 202
*The Lost Road (And Other Writings: Language and Legend before The Lord of the Rings)* 26, 44, 46, 51f., 59-65, 69f.
Lothlórien, Lórien 47, 105f., 160, 166f.
Lotophagi 160
love 5, 9, 20-22, 32, 35, 57, 63, 69, 81f., 84, 108, 113, 117, 121, 123, 140, 155, 162, 166, 181, 196, 208
Lovecraft, Howard Phillips 111
*Luke* 13, 164
*Lumen Gentium* 24
Lúthien 26, 33, 37, 41, 45f., 57f., 63, 81, 112, 208
*Lutyens and the Great War* 136
Lutyens, Edwin 135-137

# M
*Macbeth* 84
Machen, Arthur 148
Maedhros 202f.
Maggot 78
Maia 49, 124, 205
Maldon 106
Man 6, 12, 14-16, 19, 30-33, 38, 41-46, 48-50, 53f., 56, 58-68., 73, 75f., 80-82, 85, 105f., 110, 118-122, 124-127, 132, 142, 144-146, 151, 156, 158, 163, 165, 167, 170f., 173, 176-182, 182, 186-190, 193, 195f., 200f., 204-208
"The Man in the Moon came down Too Soon" 110
"The Man in the Moon stayed up Too Late" 110
Mandos 50-55, 59
Mann, Thomas 36
Manni, Franco 5, 9, 60, 75, 130, 150, 155, 184, 194, 198
Manning, Frederick 139
Manuscript Tolkien 86, 89-91, 184
Manwë 48, 53, 59, 119, 197f., 200, 208
Marcus Aurelius 27
Marring of Arda 177, 196, 198
Marvell, Andrew 11

Marx, Karl, Marxist 5, 9, 12, 27
Master Cook 112-114
*Master of Middle-earth – The Fiction of J.R.R. Tolkien* 93, 128-130, 193
Mathie, Anne 23
*Matthew* 13, 164
Mayor of Michel Delving 21
McRae, John 147
*meditatio mortis* 41, 141, 175, 181
melancholy 14, 18, 28, 80, 82, 156, 161f., 171
Melkor 12, 16, 28, 43, 47, 61, 65, 118, 124f., 129, 177f., 181-183, 188, 196-198
Memorial to the Missing of the Somme 136
*Memorials of the Great War in Britain. The Symbolism and Politics of Remembrance* 136, 138
memory 12, 14f., 18, 21, 24, 60, 66, 80, 82, 114, 121f., 133f., 136, 138-142, 145-153, 156, 159-161, 163, 165f., 168-173, 207f.
Meneldil 166
*Merchants of Hope. British Middlebrow Writers and the First World War, 1919-1939* 139
Merry 20, 131, 152f.
metaphor 19, 72f., 107, 171
metaphysics, metaphysical 8, 12, 54f., 57
"The Mewlips", "Knocking at the Door: Lines Induced by Sensations When Waiting for an Answer at the Door of an Exalted Academical Person", 111
Middle-earth 13, 15, 18f., 21-24, 28f., 31, 37, 40f., 46f., 52-54, 56f., 60, 79, 85, 90, 103f., 110, 112, 118, 120f., 123-126, 133, 141-143, 145-150, 152f., 157-161, 164, 166f., 169, 171f., 178, 202, 208
Milbank, Allison 185
Milton, John 17
Mîm 111
Minas Anor 166
Minas Tirith 29, 142, 150f., 167
*Minds at War. Poetry and Experience of the First World War* 147
Míriel 42, 52f., 57f., 63, 194
Mirkwood 161
*Mirröanwi* (Incarnates) 176, 178, 180
Mirror of Galadriel 18
"Misomythus" 98
Modena 5, 9f., 185
*Modi di morire* 58
Monda, Andrea 15, 61, 121, 132, 149, 155, 194
*Il mondo incantato. Uso, importanza e significati psicoanalitici delle fiabe* 72, 88
Mons 148
*The Monsters and the Critics and Other Essays* 144

Moore, G. E. 9
morality, moral 8, 12, 14f., 22, 28, 30f., 55, 84, 88f., 108, 138f., 141, 154
Mordor 23
Morgan, Francis Xavier 83
Morgoth 12, 17, 29, 46, 119, 142f., 202
*Morgoth's Ring* 6-8, 11f., 17, 21, 32, 44f., 47-49, 52-55, 57f., 60-65, 67f., 176-182, 190, 194, 196-198, 200f., 204, 206
Morgul 47
Moria 36, 168, 170
Morin, Edgar 39
Morris, Richard 11
Morris, William 36
*La Mort* 40
mortality, mortal 11, 15f., 19, 21-23, 29, 32, 36, 38, 55f., 48f., 57, 61, 63-66, 68, 74, 77, 79-81, 85, 94, 105, 112f., 117-122, 126-128, 130, 163, 175, 181f., 188-190, 205, 208
"Mortality and Immortality" 16
*Una morte dolcissima* 67, 79
*La Morte e l'Occidente* 39
*La Morte eroica nell'antica Grecia* 39
mound 143-149
Mounds of Mundburg 133, 146f.
Mount Doom 121, 131
Müller, Max 86
Music of the Ainur 32, 49, 61, 181f.
"The Music of the Ainur/Ainulindalë" 41, 49, 52, 59, 61, 64f.
myth, mythic 5, 8, 18, 28, 41f., 69, 86f., 91, 98, 100, 111, 118, 139, 159, 176, 188
mythology 8, 16, 35, 40, 58-60, 63, 66-68, 106, 109, 118, 121, 188, 202
mythopoeia, mythopoetics, mythopoesis 70, 85, 140, 160, 183
"Mythopoeia" 70, 84, 98f.
*Der Mythos des 20. Jahrhunderts (The Myth of the Twentieth Century)* 27

# N
Nargothrond 29, 143
narration, narrative 43, 58, 70-72, 79, 81, 104, 141, 146, 148, 151, 155, 164, 170, 191, 199
Narya 129
nationalism, national(istic) 29, 34f., 133, 135, 139, 195
*Navigatio Sancti Brendani* 109
Nazgûl (Black Riders) 14, 33, 127-131, 150, 157, 164
Nelson, Charles 10
Nenya 31
New Testament 16, 20, 188

Nicolini, Fausto 25
Nietzsche, Friedrich 15, 171
Nimloth 203
Niggle 74, 79, 88-98, 101, 107, 110, 114
Nirnaeth 143f., 149
Nodens 25
Noldor (of Fingolfin) 29, 31, 201, 205, 208
nostalgia 12, 18, 22, 161f., 168
"La Nostalgia di Legolas" 162
"Notes on Óre" 67
*The Notion Club Papers* 5, 8, 26, 65, 69
*noumenon* 5
Númenor, Númenóreans 5, 7f., 14-16, 41f., 60, 63, 65, 68, 109, 118-127, 131, 150f., 157f., 161, 164f., 168, 170, 207
nursery rhymes 110, 169
nymphs 157

## O

Octavian 28
*Odyssey* 73f.
"Of the Return of the Noldor" 202
"Of the Rings of Power and the Third Age" 127f., 166
*L'officina della guerra* 75
*Old English Homilies* 11, 184
Old Forest 19, 169
Old Man Willow 110
Old Testament 16
Old Took 162
Olórë Mallë 106
"On Fairy-stories" 7f., 10, 25, 28, 37, 62-65, 69f., 79, 82-84, 86-88, 90f., 95f., 98f., 103, 105, 107, 113, 157, 159, 184
"On Transience" 18, 77
One Ring 28, 74, 131, 168
orc 20, 142, 144f., 147, 150, 202
Original Sin 186f., 189
Oromë 206
Ósanwe-kenta 7, 124, 176
Ouboter, Cees 156
Owen, Wilfried 139, 153
Oxford 9-11, 18, 25f., 33, 73, 79, 82, 84, 86, 88, 90f., 133, 141, 171, 175, 184f.

## P

pagan 109, 122, 130f., 144, 151, 168

*Paganesimo e cristianesimo in Tolkien* 60
pain 12, 14, 21f., 84, 100, 140, 172, 178f., 186, 193f., 197, 199f., 204-207
Palantíri 18, 100, 168, 173
Paradise 59, 96, 186-189
*Paradise Lost* 17
"Pardoner's Tale" 111
Parish 70, 90-93, 95f., 98
Pascal, Blaise 76
Passaro, Errico 60
Path of Dreams 106
Paths of the Dead 74
Paul (Apostle) 12, 17, 158
peace 75, 112, 120, 135, 137, 140, 148
Pearce, Joseph 42, 200
*Pearl* 103
Pelennor 146, 152
Pembroke College 25
Pengoloð 124
*Pensare la Morte* 40
*Pensieri* 76
People of the Stars 46, 50, 56
*The Peoples of Middle-earth* 61, 66
Peregrin 153
*perennis philosophia* 5
Persephone 111
Peter 20
Petty-dwarf 111
*Per una teoria del trattamento psicoanalitico* 72
*Perché sono cattolico* 161
Perilous Realm 103, 105, 110
"Perilous Realm" 86
*Phaedo* 7, 176
philology, philological, philologist 5, 8f., 18, 25f., 34-37, 83, 85, 104, 110, 157f., 169, 184, 191
"Philomythus" 98
*Die Philosophie in der Krisis der europäischen Menschheit, Philosophy and the Crisis of European Man* 27
philosophy, philosophical, philosopher 5, 7-13, 16-19, 21, 23, 25-28, 32f., 35, 37, 42, 54f., 57, 70, 72f., 89, 129, 157, 176f., 181, 183, 185, 191
*Philosophy of Enchantment* 25
*The Philosophy of Tolkien* 14, 63
physical pain 193, 195, 200, 204f.
*Pictures by J.R.R. Tolkien* 55, 60

Pindar 74
Pippin 152f., 169
*Pitica* 74
Pius V 188
Pius X 184
Plato, Platonic, Platonism 5, 7, 11f., 21f., 26, 129, 176, 178, 205
Plotinus 7
politics, political 25f., 30
Polybius 30
Positivist 12, 27
Pope, Alexander 99
Popper, Karl 5, 18
*The Poverty of Historicism* 18
power 7, 14f., 17, 26, 32, 34, 37, 55, 64f., 69f., 80f., 84, 87f., 91, 96, 99f., 105, 117-120, 122-131, 136, 144, 156, 162-166, 168, 170f., 177-179, 184f., 189, 195f., 199, 204
*The Power of Tolkien's Prose* 46
*La prima guerra mondiale* 75
Primary World 54, 57, 66, 117, 123, 142, 147, 152, 177, 190, 206
The Problem of Pain 9
"The Problem of Ros" 61
*Il Problema della Sofferenza* 206
Prospero 100
Protestantism 184
Proverbs 184
Providence 10, 108, 167, 171
psychoanalysis 8, 13, 76
psychology, psychological 17, 25, 55, 75, 80, 86, 96, 178
Púkel 149
Purgatory 59, 91, 96
Purtill, Richard L. 89

# Q
Qerkaringa 44
Qohèlet 27
Quendi 48, 160, 196, 206
"Quenta Noldorinwa" 41, 44, 46, 51, 59-61, 64, 68
"Quenta Silmarillion" 31f., 41, 44, 46f., 51-53, 59-62, 142f., 150, 194, 196, 201-204
*A Question of Time* 50, 56, 63, 92, 105, 110, 193

# R
Ramer, Michael 8

Rateliff, John D. 15, 35f.
Rath Dínen 168
*Recovery and Transcendence for the Contemporary Mythmaker. The Spiritual Dimension in the Work of J.R.R. Tolkien* 13, 17, 32, 65
Red Book (of Westmarch) 24, 153
reincarnation 7f., 26f., 41f., 50f., 54-56
"Reincarnation" 55f.
religion, religious 8-10, 16, 21, 28, 58, 70, 72, 89, 91, 95, 125, 130f., 136-139, 147, 151, 183f.
*Religione e miti del Nord* 130
Remarque, Erich Maria 153
*Remembered. The History of the Commonwealth War Graves Mission* 135
remembrance 136-138, 140f., 143, 154
*Remembrance* 135f.
*Republic* 7, 176
resurrection 20, 58, 149, 190
*The Return of the King* 20, 73, 129, 131, 146, 149f., 152f.
*Return to Bag-End. Part Two* 55
Rialti, Edoardo 60
Rían 146
Ricoeur, Paul 72
Riders of the Mark 145-147, 151
Riders of Théoden 146
Ring 7, 14, 21, 31, 119, 127f., 131f., 154, 160-166
Ring of Fire 129
(Nine) Ring(s) of Power 8, 15, 47, 127f., 168
*The Ring of Words* 40, 85, 117
Ringwraith(s) 14, 20, 80, 118, 127-131, 156, 164-166
Rivendell 119
*The Road to Middle-earth* 10, 13, 17, 19f., 22-24, 28, 37, 69, 78f., 84, 87, 89, 92, 96, 104, 113, 129f., 152, 193
Rohan 145, 150, 152
Rohirrim 145f., 149f.
Roll of Honour 153
*Roman Britain* 25
Roman Catholic 58, 166, 113
*Romanticism Comes of Age* 86
*Roots and Branches* 8, 10f., 18, 34-36, 89, 104, 111
Rosebury, Brian 74, 95
Rosenberg, Alfred 27, 29
Ros(i)e 21
Ruin of Doriath 203
Ruling Ring 128

Ryle, Gilbert 5

## S

*Saggio sui dati immediati della coscienza* 72
salvation 12f., 21, 24, 154, 199f.
Sam 20, 73, 144, 151-154
*Le sang des autres, The Blood of Others* 79
Saramago, José 77
Saruman 124, 152, 167-169
Sassoon, Siegfried 139
Satan 129
satyrs 157
Sauron, Dark Lord 15f., 28, 34, 65, 123, 125-127, 129, 131f., 148, 153f., 161, 164-166, 170
*Sauron Defeated* 5, 8, 42, 61, 63, 65, 89
*Saving the Appearances. A Study in Idolatry* 86
Schelmhaas, Harm 16
Schiro, Herbert 117, 156
Schopenhauer, Arthur 5, 73
*Lo scrittore nel tempo* 71
*Scrittori in trincea* 75
Scull, Christina 7, 145
"The Sea Bell" 78, 112
Second Age 126, 128
Second World War, World War II 9, 27, 29, 35, 78, 90
*Secret fire* 177, 196
*Semi-immortalità* 39
Senior, W.A. 10, 29
*Il senso della morte e l'amore della vita nel Rinascimento* 39
Seventh Age 28
"Shadow-bride" 111
Shakespeare, William 9, 74, 113
*The Shaping of Middle-earth* 44, 46, 51, 59-61, 64
Shippey, Tom 5, 9, 10f., 13, 17-25, 28, 34-37, 87, 89, 91f., 96, 104, 110
Shire 11, 20f., 73, 75, 152f., 162
Siege of Angband 177
*The Silence of Memory. Armistice Day 1919-1939* 136
*The Silmarillion* 17, 28, 31-33, 37f., 44, 46, 51f., 64f., 68f., 73, 79, 81, 101, 103, 111, 114, 118-128, 142f., 147, 150, 165f., 187, 189, 194, 196f., 200-204, 207
Silmarils 31, 79
Silvestris, Bernardus 157
Sindar 205, 208
*Sir Gawain and the Green Knight* 103

*Sir Orfeo* 103
*Sirach* 117
*Sites of Memory. Sites of Mourning. The Great War in European Cultural History* 136
Sixth Age 28
Skeat, Walter W. 7
"Sketch of the Mythology" 41, 44, 46, 50f., 59-61, 64
Sméagol 86
Sméagol-Gollum 170
Smith 37, 112f.
Smith, Geoffrey 22-24, 33, 141
*Smith of Wootton Major* 37, 104f., 112f., 115
Smith, Ross 10
Snowmane 149
soul 11-13, 49-55, 60, 66f., 74, 82, 92, 108, 128, 168, 176-180, 182, 186-189, 190, 199
Southron 153
Socrates 5
*La solitudine del morente* 39f.
*La spada e il labirinto* 66
Spengler, Oswald 27, 29
spirit, spirituality, spiritual 11-14, 22, 28, 39, 46-48, 51-54, 56, 59f., 66, 86, 74f., 98, 109, 119, 121, 124, 126, 128f., 137-140, 148, 169, 171, 175-179, 182, 187f., 190, 197f., 200, 204
Spirito, Guglielmo 162
*Splintered Light. Logos and Language in Tolkien's World* 57, 105, 119, 126, 193, 207
Stalin, Josef 28
Steimel, Heidi 90, 96
Stone of Remembrance 135, 153
"The Stone Troll" 110
*La storia come pensiero e come azione* 15
*Storia della morte in Occidente* 39
*A Study of History* 27
sub-creation, sub-creative 43, 70, 79, 84f., 87f., 91f., 96, 98, 104, 107, 113, 118, 150
sub-creator, sub-create 15, 91, 93, 99, 108, 117, 152, 171
Sulis 25
*Sulla teologia della morte* 186-188
*Summa Theologiae* 6f., 17, 175, 185, 187-189
Sundering Sea 21
*Supra Epistolas ad Romanos* 189
*Supra Genesi ad Litteram* 187
Swanwick 21
sylvan elves 157
symbolism, symbol(ic) 75, 91, 114, 128, 140, 146, 148, 180, 183, 188

# T

Tacitus 30
"The Tale of Adanel" 67, 206
"The Tale of Aragorn and Arwen" 207f.
"The Tale of Finwë and Míriel" 52, 57
Tea Club Barrovian Society (TCBS) 23f., 33-35, 82
*The Tempest* 74, 100, 113
*Tempo e racconto* 72
Testi, Claudio A. 6, 11, 17, 25, 32, 39, 76, 103, 121, 141, 158, 175, 194, 198
thanatology 175, 181, 186, 188f.
Thangorodrim 143, 202
Théoden 146
theology, theological, theologian 7, 9, 11f., 24, 27, 30, 54, 59, 66f., 96, 129, 175f., 181, 183-191
Thidhrandi 130f.
Thiepval 137
Thingol 205
Third Age 28, 31, 121, 126, 164
Thor 22
Thorhall 130f.
Thorondor 202
"Thoughts for the Times on War and Death" 69, 75
Tídwald 106
*Timaeus* 7
*Time and Tide* 109
Time of the Elves 30
Tinúviel 45
Tirion 100
Tolkien, Christopher 6, 44f., 50, 59, 61, 72f., 81, 100, 103, 118, 122, 145, 185, 202
Tolkien, Edith 18, 33, 37, 83, 91
Tolkien, J. R. R., Tolkienian 5-52, 54-60, 70-75, 78-101, 103-115, 117-119, 121-123, 125f., 128-131, 133f., 137, 140-146, 148-173, 175-178, 180-191, 193-196, 198f., 201-203, 207
Tolkien, Mabel (née Suffield) 82f., 183
Tolkien, Michael 3
Tolkien, Priscilla 91, 184
*Tolkien Encyclopedia* 7, 61, 114
*Tolkien* 113
*Tolkien 2005. The Ring Goes Ever On. Proceedings* 16
*J.R.R. Tolkien. A Biography* 33, 82
*J. R.R. Tolkien. An Audio Portrait* 79
*Tolkien. A Cultural Phenomenon* 75, 95, 113, 122, 193
*Tolkien and the Gift of Mortality* 11, 23f.

*Tolkien and the Great War* 18, 22-24, 75, 82f., 133, 141
"Tolkien and Philosophy" 5, 9, 185
*Tolkien and the Silmarillion* 40, 194
*J.R.R. Tolkien. Author of the Century* 7, 9, 91, 93, 95f., 108f., 112, 144, 158
"Tolkien between Philology and Philosophy" 5
*The J. R. R. Tolkien Companion and Guide: Chronology* 7, 40
*The J. R. R. Tolkien Companion and Guide: Reader's Guide* 7, 40, 47, 56, 60, 79, 118
*J.R.R. Tolkien. A Descriptive Bibliography* 85
*Tolkien in the Land of Heroes. Discovering the Human Spirit* 80
*Tolkien in Oxford* 79
*Tolkien, Lewis, and Christian Myth* 199
*Tolkien. Man and Myth* 42, 91, 199f.
*J.R.R. Tolkien. Myth, Morality and Religion* 60, 89
*Tolkien On Fairy Stories* 8, 83-88, 91, 95, 184
*Tolkien, Race and Cultural History. From Fairies to Hobbits* 46
*The Tolkien Reader* 84
*J.R.R. Tolkien. Six Decades of Criticism* 40
*J.R.R. Tolkien's Sanctifying Myth. Understanding Middle-earth* 177
*Tolkien's Art. A Mythology for England* 88, 96
*Tolkien's Legendarium* 40, 118, 194
*Tolkien. Sur le rivage de la Terre du Milieu* 14, 24, 29, 40, 65, 84
tomb 122f., 134, 144f., 149f., 152, 165
Tolley, Clive 99
Torhthelm 106
Toynbee, Arnold 27
*Tra San Francesco e Tolkien. Una lettura spirituale del Signore degli Anelli* 162
tradition, traditional 5, 10-12, 16f., 20-22, 30, 60f., 67, 105f., 110, 113, 128, 139, 147, 149, 162, 181, 183, 187-189, 196
*The Treason of Isengard* 47, 56
"The Tree" 90
*Tree and Leaf* 69f., 84f., 88, 91f., 93-100, 107
Treebeard 47, 167, 169, 171
Tuor 81
Turgon 202
Túrin (Turambar) 41, 60, 111, 143
*The Two Towers* 47, 75, 100, 124, 127, 144f., 147, 150f., 153, 169, 204

# U

Úlairi (see also Nazgûl and Ringwraiths) 127
Ulmo 197f.
Ulysses 73f.
Undying Lands 21
*Unfinished Tales of Númenor and Middle-earth* 31

*L'universo logico* 180
Ungoliant 201
United Kingdom of Great Britain and Ireland 133
*Der Untergang des Abendlandes, The Decline of the West* 27
Unwin, Stanley 89, 91
*Unzeitgemässe Betrachtungen* 15
*L'uomo e la morte* 39
*L'uomo e la morte dal Medioevo a oggi* 39
Uruk-hai 168, 201, 204

# V

Vala 106, 118, 206
Valar 7, 31, 49, 52, 55, 59-61, 63, 65, 109, 118-126, 129, 177, 182, 196f., 201, 205-207
"Valaquenta" 200
Valië Nienna 200
Valinor 43f., 46, 51-54, 56f., 106, 109, 112, 118f., 165, 201
Vefántur 59
*Verso l'immortalità* 39
Vico, Giambattista 26
Vikings 144
Vink, Renée 17
Virgil 5
Virgin Mary 180, 183
*Vita/Morte* 57

# W

Waldman, Milton 117, 158
Walker, Steve 46
war 9, 18, 20, 23, 29f., 33, 75, 78, 81-84, 89, 123, 126f., 133-141, 143f., 148, 150-154, 170, 172
*War and the Work of J.R.R. Tolkien* 80
War of Elendil 28
*The War of the Jewels* 44, 47, 51f., 60, 62, 68, 176
War of the Ring 28, 143f., 152
*The War of the Ring* 145
War of Wrath 28
Weinreich, Frank 99
Weisman, Christopher 23f.
*Welsh Review* 108
West, Richard C. 21
White Tree 100, 166
"The Window of the West" 151

Wittgenstein, Ludwig 5
Wood, Ralph C. 11f.
Wootton 37
Wootton Major 112

# Z
Zeally, Christopher 185

# Walking Tree Publishers

Walking Tree Publishers was founded in 1997 as a forum for publication of material (books, videos, CDs, etc.) related to Tolkien and Middle-earth studies. Manuscripts and project proposals can be submitted to the board of editors (please include an SAE):

Walking Tree Publishers
CH-3052 Zollikofen
Switzerland
e-mail: info@walking-tree.org
http://www.walking-tree.org

*Cormarë Series*

The *Cormarë Series* has been the first series of studies dedicated exclusively to the exploration of Tolkien's work. Its focus is on papers and studies from a wide range of scholarly approaches. The series comprises monographs, thematic collections of essays, conference volumes, and reprints of important yet no longer (easily) accessible papers by leading scholars in the field. Manuscripts and project proposals are evaluated by members of an independent board of advisors who support the series editors in their endeavour to provide the readers with qualitatively superior yet accessible studies on Tolkien and his work.

*News from the Shire and Beyond. Studies on Tolkien*
Peter Buchs and Thomas Honegger (eds.), Zurich and Berne 2004, Reprint, First edition 1997 (Cormarë Series 1), ISBN 978-3-9521424-5-5

*Root and Branch. Approaches Towards Understanding Tolkien*
Thomas Honegger (ed.), Zurich and Berne 2005, Reprint, First edition 1999 (Cormarë Series 2), ISBN 978-3-905703-01-6

Richard Sturch, *Four Christian Fantasists. A Study of the Fantastic Writings of George MacDonald, Charles Williams, C.S. Lewis and J.R.R. Tolkien*
Zurich and Berne 2007, Reprint, First edition 2001 (Cormarë Series 3), ISBN 978-3-905703-04-7

*Tolkien in Translation*
Thomas Honegger (ed.), Zurich and Jena 2011, Reprint, First edition 2003 (Cormarë Series 4), ISBN 978-3-905703-15-3

Mark T. Hooker, *Tolkien Through Russian Eyes*
Zurich and Berne 2003 (Cormarë Series 5), ISBN 978-3-9521424-7-9

*Translating Tolkien: Text and Film*
Thomas Honegger (ed.), Zurich and Jena 2011, Reprint, First edition 2004 (Cormarë Series 6), ISBN 978-3-905703-16-0

Christopher Garbowski, *Recovery and Transcendence for the Contemporary Mythmaker. The Spiritual Dimension in the Works of J.R.R. Tolkien*
Zurich and Berne 2004, Reprint, First Edition by Marie Curie Sklodowska, University Press, Lublin 2000, (Cormarë Series 7), ISBN 978-3-9521424-8-6

*Reconsidering Tolkien*
Thomas Honegger (ed.), Zurich and Berne 2005 (Cormarë Series 8), ISBN 978-3-905703-00-9

*Tolkien and Modernity 1*
Frank Weinreich and Thomas Honegger (eds.), Zurich and Berne 2006 (Cormarë Series 9), ISBN 978-3-905703-02-3

*Tolkien and Modernity 2*
Thomas Honegger and Frank Weinreich (eds.), Zurich and Berne 2006 (Cormarë Series 10), ISBN 978-3-905703-03-0

Tom Shippey, *Roots and Branches. Selected Papers on Tolkien by Tom Shippey*
Zurich and Berne 2007 (Cormarë Series 11), ISBN 978-3-905703-05-4

Ross Smith, *Inside Language. Linguistic and Aesthetic Theory in Tolkien*
Zurich and Jena 2011, Reprint, First edition 2007 (Cormarë Series 12), ISBN 978-3-905703-20-7

*How We Became Middle-earth. A Collection of Essays on The Lord of the Rings*
Adam Lam and Nataliya Oryshchuk (eds.), Zurich and Berne 2007 (Cormarë Series 13), ISBN 978-3-905703-07-8

*Myth and Magic. Art According to the Inklings*
Eduardo Segura and Thomas Honegger (eds.), Zurich and Berne 2007 (Cormarë Series 14), ISBN 978-3-905703-08-5

*The Silmarillion - Thirty Years On*
Allan Turner (ed.), Zurich and Berne 2007 (Cormarë Series 15), ISBN 978-3-905703-10-8

Martin Simonson, *The Lord of the Rings and the Western Narrative Tradition*
Zurich and Jena 2008 (Cormarë Series 16), ISBN 978-3-905703-09-2

*Tolkien's Shorter Works. Proceedings of the 4th Seminar of the Deutsche Tolkien Gesellschaft & Walking Tree Publishers Decennial Conference*
Margaret Hiley and Frank Weinreich (eds.), Zurich and Jena 2008 (Cormarë Series 17), ISBN 978-3-905703-11-5

*Tolkien's The Lord of the Rings: Sources of Inspiration*
Stratford Caldecott and Thomas Honegger (eds.), Zurich and Jena 2008 (Cormarë Series 18), ISBN 978-3-905703-12-2

J.S. Ryan, *Tolkien's View: Windows into his World*
Zurich and Jena 2009 (Cormarë Series 19), ISBN 978-3-905703-13-9

*Music in Middle-earth*
Heidi Steimel and Friedhelm Schneidewind (eds.), Zurich and Jena 2010 (Cormarë Series 20), ISBN 978-3-905703-14-6

Liam Campbell, *The Ecological Augury in the Works of JRR Tolkien*
Zurich and Jena 2011 (Cormarë Series 21), ISBN 978-3-905703-18-4

Margaret Hiley, *The Loss and the Silence. Aspects of Modernism in the Works of C.S. Lewis, J.R.R. Tolkien and Charles Williams*
Zurich and Jena 2011 (Cormarë Series 22), ISBN 978-3-905703-19-1

Rainer Nagel, *Hobbit Place-names. A Linguistic Excursion through the Shire*
Zurich and Jena 2012 (Cormarë Series 23), ISBN 978-3-905703-22-1

Christopher MacLachlan, *Tolkien and Wagner: The Ring and Der Ring*
Zurich and Jena 2012 (Cormarë Series 24), ISBN 978-3-905703-21-4

Renée Vink, *Wagner and Tolkien: Mythmakers*
Zurich and Jena, forthcoming (Cormarë Series 25), ISBN 978-3-905703-25-2

*The Broken Scythe. Death and Immortality in the Works of J.R.R. Tolkien*
Roberto Arduini and Claudio Antonio Testi (eds.), Zurich and Jena 2012
(Cormarë Series 26), ISBN 978-3-905703-26-9

*Constructions of Authorship in and around the Works of J.R.R. Tolkien*
Judith Klinger (ed.), Zurich and Jena, forthcoming

J.S. Ryan, *In the Nameless Wood* (working title)
Zurich and Jena, forthcoming

*Tolkien's Poetry*
Julian Morton Eilmann and Allan Turner (eds.), Zurich and Jena, forthcoming

### Beowulf and the Dragon

The original Old English text of the 'Dragon Episode' of *Beowulf* is set in an authentic font and printed and bound in hardback creating a high quality art book. The text is illustrated by Anke Eissmann and accompanied by John Porter's translation. The introduction is by Tom Shippey. Limited first edition of 500 copies. 84 pages. Selected pages can be previewed on: www.walking-tree.org/beowulf
*Beowulf and the Dragon*
Zurich and Jena 2009, ISBN 978-3-905703-17-7

### Tales of Yore Series

The *Tales of Yore Series* grew out of the desire to share Kay Woollard's whimsical stories and drawings with a wider audience. The series aims at providing a platform for qualitatively superior fiction with a clear link to Tolkien's world.

Kay Woollard, *The Terror of Tatty Walk. A Frightener*
CD and Booklet, Zurich and Berne 2000, ISBN 978-3-9521424-2-4

Kay Woollard, *Wilmot's Very Strange Stone or What came of building "snobbits"*
CD and booklet, Zurich and Berne 2001, ISBN 978-3-9521424-4-8

www.ingramcontent.com/pod-product-compliance
Lightning Source LLC
Chambersburg PA
CBHW070726160426
43192CB00009B/1333